Life:
The Owner's Manual

By Alan Fensin

Life: The Owner's Manual

Published by
Way Enterprises
Box 732
Metairie, LA 70004

Copyright © 1995 by Alan Fensin
All rights reserved. No part of this book may be reproduced, stored in a retrieval system, or transmitted in any form or by any means, electronic, mechanical, photocopying, recording, or otherwise, without prior written permission of the publisher.

Printed in the United States of America.

Library of Congress Catalog Card Number 94-68119

ISBN 0-9622183-2-4

Contents

Introduction — 13

Chapter 1. Body — 19
- Overview — 21
- Nutrition — 22
  - What is Proper Nutrition? — 23
  - Proteins: Essential for Life — 24
  - Energize with Carbohydrates — 26
  - Different Types of Fats — 27
- Understand Cholesterol — 29
  - The Relationship between Fats — 30
- Vitamins and Minerals — 31
  - Understand the Vitamins — 32
  - Understand the Minerals — 35
  - What are Antioxidants — 38
  - Should We Take Vitamin Pills? — 38
- Processed Foods — 40
  - Gone is the Goodness of Grains — 41
  - Fats — 41
  - Minimize Food Processing — 42
  - Irradiated Foods — 42
- Food Additives — 42
  - Fertilizers and Pesticides — 43
  - Preservatives — 43
  - Sweeteners — 44
  - Too Much Salt? — 45
  - Other Additives — 46
- Whole Foods — 47
  - What are Health Foods — 48
  - Organic Foods — 48
  - What's for Supper Tonight — 48
  - Foods that Heal — 51
  - Foods You Should Not Eat — 52
  - Eating Out — 53
- Alternatives in Nutrition — 53
  - The Vegetarian Diet — 53
  - The Macrobiotic Diet — 55
  - Food Allergies — 57

- Your Ideal Weight — 57
  - Recommended Weight Chart — 59
  - Calories Chart — 59
  - Maintaining Your Ideal Weight — 60
  - The "Don'ts of Dieting — 63
  - Low-Calorie Frozen Dinners — 64
  - Cellulite — 65
  - Fasting — 65
  - Weight Gain — 66
- Water — 67
  - Drinking Water — 67
  - Home Purification Systems — 71
  - Flavor Variety in Drinking Water — 72
- Other Water Uses — 73
  - Cleansing Baths — 73
  - Herbal Baths — 73
  - Cold Showers and Baths — 74
  - A Gift from Finland: The Sauna — 75
- Skin — 77
  - Skin Care Products — 78
  - Some Common Skin Problems — 79
  - Methods to Treat Acne — 81
  - To Limit and Delay Wrinkles — 82
  - Sun and Skin — 83
- Hair — 85
  - Hair Care — 86
- Nails — 87
  - Nail Care — 88
- Teeth and Gums — 88
  - Cavities — 89
  - Caring for Your Teeth — 90
- Clothing — 91
  - Synthetic Fibers — 92
  - Natural fibers — 94
  - The Comfort of Clothes — 95
- Shoes — 96
  - The Right Fit — 97
- The Environment — 98
  - Toxins — 99
  - Exposure to Toxins — 99
  - Sources of Toxins in the Home — 101
  - Symptoms of Indoor Air Pollution — 105
  - Temperature and Humidity — 105

Chapter 2. Body–Mind   107

- Overview   109
- The Immune System   110
  - Parts of the Immune System   110
  - Stress and the Immune System   112
  - Vitamins and the Immune System   112
  - Exercise and the Immune System   112
  - The Mind and the Immune System   113
- Cancer   113
  - Tumor Growth   114
  - Physical Causes of Cancer   114
  - Cancer and Nutrition   115
  - Cancer and Exercise   115
  - Cancer Prevention   115
  - Early Warning Signs of Cancer   116
  - The Battle Against Cancer   117
  - New Hope for Cancer Treatment   118
- Heart Disease   119
  - Blood Pressure   119
  - Stroke   120
  - Hardening of the Arteries   120
  - Heart Attack   121
  - Treatments for Cardiovascular Disease   122
  - Preventing Heart Disease   123
- Organ Transplants   123
- Diabetes   124
  - Type 1: Insulin-Dependent   124
  - Type 2: Non-Insulin-Dependent   125
  - Who's at Risk?   125
  - Precautions   125
  - Taking Control of Diabetes   126
- Colds and Flu   127
  - Catching the Bug   128
  - When a cold Strikes   128
  - Influenza   129
  - Prevention is the Best Remedy   129
  - If You do Get Cold or Flu   129
  - Who Gets a Flu Shot   130
- Asthma   130
  - Treatment and Prevention   131
- Back Pain   132
  - What's in a Back?   132
  - Causes of Backaches   132
- Preventing and Treating Back Pain   133

- — Exercising for a Healthy Back ... 133
- — Posture ... 134
- — First Aid for Backaches ... 136
- — Chiropractic: The Touch that Heals ... 137
- Headaches ... 138
  - — Types and Causes of Headaches ... 138
  - — Tension Headaches ... 139
- Pain and Pain Management ... 141
  - — Pain Relievers ... 141
  - — Pain Clinics ... 142
- Stress ... 143
  - — The Fight or Flight Response ... 143
  - — How Stress Influences Body Functions ... 144
  - — Who's at Risk? ... 144
  - — Assessing Your Level of Stress ... 145
  - — Performing Under Stress ... 147
  - — Stress Management ... 147
  - — Physical Exercise to Lower Stress ... 148
- Meditation ... 150
- Biofeedback ... 152
  - — Biofeedback to Relieve Stress ... 153
- Massage ... 154
  - — Different Types of Massage ... 156
- Exercise ... 157
  - — Elements of Fitness ... 158
  - — Before Starting any Exercise Program ... 159
  - — Warm-up and Cool-down ... 159
  - — Types of Exercise ... 160
  - — The Key to Staying Active and Fit ... 163
- Yoga ... 165
- Tai Chi ... 166
- Sleep ... 166
  - — Our Sleep Rhythms ... 167
  - — Sleep Disorders ... 168
  - — The Case Against Sleeping Pills ... 170
- Dreams ... 171
- Aging and Longevity ... 172
  - — Disorders Associated with Aging ... 174
  - — Increase Your Life Expectancy ... 175
  - — Who Lives Longer ... 177
  - — Your Life Expectancy ... 178
- Secrets to the Fountain of Youth ... 179
- Menopause ... 179
  - — Sex and Menopause ... 180
  - — Treatments ... 181

- — Osteoporosis and Menopause — 181
- — Male Menopause — 182
- Sexuality — 182
  - — Our Sexual Organs — 182
  - — Sexual Functions and Responses — 182
  - — Sexual Behavior — 183
  - — Sex in Society — 183
  - — Sexual Malfunctions — 184
  - — Sexual Ecstasy — 185
  - — Birth Control — 187
- Sexually Transmitted Diseases — 188
- AIDS — 190
  - — Who;s at Risk? — 190
  - — AIDS Prevention — 192
  - — AIDS Testing — 193
- Doctors — 194
  - — Choosing a Physician — 194
  - — The Medical Check-up — 195
- Modern and Traditional Medicine — 195
  - — Alternative Therapies — 196
- Herbal Medicine — 197
- Drugs — 200
  - — Over-the-counter Drugs — 200
  - — Prescription Drugs — 202
  - — Drugs and Pregnancy — 204
  - — Drugs and Alcohol — 204
  - — Interactions between Drugs and Foods — 206
  - — Generic Drugs — 206
- Smoking — 207
  - — The Effects of Tobacco Smoke — 208
  - — Quitting — 209
- Alcohol — 211
  - — Alcohol Intoxication — 211
  - — The Health Risks — 212
  - — Fetal Alcohol Syndrome — 213
  - — Reducing Your Alcohol Intake — 214
- Recreational Drugs and Substance Abuse — 215
  - — Narcotics — 218
  - — Hallucinogens — 219
  - — Pills — 221
- Light, Color and Sound — 223
  - — Light — 223
  - — Color — 225
  - — Sound — 226

Chapter 3. Mind　229

- Your Brain and Your Mind　231
  - So Where is Your Mind?　231
  - The Parts of the Mind　232
- Psychology　232
  - How Does Psychoanalysis Work?　233
  - Other Contributors to Psychology　235
  - The Enneagram　237
  - Psychological Counseling　239
  - Mental Health Professionals　239
  - Different Types of Therapy　240
  - Support Groups and Self-Help　241
- Mental Illness　242
  - What are the Causes of Mental Illness　243
  - Stress and Adjustment Disorders　244
  - Anxiety-based Disorders　245
  - Understand Burn-out　246
  - Personality Disorders　248
  - Mood Disorders and Suicide　249
  - Suicide Potential　252
  - Delusional Disorder　253
  - Schizophrenia　254
- Common Emotional Issues　256
  - Common Fears　256
  - Anxiety　258
  - Envy　259
  - Death, Loss and Grief　261
  - Overcome Loneliness　263
  - How to Make Friends　264
  - Are You Co-Dependent?　264
  - Escape and Addictions　265
- Health and Wellness　267
  - How to Maintain Mental Health　268
  - How to be Happy　268
  - The Secret of Happiness　268
  - Communication　270
  - Learn to Say No　272
  - Have Better Relationships　274
  - Forgiveness　275
  - Change　276
- Improve Your Memory　277
- Create Prosperity in Your Life　277

- Positive Thinking — 279
  - Thought Patterns — 280
  - Affirmations — 282
  - Daily Practice — 285
  - Hypnosis — 286
  - The Law of Attraction — 287
  - The Flip-Flop Technique — 288
  - You Can Succeed — 289
  - Increase Your Personal Power — 290
- Your Psychological Growth — 290
  - Freedom — 291
  - Mental Wellness — 293
  - Be the Master of Your Own Life — 294

Chapter 4. Mind–Spirit   207

- Overview — 299
- Why a Spiritual Quest? — 300
  - Why a God? — 301
  - The Proofs of God — 302
  - Why a Religion? — 303
- Origins and Development of Religions — 304
  - Common Elements of Religions — 305
  - The Holy Ones — 307
  - Common Elements of Great Religions — 307
- The Great Living Religions — 308
- Hinduism — 310
  - The Sacred Hindu Texts — 310
  - Asceticism and Moksha — 311
  - The Law of Karma — 312
  - The Hindu God — 313
- Buddhism — 314
  - The Buddha's Life — 314
  - The Buddhist Doctrine — 315
  - Divisions of Buddhism — 316
  - Zen Buddhism — 319
- Taoism — 321
  - Tao Te Ching — 322
- Judaism — 324
  - Abraham and the Origins of Judaism — 326
  - The Torah — 326
  - The Ten Commandments — 327
  - The Hallowed Life — 328

- Islam — 329
  - The Life of Mohammed — 330
  - The Koran — 331
  - Divisions in Islam — 332
  - Sufis and Whirling Dervishes — 332
- Christianity — 334
  - The Life of Jesus — 334
  - the Gospels — 335
  - The Sermon on the Mount — 335
  - The Christian Church — 338
  - Divisions of Christianity — 339
- Spiritual Choices and Practices — 341
  - Choosing a Religion — 341
  - Practices to Strengthen the Spirit — 343
- Letting Spirit Heal — 346
  - Spiritual Decision — 348

Chapter 5. Spirit — 349

- Overview — 351
- Spiritual Meditations — 351
- One Year Spiritual Training — 353
- Reality — 353
- I am — 358
- One Spirit — 362
- Love — 364
- Trust — 364
- Error — 365
- Forgiveness — 372
- Love–Peace — 378
- Abundance — 380
- Present — 381
- Prayer — 381
- Listen — 384
- Purpose — 385
- Healing — 387
- One — 388
- Teacher — 389
- Daily Meditations — 390
- Recovery Work — 391

Index — 393

Acknowledgments

I would like the thank the following people for their help on this book:

- **Severine Singh** for her major work in researching and writing sections of this book.

- **Michelle Guirard** for her help in major editing of this book.

- **Peggy Gelpi** for her help in major editing of this book.

- **Hal Pluche** for his help on the artwork of this book.

- I also want to thank the following people for their assistance: Lolita Roy, Leslie Fensin and Fran Randal.

INTRODUCTION

Life: The Owner's Manual is so named because it offers all the information needed for the individual to design his or her own plan for a lifetime of good health, peace, happiness and holiness.

Introduction

When we think of health, we think of a joyous being in a strong body and a clear mind. However we also immediately think of its opposite: disease and its cures, doctors, medicines and hospitals.

We can assure ourselves of the basic needs to sustain our wellness: good food, adequate shelter, appropriate clothing and proper environment.

But do you know which foods provide what? What is a good diet? What is good nutrition? Which are nutrient-packed foods? What about our water: is it safe to drink?

Are there healthier ways to relate to each other that we can learn? Can we learn to maintain a personal inner space as well? How do we enrich our lives?

In other words how do we make sense of it all?

Let's face it. Today's world can appear fraught with problems: global air and water pollution, population explosion and many other problems. Yet through our own creativity we can resolve these situations and live in joy. Still, to begin to be joyful in the world, one must begin to be creative at home, by creating one's own environment to best fit one's own needs. In other words, one must begin creating one's own life-style by determining a sound plan for nutrition, health and all-around wellness.

Since the discovery of cells and molecules, it has become more and more evident that a human being is a complicated life form, which functions best when in total harmony. We are all microcosmic universes intermingling on a small planet. As the world changes around us, we too make constant changes, conscious or not, to adapt and maintain our physical, mental, emotional and spiritual balance. We function as a whole. At any one time, each part of our body is assisting the whole, and being helped by every other part.

Our minds are powerful and can control our bodies.

We feel better when we learn to think better and we end up looking better. A self-propelling system is started that ensures the individual wholeness and wellness. To achieve this, each of us needs to determine and draw up a constructive and practical program for living. But what about our spirit? Isn't the spirit a part of the whole as well? Can a sense of holiness, of communion with the divine, help us achieve overall well-being?

In his book *Motivation and Personality*, Abraham Maslow categorizes human needs into seven levels. Known collectively as the *Maslow Need Hierarchy*, the seven levels encompass physiological needs such as food and shelter, the very basic needs; needs for shelter and security, love, sex and social contacts; for self-actualization; and finally, needs for knowledge about life and God, as well as aesthetic needs. Therefore it seems that in order to achieve wholeness, we must determine a proper and practical way of satisfying each of these categories of needs, including the need for spiritual beliefs and practices.

Since the advent of rapid global communications, many religious paths have been opened to us. We may also choose from hundreds of foods offered to us each day for maintenance of our bodies, dozens of methods of exercises and sports, thousands of medicines and hundreds of natural therapies: therapies for the body, therapies for the mind; religions and cults for the spirit. How do we make an educated choice? How can we know what will work for us?

Most of us bounce through life haphazardly, guided by our likes and dislikes and our old familiar patterns. For instance, we know which foods we like to consume but we seldom follow a nutritional plan. We are influenced by advertisements and by our friends in our choices of habits, activities and foods. What if we could be truly and impartially informed – even in a general way – about the options available to us in each category of our life? What if we could construct for ourselves a truly unique and wholesome "life plan"?

This book aims to give such information and choices: information about nutrition and guidelines for planning a healthy nutrition program based on your particular needs and preferences; information and choices among major forms of physical exercises and fitness; choices to develop a sound, active, open and stress-free mind; information and choices for growing on the spiritual level.

Life: The Owner's Manual contains five parts:
- *Body*
- *Body-Mind*
- *Mind*
- *Mind-Spirit*
- *Spirit*

Using this book as a resource, each one of us can build his or her own unique system by choosing the most appropriate elements from among the many options available. The key here is *informed choices*. *Life: The Owner's Manual* offers general yet comprehensive information about the many elements impacting our lives.

This book can become a life-time source of vital information.

As you grow older, you may want to change some aspects of your life. The choice is ultimately yours, yet it will depend on many different elements: your personality, preferences, present health and needs, life-style, etc. This book is here to suggest alternatives and comment on their assets.

But of course in the end, the choices remain yours. We each travel a very unique path on this earth, and we must each take full responsibility for achieving the optimum results with the gifts we have been given. Choosing the right plan for a lifetime can lead you to wholeness and holiness.

CHAPTER 1
BODY

Nothing in the world exists that is more wonderful than the human body. Each and every anatomical structure of the body is perfectly designed to accomplish its own functions and tasks.

Overview of Chapter 1

Our entire body is made up of nearly 100 trillion living cells, which are invisible to the naked eye. These cells are grouped and structured into tissues that perform the various functions necessary to our growth and survival.
- The cells are composed primarily of four elements: hydrogen, oxygen, carbon and nitrogen. They also contain other trace elements.
- The four major elements in the cells combine in different ways to form water, carbohydrates, fats and proteins.
- Carbohydrates are used for energy, while fats store food and insulate the body.
- Proteins transport substances as well as information via the circulatory and lymph systems.
- Trace elements, of which there are about twenty, are present only in very small quantities, but they are vital to certain functions of the body. Calcium, iron, phosphorus and iodine are such trace elements.

There are four different kinds of body tissues:
- Protective (*epithelial*) tissue forms the surface of the skin, which protects the other tissues of the body.
- Connective tissues, such as tendons and ligaments, hold the other tissues in place.
- Muscular tissues form the different muscles of the body.
- Nerve tissues make up the different parts of the nervous system, including the brain and the spinal cord.

Hydrogen →
Oxygen →
Carbon → Cells → Tissues → Organs → Body
Nitrogen →
Trace Elements →

The body's organs are made of different kinds and combinations of tissues. The organs are arranged in systems which perform the complex functions necessary to human life. The major organ systems are the *respiratory, circulatory, gastro-intestinal, genito-urinary, nervous,* and *immune systems.* The health and functioning of the entire body depends on the health of the cells within these separate systems.

Nutrition

Food is the fuel that keeps the body running smoothly.

In 1734, an English sailor who had contracted scurvy was abandoned on an island in order to protect the rest of his crew from infection. With nothing to eat but grass, he eventually recovered. The sailor was rescued and returned to England, where his case caught the attention of Dr. James Lind. The first known study of nutrition began with Dr. Lind's subsequent investigation of the relationship between certain foods and scurvy.

Dr. Lind's work was ridiculed and many more sailors died. However, in 1753, soon after Dr. Lind's death, British sailors began taking lime juice aboard ship. They remained free of scurvy, and came to be known as "limeys."

The first known connection between foods and good health had been made. But it took the advent of modern chemistry to unravel the complex relationships between the nutrients in our foods and the growth and health of the human body, and today there is still much to learn about nutrition.

Most of us know the names of the major organs and systems of the body, the names of certain diseases, and many terms associated with health and nutrition. We know of proteins, fats, carbohydrates, vitamins and calories; we know that we need some of these things, and that we should avoid others. We know that fiber is good and cholesterol is bad. Yet the majority of us could not accurately define most of these terms. We would find it difficult to explain how the organs function, how the body processes nutrients, and how all of the workings of the body relate to each other.

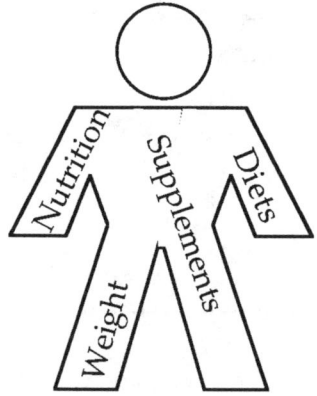

What is Proper Nutrition?

Nutrition involves all of the complex processes through which the body breaks down and utilizes the *nutrients*. These include:
- Intake of the necessary variety of foods in the right quantities and combinations.
- The proper digestion of those foods.
- Extraction of nutrients from the foods.
- Absorption of the nutrients into the bloodstream.
- Utilization of the nutrients by the individual cells.

These processes themselves depend upon a minimal presence of certain nutrients in the body, so that even a mild case of malnutrition cannot be instantly cured with the ingestion of a specific food or vitamin pill. A nutritional deficiency can only be remedied with a highly varied and nutritious diet and added supplements.

For optimal health, the essential nutrients need to be present at the same time and in the right amounts.

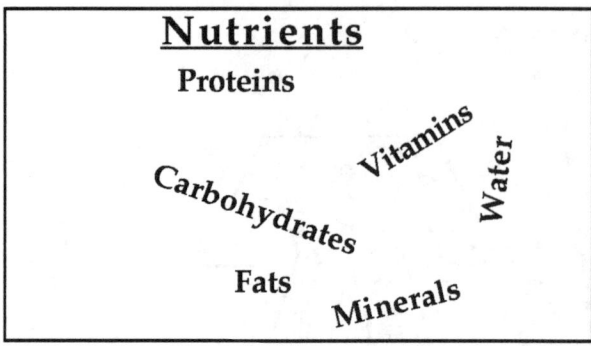

Fortunately, most of the foods we eat provide us with several nutrients at once. For instance, we all know that red meat is a great source of protein, but it also contains some fat, and is a good source of iron. Our task, therefore, is to eat a variety of nutritious foods each day, which together supply everything that we need in a balanced way.

Furthermore, we each have a unique body chemistry, lifestyle and range of tastes, which is why diets seldom work. So we need to make up our own diet based on a clear understanding of personal nutritional requirements, and the categories of foods that can fulfill those requirements, while keeping taste preferences in mind.

Proteins: Essential for Life

- Proteins build and repair cells in all the body's tissues.
- They help renew and fortify the tissues which form our bones, connective tissues and muscles.
- Proteins build antibodies to fight infections, and hormones and enzymes to regulate body functions.
- Proteins themselves are made up of twenty-two substances called *amino-acids*.
- Chains of tens of thousands of the twenty-two amino-acids, linked in different sequences, form the specific proteins which are needed by the body to grow, to function and to remain healthy.
- The body itself can manufacture most of these amino-acids itself but eight of the amino-acids cannot be made by the body. They must be supplied by the foods we eat. These are called *essential amino-acids*.

A *complete protein* is one which contains all of the essential amino-acids. Foods which have some essential

amino-acids are called *incomplete proteins*. These must be eaten together in certain combinations in order to form a complete protein.
* Complete proteins almost always come from animal products.
* Incomplete proteins generally come from vegetable sources.

Proteins	Incomplete Proteins
Meat	Grains (wheat, millet, corn, rice, etc.)
Fish	Beans
Eggs	Nuts (peanut butter, etc.)
Cheese	Seeds
Yogurt	Many Vegetables

Combinations that Make Complete Proteins
In many countries throughout the world where meat is not available on a daily basis, other foods are combined to provide complete protein:
* Corn or wheat flour tortilla with beans in Central America.
* Rice with beans almost everywhere.
* Soybean products with vegetables in India and China.
* Couscous (wheat) with vegetables and chick-peas in North Africa.

The recommended daily protein intake for average adults is 56 grams for males and 46 grams for females.

Protein is not stored as such by the body. We all need an adequate protein intake every day, otherwise the body will draw protein away from muscles and other tissues. However, it is also possible to consume too much protein.
* Excess protein is stored as fat, and can cause stress on the liver and kidneys. Americans tend to eat more protein than they need.
* Although animal proteins are complete proteins, they often contain high levels of saturated fat, which is believed to add to the cholesterol level and to thereby increase the risk of heart disease. Animal proteins should be consumed only in moderation.

- Vegetable proteins do not contain saturated fat, but need to be complemented by combining various incomplete proteins.

Energize with Carbohydrates

Carbohydrates are the main source of energy for the body. They are used to fuel the muscles, the nervous system and even the brain. They are divided in two categories: *simple* and *complex* carbohydrates. Complex carbohydrates also provide fiber, which is an essential part of any healthy diet.

Simple Carbohydrates
- Simple carbohydrates provide calories which are burned by the body for energy.
- All forms of sugars are simple carbohydrates: cane sugar, beet sugar, honey, syrups, and the sugars in fruits and vegetables.
- Simple sugars include *fructose* (from honey, fruits and vegetables), *maltose* (from milk products), *glucose* and *sucrose* (raw sugar and sorghum).

Why You Should Reduce Your Sugar Intake
- Simple sugars should be avoided as much as possible. They give a sudden boost of energy, but little else.
- The body's own store of minerals is depleted to help break down the carbonic acid created by simple sugars.
- If great quantities of simple sugars are eaten habitually, they may cause hypoglycemia, (a pre-condition to diabetes) and even kidney damage.

Complex Carbohydrates
- Complex carbohydrates are also known as *starches*.
- They take longer to digest than simple carbohydrates, and come from many sources: grains, beans, peas, seeds, and some vegetables, especially potatoes.
- Complex carbohydrates are much healthier than simple carbohydrates because they are digested more slowly and contain more nutrients.

- Whole grains, pastas, legumes and many vegetables provide not only complex carbohydrates, but also contain protein, some minerals and some vitamins.
- Most complex carbohydrates also contain *fiber*.

The Case for Fiber
- Fiber is plant material that the body cannot digest. It is also known as *roughage*.
- Fiber helps elimination by adding bulk to the stools and removing some of the toxic matter in the intestines.
- When cooked, vegetables retain their fiber.
- In cultures in which a lot of roughage is naturally present in the food, there is a very low rate of colon cancer.
- When whole grains are refined (into white flour, for instance), the fiber is taken out, along with most of the nutrients. So even if the vitamins and minerals are added later (the flour is then called enriched), the grain is still less nutritious than the unrefined product.

Complex carbohydrates are essential to a good diet: they provide long-lasting energy, and in their natural form, provide adequate roughage as well.

However, to simply add wheat bran to everything one cooks is not sufficient to provide the different kinds of fiber which we need. A wide variety of grains, vegetables and beans is necessary for good health.

Different Types of Fats
- We need a certain amount of fat for protection and insulation of the body and maintenance of adequate body temperature.
- Fats contain some fat-soluble vitamins, such as vitamins A, D, E and K.
- Fats provide the elements needed for their own digestion, such as *cholesterol, lecithin* and vitamin E.
- Too much fat in the diet can be detrimental to one's health. Excess of fats has been linked to breast and colon cancers.
- Excess fat also contributes to thickening of the lymph fluid, which causes it to become more sluggish.
- Controlling weight or maintaining the ideal weight is difficult with a high-fat diet.

- There are several kinds of fats present in foods: *saturated fats, polyunsaturated fats* and *monounsaturated fats.*

Saturated Fats
- Fats which turn solid when stored at room temperature are saturated fats. This includes animal fats such as lard, butter, and some vegetable fats.
- Saturated fats increase the level of cholesterol in the bloodstream. Cholesterol deposits can lead to clogging of the arteries, which increases the risk of heart disease.
- No oil derived from plants contains any cholesterol. (See *Cholesterol.*)

Degree of Saturation in some Vegetable Oils

Cottonseed oil	26%	Palm kernel oil	86%
Palm oil	51%	Coconut oil	92%

Polyunsaturated Fats
- Most vegetable oils which remain in liquid form at room temperature are polyunsaturated fats.
- Some polyunsaturated oils are safflower, sunflower, wheat germ, corn and soybean oils.
- Eating some small amount of polyunsaturated fats might be necessary since they are good sources of linoleic acid and linolenic acid which are vital to healthy cell membranes.

Monounsaturated Fats
- There is evidence that monounsaturated fats are the healthiest. Still, it is best to avoid large intake of any fats.
- Some monounsaturated oils are olive oil, peanut oil, avocado oil and canola oil (rape seed).

Is there a Right Kind of Fat?
- Use cold-pressed, polyunsaturated or monounsaturated oils.
- Beware of "partially hydrogenated" vegetable oils. (See *Processed Foods.*)
- Olive oil has special healing properties because of its potassium and calcium content.
- All animal products have some saturated fats and some cholesterol. Fish, however, is the lowest in fats and cholesterol, and contains fatty acids that have been

shown to help break down cholesterol. (See *The Case for Fish*.)

Fats and Calories

One gram of fat is roughly equal to 9 calories. If a food contains 10 grams of fat, this equals about 90 calories. So, if this food contains a total of 100 calories, then 90% of these calories come from fat.

| Grams of Fat x 9 = Calories of Fat |
| Calories of Fat ÷ Total Calories = % of Calories from Fat |

How You Can Reduce Fat in Your Diet
- Meats labeled "prime cut" are the most tender, but also contain the most fat. Choose meats labeled "good."
- Cut away all visible fat from steak, roast and chops. Take the skin off of poultry.
- Stew, braise, or sauté meats in seasoned stock instead of oil or butter.
- Marinate foods in stock, herbs, wines or fruit juices instead of oil.
- Choose canned fish packed in water rather than oil.
- Add tomatoes, onions, garlic, peppers and herbs to flavor, instead of rich cream or cheese sauces.
- Steam vegetables instead of frying in fat.
- Refrigerate stews, stocks and soups so you can skim the solid fat layer before re-heating to serve.

Understand Cholesterol

A 1% drop in a person's total cholesterol level can lower the chance of developing heart disease by 2%!

- A high level of cholesterol in the blood – 200MG or above – appears to be associated with fat deposits in the arteries, which can cause blockage and lead to heart problems.
- Yet cholesterol is an essential element in the human body. It is a steroid that is present in every cell of the body.

- Cholesterol is necessary for the digestion of fats, proper brain function, menstruation, and the production of sex hormones.
- The body manufactures some of the cholesterol it needs, but the rest must be obtained from the foods we eat.
- Cholesterol is found mostly in animal products.
- If your blood cholesterol level is below 200, you can safely eat high-cholesterol foods in moderation.
- If your cholesterol level is over 200, your doctor should test you for levels of good cholesterol, known as *high-density lipoprotein* (HDL), and bad cholesterol, which includes *low-density lipoprotein* (LDL) and *very low-density lipoprotein* (VLDL). These last two forms of cholesterol differ in the way they combine with proteins as they pass through the bloodstream.

High Cholesterol Foods	Lower Cholesterol Substitutes
egg yolks	egg whites
pork meats and bacon	tofu and beans
luncheon meats	sliced turkey breast
organ meats (liver, heart, kidney)	fish (perch, cod, haddock)
lard and animal fat	liquid vegetable oils
whole milk, cheese, butter, cream	low-fat dairy products, soy milk

The Relationship between Fat and Cholesterol

- A product can be cholesterol-free and still have a high fat content. Only animal products contain cholesterol, but many other products, such as potato chips and other snack foods, are loaded with saturated fats.
- Monounsaturated oils such as olive oil and canola oil can help lower bad cholesterol levels, but these must take the place of (rather than add to) other fats in the diet.
- Saturated fats in the diet prevent the reduction of cholesterol levels in the blood.
- Cholesterol levels depend on many factors, including genetic predisposition.

Understanding Labels: Cholesterol
- Cholesterol-free: less than 2 mg per serving.
- Low cholesterol: less than 20 mg per serving.
- Cholesterol-reduced: the food has been reformulated or processed to reduce cholesterol levels by 75% or more.

Ways To Reduce Your Cholesterol
- Exercise is first and foremost. Regular, active exercise helps control cholesterol levels and helps decrease your levels of LDL and VLDL.
- Reduce high-cholesterol foods (meat, eggs, shellfish, saturated oils).
- Eliminate smoking and drinking. Smoking has a serious detrimental effect on cholesterol levels.
- Maintain a proper weight for your height and frame.
- Eat more fish. Certain fatty acids from fish oils (especially from mackerel, salmon, sardines, tuna, trout, pompano and mullet) help lower blood cholesterol levels. (See *The Case for Fish*.)
- Eat whole grains and vegetables for adequate fiber.
- Eat more vegetables and fruits with pectin (apples, grapefruits).
- Supplement your diet with lecithin (available from health food stores) which helps break down cholesterol.

The American Heart Association recommends that you avoid cholesterol altogether.

Vitamins and Minerals

To function well and remain healthy, our bodies need a specific balance of all the minimum required nutrients to be present at the same time.

Even though vitamins and minerals are needed only in small quantities, their functions are vital. A few millionths of a gram of vitamin B12, for instance, can prevent pernicious anemia.

The more varied our food sources, the more likely we are to meet our individual requirements of vitamins and minerals.

Most nutrients are destroyed or depleted when our food is processed, refined, handled excessively or overcooked. By the time our food reaches the table, it may have very little nutritional value. We may therefore choose to supplement our diet with a multi-vitamin, multi-mineral tablet.

Supplements should never take the place of a sound and varied nutritional plan.

Supplements have only been developed for the fifty essential nutrients which have been identified. It is very probable that we need and get other essential elements from our foods. This is one reason why it may be best to choose a supplement derived entirely from natural sources, as opposed to a chemically synthesized supplement.

Understand the Vitamins

Vitamins are necessary to the formation and strength of the body tissues. They can be found mostly in fruits and vegetables.
- Vitamin C and the B vitamins dissolve in water. Excess quantities are excreted in the urine, so these vitamins must be replaced on a daily basis.
- Vitamins A, D, E and K are fat-soluble and are stored in the fatty tissues. If vitamins A and D are present in the body in excess, they can become toxic.

Vitamin A
- The human body can manufacture a certain amount of vitamin A by using *beta-carotene*, a substance found in fruits and vegetables such as squash, carrots, yams (yellow vegetables), cantaloupes, apricots, spinach, broccoli, okra, mustard greens, alfalfa and cranberries.
- Vitamin A is also present in eggs, liver and fish liver oils.
- It is essential to the formation and health of bones, skin, hair, nails, eyes, mucous tissues, blood, and milk for nursing mothers. It may offer some protection against heart disease.
- Recommended daily intake of vitamin A is 5,000 IUs.

- More than 25,000 IUs daily can cause liver damage, blurred vision, headaches and hair loss.

B Vitamins

There are several B vitamins, but they work as a team.

B1: Known as *thiamin*, it is found in whole grains, brewer's yeast, legumes, nuts, beef and liver.
- B1 is essential for the production of energy from complex carbohydrates and for the strength of the heart, muscles and nerves.
- Recommended daily intake of vitamin B1 is 2 mg.

B2: Known as *riboflavin*, it is obtained from beef, eggs, yogurt and other dairy products, brewer's yeast and vegetables.
- It helps release energy and is necessary for healthy eyes, skin and hair.
- Recommended daily intake of vitamin B2 is 2 mg.

B3: Known as *niacin*, it is obtained from fish, liver, kidneys, whole grains, legumes and peanuts.
- B3 prevents pellagra, and may prevent cancer. It helps lower cholesterol, if taken in large doses.
- Note: excessively large doses can cause liver damage.
- Recommended daily intake of vitamin B3 is 20 mg.

B5: Known as *pantothenic acid*, it is found in liver, kidney, fish, eggs, brewer's yeast, legumes, vegetables and the royal jelly of bees.
- It keeps hair and skin healthy and helps the body cope with stress.
- Recommended daily intake of vitamin B5 is 20 mg.

B6: Known as *pyridoxine*, it is contained in liver, eggs, milk, brewer's yeast, cereals, legumes, nuts, vegetables and bananas.
- It helps release the amino-acids from protein, and also aids in the production of blood, and in the absorption of vitamin B3.
- Recommended daily intake of vitamin B6 is 3 mg.
- Note: more than 400 mg daily can cause numbness.

B12: This vitamin is found in liver, fish, dairy products and brewer's yeast.
- It is essential for the production of blood and nervous tissues.
- Recommended daily intake of vitamin B12 is 2 mcg.

Folic Acid: Folic acid is found in liver, legumes, dark green leafy vegetables and fruits.
- It works in conjunction with vitamin B12 and is essential for the production and health of the blood cells. It may prevent cervical cancer.
- Low levels of folic acid are often associated with certain birth defects.

Biotin: This B vitamin is found in liver, kidney, legumes, nuts, yeast and some vegetables.
- It helps metabolize (draw the energy from) the foods we eat, and aids in the digestion of fats.

Vitamin C
- Also known as *ascorbic acid*, vitamin C is found in most vegetables and fruits, particularly citrus fruits and potatoes.
- It is essential to the maintenance of strong teeth and bones, as well as healthy skin and gums. Vitamin C helps the body fight infection, fatigue and stress and may offer some protection against cancer.
- The RDA of vitamin C is 60 mg.
- Too much vitamin C can cause diarrhea and stomach pains.

Vitamin D
- The body manufactures its own vitamin D when exposed to sunlight.
- It is found in fish, cod liver oil and eggs. It is also added to pasteurized milk.
- Vitamin D helps build strong bones and teeth by maintaining the right levels of calcium and phosphorus.
- The RDA of vitamin D is 400 IUs.

Vitamin E
- Known as *tocopherol*, it allows and increases the absorption of vitamin C and fats.
- It promotes healthy cells in general, and healthy skin cells in particular. Also vitamin E is a key element in the proper functioning of the reproductive system, and it helps strengthen the immune system.
- The RDA of vitamin E is 10 mg.

Vitamin K
- It is usually produced by the body itself, by the bacteria present in the intestines.
- It is also found in liver, whole grains, peas, leafy green vegetables, cabbage, cauliflower, yogurt and molasses.
- Vitamin K is a key element affecting the ability of the body's blood to clot.
- The RDA of vitamin K is 60 mcg.

Understand the Minerals

There are seven *macro-minerals*: potassium, chlorine, sodium, calcium, phosphorus, magnesium and sulfur.
- Some of the macro-minerals help form *acids* in the body, while others form *bases*; together they maintain the cell acid or alkaline levels, which in turn allow particular enzymes to be formed, released and activated. For instance, sodium is concentrated in the extra-cellular fluid, while potassium is contained within the cells. By remaining in balance, these two minerals work together to regulate the passage of nutrients into the cells.
- Acid-forming minerals come mostly from whole grains, meat, poultry and fish. They are calcium, potassium, magnesium and sodium.
- Chlorine, phosphorus and sulfur, which form bases, come mostly from vegetables and fruits.
- Dairy products contain both base-forming and acid-forming minerals.

Trace elements, so named because the body needs only traces of them, are just as important as the other minerals described above.
- The body uses at least fourteen different trace minerals.
- A trace of iodine is needed to prevent goiter, a malfunction of the thyroid gland.
- Fluoride helps bones and teeth remain strong.
- Selenium is now believed to play a major role in cancer prevention.

Some essential minerals are present in most foods, and many foods contain several of these minerals. Two minerals which are needed in the body in fairly large quantities are calcium and iron. Potassium and sulfur are required on a daily basis.

Calcium

- During childhood, our bodies deposit calcium and other minerals into our bones, which helps the bones grow bigger and stronger. Eventually the mineral deposits balance with our body's needs.
- As older adults, we begin to draw more calcium out of our bones than we add. If we continue this trend unchecked and lose over 30% of our bone mass, we develop *osteoporosis*, a brittle bone condition for which there is no cure.
- Our bones contain 99% of the body's calcium.
- Our bones need calcium daily for the rest of our lives.

> **Osteoporosis means "porous bones."**
> Even though it is normal to lose some bone mass as we age, certain groups are at greater risk of developing osteoporosis. Elderly women are at especially high risk.

There are many ways to increase your calcium intake:
- Drink plenty of milk. One eight-ounce glass of milk supplies one third of the average daily calcium requirement.
- Eat other dairy products such as yogurt, cheddar cheese, cottage cheese and ice-cream, which are also good sources of protein. Choose low-fat dairy products.
- Eat lots of dark green vegetables from the cabbage family. Spinach while also rich in calcium, contains other minerals which decrease the body's absorption of calcium.
- Make sure you have enough vitamin D, which facilitates absorption of calcium. A little sun every day or a vitamin D supplement can help.
- Menopausal women are especially at risk for calcium loss and may choose to go on estrogen replacement therapy (ERT) within one year of their last period. (See *Menopause*.)

You can also take active measures to prevent calcium loss:
- Eliminate alcohol, cigarettes and caffeine, all of which rob the body of various minerals.
- Cut down on animal proteins, which bind with the calcium in the digestive tract.

- Avoid soft drinks. The phosphate they contain leaches calcium from the body.

> *The average calcium intake per day for older America is about 500 mg. However the recommended average intake per day is 500 to 1200 mg.*

Iron
- Iron is essential for the manufacture of red blood cells and the transportation of oxygen to the cells. Lack of iron leads to *anemia*, one symptom of which is fatigue. An excess of iron may be associated with certain heart ailments.
- Iron can be obtained from meat, fish and poultry, as well as from whole grains, dark green leafy vegetables, dried fruits, raisins and nuts.
- Iron can also be obtained from cooking in cast iron pots.
- Vitamin C facilitates the body's absorption of iron.
- Women need more iron than men, because of menstruation.
- **Note: Too much iron may be bad for the heart.**

Recommended Daily Iron Intake		
	Age	Mg Daily
Men	11 to 18 years	12
	19 and older	10
Women	11 to 50 years	15
	51 and older	10
	During pregnancy	30

Potassium
- Potassium is present in rice, wheat germ, almonds, spinach, lettuce, celery, figs, papaya, cherries, watermelon and bananas.
- Potassium promotes muscle strength and mental activity.
- Potassium counteracts excess sodium.

Sulfur
- Sulfur is found in beans, nuts, onions, garlic, cabbage and watercress.

- Sulfur is needed for normal bone and muscle development and also to help the blood to clot normally.

What are Antioxidants?

Antioxidants are certain vitamins and minerals that seem to protect you from cancer and heart disease, and may even slow the aging process. They work by combining with and neutralizing the free radicals which might otherwise damage your cells. The antioxidants include:
- Vitamin A (beta-carotene)
- Vitamin C
- Vitamin E
- The mineral selenium

Should We Take Vitamin Pills?

Two thirds of Americans use supplements.

The Food and Drug Administration (FDA) has established recommended daily allowances (RDA) for protein and 19 minerals and vitamins. The RDA was established for application to population groups and not to individuals. Yet today it is widely used by food manufacturers as their basis for establishing nutritional standards. Using supplements at the RDA levels is perfectly safe.
- Some experts recommend supplement levels far higher than the RDA.
- Pregnant women often need extra iron, as do most women during their child-bearing years because of menstruation.
- People who are very inactive and therefore cannot eat much food will definitely need supplements.
- People who take medicines that interfere with the absorption of nutrients may need supplementation on a regular basis. This often applies to elderly persons who are frequently medicated.

Remember RDA guidelines do not apply to infants, children under the age of four, pregnant or lactating women, or persons with other special needs.

Guidelines for Vitamins

The following table is suggested guidelines from various authorities for supplementation of vitamins and some minerals:

	Dr. Roger J. Williams	"Complete Book of Vitamins"	Jeffrey Bland
Vitamin A	7,500 IU	10,000 IU	2,500-10,000 IU
Vitamin D	500 IU	400 IU	200-1,000 IU
Vitamin C	100 mg	100-200 mg	100-6,000 mg
Vitamin B1	2 mg	10 mg	5-100 mg
Vitamin B2	2 mg	2 mg	5-100 mg
Vitamin B3	20 mg	10 mg	10-1000 mg
Vitamin B6	3 mg	5-10 mg	10-1000 mg
Vitamin B12	5 mcg	6-8 mcg	10-1000 mcg
Vitamin E	40 IU	100 IU	50-1000 IU
Inositol	100 mg		
Choline	100 mg		
Calcium	300 mg	600-800 mg	500-1,200 mg
Phosphate	250 mg		
Magnesium	200 mg	400 mg	300-600 mg
Cobalt	0.1 mg		
Copper	2 mg	2 mg	2-5 mg
Iodine	100 mcg	100-150 mcg	
Iron	10 mg	10-18 mg	10-30 mg
Manganese	1 mg	2 mg	2-10 mg
Molybdenum	200 mcg		5-200 mcg
Zinc	5 mg	30 mg	10-30 mg

We only know of 50 nutrients that the body needs, but it is most probable that others – yet unknown – come with most unprocessed foods. Balanced meals with a variety of foods is the only sure way to obtain all the nutrients needed each day. Supplements are just what their name implies.
- Take your supplements with meals, unless otherwise directed. It is easier for the body to absorb vitamins A, D and E when they are combined with the fats in your foods.
- Supplements are not a replacement for nutritious meals.
- Remember that some supplements taken in large amounts may be harmful.

Processed Foods

In the last hundred years or so, packaging techniques and chemical additives have been developed to preserve food and to keep it free of bacteria and parasites. In addition to chemical preservatives, the foods we eat may contain ingredients such as emulsifiers, thickeners, sweeteners, and artificial flavors and colors. Every day new chemical additives are developed and tested.

While food preservation and safety provide us with a tremendous variety of foods throughout the year, many refining processes do nothing more than deplete the natural nutrients of the foods for the sake of appearance or taste. Furthermore, our bodies have had no time to adapt to the multitude of additives we encounter, and do not always possess the enzymes necessary to break down these new chemical compounds. These chemical additives may affect our health. We do not yet know the long term effects of many food additives.

It would be very difficult to find a food which has not been processed in some way. While processing often serves to make food safer, more widely available, longer-lasting, more convenient, or more appealing in some way, it can also deplete or destroy the nutritional value of the food. Of course, some processing is unavoidable, unless we grow all of our own food.

- Vegetables and fruits are routinely harvested before they are fully ripe, as they will be shipped long distances and travel better while unripe. Yet for most vegetables and fruits, the mineral and vitamin contents increase most during the maturation period, and under the natural action of the sun.
- Vegetables and fruits lose nutrients as they are stored, handled repeatedly, and moved through different temperatures and humidity levels.
- Freeze-drying, dehydrating and cooking also deplete the nutritional value of foods. Potatoes, for example, are rich in vitamin C, but instant potato flakes have no vitamin C. Reconstituted fruit juices and frozen concentrates are also a poor source of nutrients.

It is always preferable to shop for vegetables and fruits that are locally produced and in season.

Gone is the Goodness of Grains
- Wheat loses over two thirds of its vitamins B1, B2 and B3, and as much as 90% of its mineral content as it is milled into white flour.
- The white flour which is left has lost its germ (the core of the wheat grain) and its bran (the outer shell), the parts which contain most of the nutrients.
- White flour has no dietary fiber at all. (See *Fiber*.)
- Rice loses over two thirds of its vitamin B1 when the outer brown layer is milled.
- Corn loses most of its nutrients through refining, becoming particularly deficient in vitamin B3.

Fats
- Fats and oils lose their nutrients quite easily during processing.
- Oils are often extracted by a combination of heat and pressure, or by chemical extraction that involves the addition of such compounds as hexane, benzene, ethyl ether, carbon compounds and methylene chloride. The solvent is then separated from the oil by steaming.
- After extraction, the oil is further treated with heat, a lye solution, an antioxidant, and more heat. These processes destroy most or all of the vitamins A, E, K and B12, and the trace elements such as copper, cobalt, manganese and chromium that were present in the original whole fatty seeds.

The Case Against Hydrogenated Oil
The worst case of processing of oils results in what is called "partially hydrogenated vegetable oil." In this process, the oil is heated in the presence of hydrogen gas and a nickel catalyst so that the oil becomes saturated with hydrogen atoms. This results in a firm product which is usually sold as margarine or shortening.

We can find hydrogenated oils in nearly every bread, cake, pie, bun, donut, pastry, cracker, cookie, muffin, cereal, and almost every other prepared food we purchase.
- Hydrogenated oils have no cholesterol, but they break down very differently in the body than do saturated oils.
- They have been proven to increase the risks of heart attack, high blood pressure and arterial disease.

- Another dangerous aspect of hydrogenated oils is that they release free radicals in the body. Free radicals are known to damage cells and start chain reactions that may cause cancerous growths. (See *Cancer*.)

Minimize Food Processing

It is necessary to do some handling of food, as we cannot grow our own foods in urban areas. Washing and peeling produce does improve appearance, as well as removing dirt, toxic pesticides and bacteria. Cooking may improve texture and taste. Yet even the simplest steps in food processing such as slicing and peeling can deplete the essential nutrients in our foods:

- Milk loses vitamins A and B2 when exposed to light. It is best to buy milk in cartons or opaque containers.
- Oils should be tightly closed and refrigerated, otherwise they will lose vitamin A and fatty acids.
- Most fruits and vegetables are best eaten raw. Boiled fruits may lose up to two thirds of their vitamin C. When you must cook them, light steaming is best.
- Wash, peel and slice only when necessary and just before serving.
- Quick sautéing in light oil is better than deep frying at very high temperatures.

Irradiated Foods

Irradiation is used as a means to disinfect foods: insects, bacteria and parasites are destroyed by irradiation. While irradiated food is not radioactive, and the procedure has been accepted by the Food and Drug Administration, there is major controversy over its safety. Studies so far have remained inconclusive.

- Irradiated food cannot be eaten within twenty-four hours after the process is performed.
- The irradiation process requires the addition of certain chemicals, and causes the loss of certain vitamins.

Food Additives

Most of our foods absorb harmful additives while they are being grown, in the form of chemical fertilizers and pesticides. Preservatives and other additives are also used in processing most foods. The two most common food additives are sweeteners and salt.

In the last twenty years, consumer awareness has prodded the food industry to limit its use of preservatives and other additives. Over ten coloring agents have been banned since 1960.

Unfortunately, food additives can be used at the discretion of the manufacturer, unless there is conclusive proof that they cause harm to animals or humans. The manufacturer is not required to show that the additives carry any nutritional benefits.

Fertilizers and Pesticides

Less than 5% of the foods that reach our tables are free of pesticides.

- Many of these chemical compounds are proven to be carcinogenic to laboratory animals.
- Even those that are found to be non-carcinogenic increase the body's need for vitamins.

Preservatives

Preservatives prevent food from spoiling and becoming toxic, so that we can keep them on our shelves and in our refrigerators for days, weeks, or even months.
- Various methods of preserving foods, such as smoking, salting, and dehydrating, have been widely used throughout human history.
- Today *nitrites* are used as preservatives for lunch-meats, sausages, bacon and other meats and foods. Nitrites help destroy the spores that cause botulism, a potentially fatal condition. Nitrites also release a red color in meat which makes it look more fresh.
- Nitrites are not harmless to humans. They can combine with other elements in the human body (such as tobacco, some medicines, or even saliva) to become carcinogenic.
- Other commonly used preservatives are *sulfites*, which prevent cut fruits and vegetables from turning brown. Many restaurants and grocery stores use sulfites to keep cut produce looking fresh, especially in salad bars. Frozen potatoes are also usually treated with sulfites.

- Some individuals are highly sensitive to the sulfite compounds. Sulfites have been proven to be directly responsible for several human deaths.

Sweeteners

Sweeteners are added to all sorts of foods, including canned vegetables and even some meat products. Even products labeled "all natural" may contain considerable amounts of sugar. There is very little nutritional benefit to be gained from any type of sweetener, and most are detrimental to your health.

What's the Problem with Sugar?

Sugar is added to thousands of food products. The average consumption for Americans now tops 100 pounds per person per year. Sugar content is not always listed on food labels. It can simply be included in the total carbohydrate content. Sugar is present in many products which we consume every day.

Sugar is routinely added to condiments, milk products, cheese foods, soft drinks, vegetable juices, baby foods, alcoholic beverages, baby formula, canned vegetables and fruits, sauces, and many other products.

Simple sugars should be avoided as much as possible. They give a sudden boost of energy, but little else. The body's own store of minerals is depleted to help break down the carbonic acid created by simple sugars.

Over-consumption of sugar can lead to the following:
- Vitamin and mineral deficiencies.
- If large quantities of simple sugars are eaten on a regular basis, *hypoglycemia*, a pre-condition to diabetes, may result.
- Kidney damage is another possible result of long-term, excessive consumption of simple sugars.

The Case for Honey
- Honey is over one third fructose, which is released slowly into the bloodstream.
- It is easy to digest, yet packed with nutrients: B vitamins, vitamin C, and at least a dozen minerals. Bee pollen is rich in protein, and is also useful to hay fever suffers by desensitizing them to the pollen that is in the air. Always begin with a small amount and increase during the following days if there is no adverse reaction.

Chapter 1 Body

- Because honey comes with its own nutrients, it does not need to deplete the body's supply during digestion.
- It provides an even greater store of energy if used with whole grains in breads or cereals.
- Honey is twice as sweet as sugar, so the amount used should be cut in half in all recipes.
- Babies under one year of age should not be given honey.

Alternative Sweeteners
- Nutritive sweeteners or caloric sweeteners include *fructose* (from fruits and honey), *sorbitol, manitol* and *xyletol*.
- Low-calorie sweeteners include *aspartame*, which was approved by the FDA in 1981. One trade name is Equal, and it is listed on labels as Nutra-sweet. Aspartame is made of two amino-acids, and is digested like a protein. It can lose its sweetness if heated.
- Corn syrup and *dextrose* are the third and fourth most highly consumed additives in the U.S. The average yearly consumption for corn syrup is eight and a half pounds per person, and four pounds per person for dextrose.

Too Much Salt?
Salt is the second most highly consumed additive, after sugar. The average American consumption of salt is now fifteen pounds per person per year. While we need 1.1 grams to 3.3 grams of salt each day, the average diet provides each of us with 10 to 20 grams per day.
- There is enough natural sodium in our foods for us to omit all added salt during cooking or at the table.
- Too much salt can raise the blood pressure to dangerous levels.
- There are some good salt substitutes at health food stores that combine herbs, kelp or seaweed, and other spices.
- Only pure sea salt should be used, as other types often contain additives such as aluminum or dextrose. Real sea salt also contains trace minerals from the sea such as potassium and iodine.

Hidden Salt
Salt is not always mentioned as such on a label. It is included in all of the following:

Brine (water and salt)	Sodium alginate
Sodium benzoate	Sodium caseinate
Sodium glutamate	Monosodium glutamate
Sodium hydroxide	Sodium phosphate
Sodium propionate	Sodium sulfite

Excess Salt

The following foods usually contain very large quantities of salt:

Potato chips	Pretzels	Crackers
Salad dressing	Salted nuts	Pastrami
Olives	Sausages	Pickles
Mustard	Soy sauce	Corn chips

Other Additives

Artificial flavorings and colors are a food additive with no nutritional value whatsoever. Many artificial coloring agents and other additives currently in use may even be harmful to humans:

- Blue #1 and #2, citrus red #2, green #3, red #3 and #40, yellow #5 and #6 can be found in products in your local supermarket.
- Yellow #6 should definitely be avoided whenever possible.
- Red #40 and yellow #5 are not currently known to be harmful in small quantities. However, it is important to note that they tend to be found in products which people consume in large quantities, such as soft drinks, candies, desserts and baked goods.
- Artificial flavorings, brominated vegetable oils, BHA and BHT (two antioxidants that keep oils from turning rancid), saccharin, sodium nitrate and sodium nitrite should all be avoided.

Dozens more additives are still being investigated as possible health risks. It is best to avoid all additives and preservatives whenever possible.

You can buy a product that says "all natural" and that is still loaded with additives: sugar, salt, corn syrup, processed oils and others.

Another generally unsuspected danger to humans comes from beef, poultry, and some other meats. Livestock and poultry are routinely fed hormones and antibiotics. Many of these animals develop bacteria which becomes resistant to the antibiotics. These new, more resistant bacteria can be passed on to human consumers.

Understanding Labels: Additives
- The ingredients are listed on the label in the descending order of weight in the contents.
- All additives must be listed, except in butter, cheese and ice-cream.
- Yellow #5 must be listed in all products, because it causes allergic reactions in some individuals.
- Look out for several sugars which, added together, make up the main ingredient in total weight.
- Nutritional information may be given, but it may not be very helpful. For example, carbohydrates may not be listed separately as simple sugars and complex carbohydrates.
- Fiber content may include crude fiber and dietary fiber listed together, though we can only use the dietary fiber.
- Beware of serving sizes which are not standardized: some products have a one cup serving size, while others provide information based on a four ounce or even a two ounce serving size, making nutritional comparisons difficult.
- Beware of claims that advertise "only one gram of sodium," or any other substance that would normally be measured in milligrams. A gram of sodium is quite a lot!
- A product's name may include the word "natural" because it describes one of its ingredients, yet the total product may still contain preservatives or other additives.

Whole Foods and Health Foods

Whole foods are, in essence, unrefined foods. Many foods need to be shelled, peeled, seeded or cored to be edible, but whole foods are processed as little as possible, so that they stay close to their natural state, and therefore

retain more of their nutrients. Brown rice is a whole food, as are oranges, bananas, whole wheat flour and rolled oats.
- By definition, whole foods contain no preservatives or other additives.
- They are always preferable to highly refined or processed foods.

What are Health Foods?

The term "health food" refers to whole foods, or foods that keep you healthy. But of course, a great variety of good foods should keep you healthy. However, it is fair to say that health food stores usually provide nutritious products such as whole-grain cookies, breads and cereals; products sweetened with fructose (sugar from fruits) or honey instead of refined sugar; cold-pressed, polyunsaturated and monounsaturated oils; organic meat and produce, and more. Read the labels and determine the best foods for you.

Organic Foods

Organic foods are plant and animal products that have been grown and harvested without the use of fertilizers, pesticides or any chemical additives.
- Organic produce almost always tastes better, especially if it has been allowed to ripen naturally before being picked.
- Organic produce often looks more like real garden vegetables and fruits: they may be of uneven sizes and colors, without the perfect look of conformity achieved by supermarket produce.
- In general, the soil may only be fertilized naturally (with mulch and manure), and the land must remain free of chemicals for several years, before it can be fully restored and its produce considered organic.
- Whenever buying organic produce or animal products from a market, you can inquire about its source and area of provenance. There are certification programs for organic farmers, and you can ask to see proof of certification.

What's for Supper Tonight?

There are many things that you can do to improve your diet:

- Avoid eating only one large meal per day. Eat two or three balanced meals. Frequent, small meals help prevent peptic ulcers, help keep your blood sugar levels more constant, and keep you from getting hungry.
- Identify your specific needs by carefully assessing your state of health, environment and life-style.
- Eat slowly and chew well, to avoid over-eating and to aid digestion.
- Eat with family or friends at least once a day. A pleasant meal is more satisfying.
- Construct your diet around high nutrient-density foods.
- Include high-fiber foods such as whole grains, beans, fresh vegetables and fruits.
- Use brown rice and whole grains breads, crackers and cereals.
- Replace iceberg lettuce with dark leafy vegetables.
- Choose foods that are fresh, unrefined and unprocessed.
- Eat a wide variety of foods.
- Keep skins on potatoes and other fruits and vegetables.
- Reduce salt by one third in all recipes. Replace with a natural substitute.
- Use only low-fat dairy products.
- Use yogurt in place of sour cream or mayonnaise.
- Cut skin and fat off of meats and poultry.
- Eat different types of fish two or three times a week.
- Add cooked beans, seeds or nuts to salads.
- Learn to read and understand food labels.
- Avoid empty calorie foods.
- Avoid highly processed or refined foods.
- Limit your consumption of commercially prepared foods.
- Avoid hydrogenated oils.
- Use less sugar, and substitute with honey.
- Do not overcook foods.

The Case For Fish

- Fish is very easily digested. It is high in protein and other essential nutrients, and provides essential fatty acids.
- Fish is low in overall fat, particularly in saturated fat, and is low in calories.
- Fish oils appear to lower the risk of heart disease, based on discoveries made about fifteen years ago by two Danish doctors. They found that Eskimos, whose diet is

very high in animal fats, nevertheless have a very low rate of heart disease. This is thought to be due to *Omega-3 Essential Fatty Acids* (EFA), which are found in fish and some marine plants. The addition of Omega-3 EFA to a low fat, high fiber diet has actually been shown to decrease LDL (bad cholesterol) and increase HDL (good cholesterol), as well as reduce blood triglycerides and diastolic blood pressure.
- Fresh water fish from our lakes and rivers can be contaminated by organic or industrial pollutants.
- Deep sea fish and small fish are the least likely to be toxic.

The Case For Eggs
- Eggs may well be the most complete food available to humans.
- They provide complete proteins, vitamins, minerals and unsaturated fatty acids.
- Vegetarians in particular can benefit from a small weekly intake of eggs, which are high in vitamin B12.
- People with high cholesterol levels can refrain from eating the yolk of the egg, and just eat the whites.

> Because of increasing risks of *salmonella poisoning*, it is recommended that all eggs be cooked until well done.

The Case For and Against Dairy Products
- All dairy products (milk, cheese, yogurt) constitute a good source of complete protein.
- They are also rich in calcium, and contribute to the formation of strong and healthy bones.
- Cultured milks like buttermilk, kefir, and yogurt are easier to digest than other milk products.
- Yogurt and kefir also contain bacteria which is beneficial to the colon (*acidophilus*). Anyone taking antibiotics should eat a small amount of yogurt each day. Some yogurt, however, is made with gelatin, and does not contain the live bacteria. Look on the label for the following words: live bacteria, acidophilus, or viable culture.
- Dairy products can provoke allergic reactions.

- Milk products contribute to the formation of mucus, and should be avoided when there is a problem with congestion.

The Most Nutritious Vegetables and Fruits, Listed in Order of Density of Nutrients	
1. Red Peppers (raw)	13. Corn
2. Green Peppers (raw)	14. Strawberries
3. Broccoli (cooked)	15. Cantaloupe
4. Spinach (raw)	16. Potatoes
5. Brussels Sprouts	17. Cabbage
6. Lima Beans	18. Tomatoes
7. Peas	19. Bananas
8. Asparagus	20. Lettuce
9. Artichokes	21. Onions
10. Cauliflower (cooked)	22. Oranges
11. Sweet Potatoes	23. Grapefruit
12. Carrots	24. Grapes

Foods that Heal

- Use barley in place of rice or pasta. Add to vegetable or mushroom soup, salads or casseroles. Barley contains soluble fiber that can help lower your cholesterol.
- The beta-carotene that makes carrots orange can help strengthen your immune system. It gives protection against cancer and against heart disease.
- *Capsaicin* is the ingredient that makes chili peppers hot. Eating hot, spicy foods can help speed up your metabolism if you are on a diet. It is also good for anyone with a weak respiratory system: a mouth-burning meal causes extra fluid that can thin the mucus in the nose, throat and bronchial passages.
- Garlic is a natural antibiotic. It can also lower your blood pressure, reduce your risk of heart disease, and help prevent stomach cancer. Use raw or lightly sautéed garlic. Garlic powder is usually processed under high heat, which eliminates its healing properties.
- One of our best sources of absorbable calcium is kale. Other dark leafy green vegetables also have calcium, but it is less readily absorbed. Kale and other vegetables of the cabbage family also help break down extra estrogen in the blood and may help prevent breast cancer. Kale also contains beta-carotene.

- Prunes are well known for their natural laxative ability. They may also help lower cholesterol levels. Prunes are very rich in pectin, a type of soluble fiber also found in apples.
- Spicing up your food with cinnamon, turmeric and cloves may help keep your blood sugar levels more even.
- Ginger helps digestion and prevents motion sickness.
- Yogurt (with live *lactobacillus acidophilus*) is a healing food for the gastro-intestinal tract. It is rich in calcium and helps prevent colon cancer and yeast infections, and strengthens the immune system.
- Oranges, lemons and persimmons are high in vitamin C, which helps reduce blood pressure and may prevent cataracts and cancer as well.

Arthritis

Certain vegetables in the nightshade family may aggravate existing arthritis conditions. Those suffering from arthritis might experiment with avoiding the following vegetables: tomatoes, bell peppers, eggplant, white onions, squash and potatoes.

Some sufferers are relieved by eating cartilage from shark or chicken. The theory is that our bodies become allergic to and attack the cartilage in our joints. This creates an inflammation, with resulting pain. By eating cartilage our bodies build up a tolerance to cartilage so that our immune systems do not attack it.

Foods You Should Not Eat

Certain foods should be avoided when ever possible.
- Popcorn at the movies is often popped in coconut oil or some other unhealthy oil. Just a small portion contains a day's worth of saturated fat.
- Doughnuts are cooked in hydrogenated shortening that adds an extremely high amount of saturated fat.
- Ice cream has very high fat content, which comes from cream and added flavorings such as fudge.
- Cold cuts and heavily processed meats are usually very high in artery-clogging fat.

Eating Out

- Try ethnic restaurants such as Indian, middle Eastern or Oriental. They will usually have many options among chicken, fish or vegetarian dishes.
- In Chinese restaurants, specify that no MSG is to be used in your food.
- Mexican food can also be a good alternative if you make sure that the corn tortillas are not fried and the beans are not cooked in lard.
- Frequent salad bars, after making sure that no sulfites are used.
- Try a natural or health food restaurant.
- Choose a salad platter as a main course (chef's salad or fruit salad). Have the ham omitted from the chef's salad.
- Request whole grain breads and cereals.
- Choose plain baked potatoes instead of fried or mashed potatoes.
- Select lemon or vinegar and olive oil dressings. Ask that sauces, toppings and dressings be served on the side so that you can put on the desired amount.
- Skip dessert in favor of fresh fruits.
- Do not add salt to your food.

Alternatives in Nutrition

Vegetarianism is becoming more popular in the U.S., as is the macrobiotic diet. If care is taken to insure that all the necessary nutrients are included, both of these diets present great health benefits.

The Vegetarian Diet

Many people throughout the world follow a vegetarian diet for a variety of reasons:
- There are spiritual reasons, as in many Eastern cultures, where there are strong taboos against eating animal flesh. Many people feel that vegetarianism encourages a spiritual life, and it has traditionally been the diet of choice of most ascetics, mystics and saints.
- Some do not want to take part in the suffering of animals.

- For many millions of vegetarians throughout the world, poverty is the determining factor: there simply is no animal protein available, or no money to buy it with.

In America today, the main deciding factor in becoming a vegetarian is health. Many studies have conclusively shown that a varied and wholesome vegetarian diet can easily maintain the ideal levels of nutrients needed by the body.

- Vegetarians are much more likely to have low blood cholesterol, low blood pressure, low uric acid levels and low toxicity of the liver and kidneys.
- A diet rich in fruits and vegetables appears to protect one against kidney stones.
- Vegetarians have a lower white blood cell count.
- They have little or no problem with weight control. A high-fiber diet helps excrete fats from the body.
- Seventh Day Adventists, who are vegetarians, operate several major hospitals where all patients are fed vegetarian fare. Their patients have consistently faster rates of recovery.
- The aging process is somewhat slowed, particularly regarding hair and skin.
- Anti-oxidants like selenium and vitamins C and E are found more abundantly in a vegetarian diet, and help reduce the effects of aging.
- Post-menopausal women who follow vegetarian diets seem less prone to osteoporosis than other post-menopausal women.
- In general, vegetarians have a lower incidence of cancer, particularly breast and colon cancers. Breast cancer has been associated with a diet rich in fats, and as we have seen, a high-fiber diet helps reduce the absorption of fats by the body. Fiber also helps eliminate many of the toxic substances that otherwise may stay in the colon and contribute to disease.
- Diabetes occurs less among vegetarians.
- The incidence of heart attacks is lower among vegetarians.

What about Protein?

The concern that one may not get enough protein from a vegetarian diet is largely unfounded. Generally,

Americans eat much more protein than their life-style requires.

The average adult thrives on about 46 – 56 grams of protein per day, and a comprehensive vegetarian diet with plenty of whole grains, legumes, vegetables and fruits will provide this amount.

Remember that if you include milk, cheese or eggs in your vegetarian diet, you are getting all the essential amino-acids you need from them.

The Macrobiotic Diet

This diet is based on a philosophy which relates all of our wellness to the universe. In this view, a person's diet must take into consideration such environmental factors as local climate, seasonal changes and even personal life-style.
- A macrobiotic diet can be flexible to the individual's needs, as long as it remains in harmony with planetary needs.
- We can become more harmonious within the world, within our own family, and within ourselves by adjusting our diet to include more natural and balanced foods.
- This balance is established in terms of yin and yang, ancient Chinese terms which describe the essential qualities of all known elements in the universe, including foods.

A standard macrobiotic meal for a temperate climate, such as is prevalent in North America, may include:
- One–half whole grains cooked in a variety of ways, and including brown rice, whole wheat breads or noodles, millet, corn, oats, barley, and other grains.
- One–fourth to one–third fresh vegetables which can also be cooked in a variety of ways, possibly with a small portion eaten raw, as in a salad.
- The remainder of the meal is divided between a light broth or soup of miso (a fermented soybean paste) with vegetables, grains, beans or seaweed, and a dish of cooked beans with seaweed.

This is actually a specialized vegetarian diet, based on a belief in the importance of sea products. Fish or shellfish can be included once or twice a week; seaweed, sea salt, seeds and certain condiments of Japanese origin are also part of this diet.

Note that the macrobiotic diet consists primarily of whole grains and high fiber foods, which are both essential to good health. However, it may be too restrictive for many to follow without the guidance of a professional nutritionist who is experienced with macrobiotics.

The Case for Tofu and Tempeh

Tofu is made from soybeans, water and a coagulating agent that are pressed in vats lined with cloth. It is also known as bean curd or bean cake. It is a main staple of the Japanese diet, and is eaten regularly by many other people worldwide.

- Tofu has no cholesterol and lots of easily digestible protein. It contains about half the protein of a similar portion of steak.
- To yield even more protein, tofu can be complemented by whole grains.
- It is also low in fat and sodium, and contains only 120 calories per quarter pound.
- Tofu comes in pound cakes that are sold refrigerated. They should be kept in your refrigerator, and after opening, any left-over portions can be kept for a couple of days in water in the refrigerator (change the water once a day). Some tofu is sold in aseptic packs that can be kept unrefrigerated.
- Tofu has little taste of its own, so it takes on the taste of the food it is cooked with, or can be flavored with spices and marinades (ginger, soy sauce, etc.).

Tempeh is also a soybean cake, this one pressed and fermented. It originated in Indonesia. The fermentation process is done with the use of a friendly bacteria which gives the soybean a very pleasant, nutty flavor.
- Tempeh is also very easy to digest.
- It is high in proteins, B vitamins and calcium.
- Like tofu, it is low in fat and sodium, and has no cholesterol.
- It can be baked, broiled, fried or simmered in stew and soups. It can also be added to salads, sandwiches and sauces.

Food Allergies

Some people must follow special diets due to food allergies. They affect less than one percent of all American children, and their incidence decreases as children grow older. However, food allergies can sometimes last into adulthood, and allergic reactions can be quite discomforting for those who suffer them.
- Food allergies are commonly caused by milk products, eggs, wheat, corn, potatoes, tomatoes, citrus fruits, peanuts, oats, soy, yeast, green beans, apples, carrots, chicken, beef and chocolate.
- If you suspect a food allergy, you can be tested, however most tests are lengthy and expensive.
- You can test yourself for allergies by eliminating the suspected food or foods from your diet for at least a month. Then reintroduce the food for four days and note any changes or symptoms.
- Be careful to wait at least four days before reintroducing a second food.
- Only reintroduce one suspected food at a time.

Your Ideal Weight

The USDA has found that the average caloric intake for Americans has remained the same over the last few decades. However, today most Americans lead a much more sedentary life-style than did their ancestors. We no longer do enough physical labor to burn all the calories we consume.

Learn to increase your activity level while eating a healthy and varied diet to maintain your ideal weight.

Obesity

While an overweight person simply carries more weight than is recommended (athletes, for instance, usually carry extra muscle), an obese person carries an excessive amount of body fat. Obesity increases the risks of:
- High blood pressure.
- Heart ailments.
- Stroke.
- Diabetes.
- Cancer.

Diets are Hazardous to Your Health

If you lose weight fast, you are probably losing mostly water and tissue, rather than fat. Losing weight slowly is safer and more effective.

No one should try to lose more than two pounds per week, or reduce their caloric intake to less than 1000 calories per day.

Just as it took a certain amount of time (and overeating) for you to gain extra body fat, it will take time and careful planning of your daily menu to regain your health and vitality.
- Once you have established a plan of good nutrition, you may want to acquire a vitamin and mineral supplement.
- Learn to distinguish between high nutrient-density and low nutrient-density foods.
- Lose a certain amount of weight simply by reducing or eliminating all sugar and salt from your diet. Not only do added sugar and salt take the place of valuable nutrients, they also stimulate the appetite.
- Learn to recognize any habit of unconscious eating; such as habitual snacking while you work or watch television, or eating to relieve tension in stressful situations.
- Determine your ideal weight, taking into consideration your body build.
- Establish an exercise plan that you feel you can stick to. (See *Exercise*.)

Recommended Height and Weight Range

Height: Feet/Inches	Men: Weight Range	Women: Weight Range
4/10	102 – 129	92 – 119
4/11	104 – 132	94 – 122
5/0	106 – 135	96 – 125
5/1	109 – 138	99 – 128
5/2	112 – 141	102 – 131
5/3	115 – 144	105 – 134
5/4	118 – 148	108 – 138
5/5	121 – 152	111 – 142
5/6	124 – 156	114 – 146
5/7	128 – 161	118 – 150
5/8	132 – 166	122 – 154
5/9	136 – 170	126 – 158
5/10	140 – 174	130 – 163
5/11	144 – 179	134 – 168
6/0	148 – 184	138 – 173
6/1	152 – 189	142 – 170
6/2	156 – 194	146 – 184
6/3	160 – 199	150 – 189
6/4	164 – 204	154 – 194

- Recent research suggests that people can be a little heavier as they grow older (35 years and above), without any risk to their health.
- Remember that the higher weights in the table are for people who have larger builds or more muscles than average, while the lower weights are for more lightly built individuals of the same height.

Calories in some Popular Foods

Banana (1 cup)	90	Beans, Lima (1 cup)	100
Beans, Green (1 cup)	25	Beef Sirloin (3 oz.)	250
Beer (8 oz.)	120	Bread, Whole Wheat (1 slice)	75
Broccoli (1 cup)	200	Brussels Sprouts (1 cup)	100
Butter (1 tablespoon)	95	Cabbage (1 cup)	80
Cantaloupe (1/2)	50	Carrots (1 cup)	50

Cauliflower (1 cup)	50	Cheese, American (1 oz.)	110
Cottage Cheese (1/2 cup)	150	Cream (2 tablespoons)	100
Chicken, Broiled (1/2)	270	Cucumber (1/2)	10
Egg (1 medium)	75	Eggplant (1 cup)	150
Frankfurter (1)	125	Grapefruit (1)	100
Honey (1 tablespoon)	100	Lettuce (2 leaves)	10
Margarine (1 tablespoon)	100	Milk, Skim (8 oz.)	85
Milk, Whole (8 oz.)	170	Mushrooms (1 cup)	20
Orange Juice (8 oz.)	125	Peanut Butter (1 tablespoon)	100
Pear (1)	50	Potato Chips (10)	100
Raisins (1/2 cup)	180	Rice (1 cup)	150
Spinach (1 cup)	40	Strawberries (1 cup)	90
Sugar (1 cup)	800	Tomato (1 cup)	50
Turkey (1 slice)	100	Turnip Greens (1 cup)	60
Watermelon (1 cup)	190	Wheat Flakes (1 cup)	130

The Human Nutrition Information Service (HNIS), a division of the U.S. Department of Agriculture, provides dietary guidelines and a pocket guide listing the caloric contents of most foods.

Maintaining Your Ideal Weight

Some researchers believe that each of us has a "set point," a certain weight that the body tries to maintain. As soon as a person begins a new diet, the body starts to store fats and lower its metabolism, in an effort to maintain its set point.

The only effective, lasting approach to weight loss is a comprehensive program of exercise, and a serious and continuous effort to replace high calorie foods with high nutrient-density, low calorie foods.

Reaching and maintaining your ideal weight will take careful planning. You must become aware of your eating habits, and understand the relationships between calories, exercise and weight. A familiarity with the basics of nutrition is also required.

To calculate the amount of calories you consume, and to identify problem areas in your diet, establish a food diary as follows:

Food Diary

	Foods	Calories
Day 1: Breakfast: Lunch: Dinner: All Snacks: All Drinks:		
Day 1 Total	------------------------>	
Day 2: Breakfast (etc.)		
Day 2 Total	------------------------>	
Week Total	------------------------>	

- Repeat for days 2 through 7.
- Make sure you list *everything* that you eat and drink each day, unless it has zero calories, like plain water.
- If your diet varies little from day to day, you can keep the diary for only three or four days.
- Do not omit anything, not even the smallest snack.
- Add together all the daily totals of calories.
- To determine your average caloric intake, divide the week's total calories by the number of days recorded, as shown below:

Average Caloric Intake =
Total Calories (from Food Diary) ÷ 7 Days

- Once you have determined your ideal weight and created a food diary, you will be able to see the areas of your diet which need adjustment, such as excess snacks or high calorie lunches.

- Now you must determine the amount of calories you should be consuming every day. Rate yourself according to your level of activity from the activity scale below:

Activity Scale

	Activity Level
13	Very Inactive: You drive to work and return home to the couch.
14	Inactive: You walk to work or shop but little else.
15	Somewhat Active: You exercise 2 or 3 times a week and walk some every day.
16	Very Active: You are always on the go and exercise regularly.
17	Greatly Active: You are an athlete in training, a ballet dancer, a construction worker, etc.

- Multiply your activity number (from activity scale) with your ideal weight (from the recommended height and weight chart).
- This will determine your daily caloric requirement, the amount of calories you should ingest each day in order to reach and maintain your ideal weight.

Daily Caloric Requirement =
Activity Number (from Activity Scale) x Ideal Weight, in pounds (from chart)

Compare your daily caloric requirement to your average caloric intake:
- Once you have established the adequate amount of calories required to stay healthy and energetic, eliminate the high-calorie, low-nutrient foods from your diet, and burn up excess calories by exercising more.
- Any good, comprehensive weight loss diet should contain lots of fiber from complex carbohydrates.
- You still need vitamins, minerals, and other nutrients to keep yourself fit and healthy.
- Make sure that you're getting enough protein every day by calculating your protein requirement:

Minimum Daily Protein Requirement =
Ideal Weight, in pounds x 0.5 Grams

Fats contain nine calories per gram, while complex carbohydrates and protein contain only half as much.

Understanding Labels: Calories
- Products are often labeled "light" (or "lite") if they are intended to be useful in reducing weight or caloric intake. Manufacturers must still provide full nutritional information on the label.
- A product labeled "low calorie" should not contain more than 40 calories per serving, or 0.4 calories per gram.
- A "reduced calorie" food must be at least one third lower in calorie content than the food to which it is being compared.
- "Diet" or "dietetic" foods must meet the requirements for low or reduced calorie foods, and must have some added dietary purpose as well.

Weight Control with Water
- You can help control your weight by drinking five to eight tall (8 oz.) glasses of water each day.
- Water lessens fluid retention by improving your kidneys' efficiency.
- Water helps prevent dehydration, and keeps the muscles and skin better toned while losing weight.
- Water helps flush out stored fats from the body.
- Water prevents constipation.

The "Don'ts" of Dieting
- Don't ever go on a starvation diet. Starvation lowers the metabolism and causes even greater weight gain when normal eating resumes.
- Don't go on a fad diet. Fad diets are known to increase the incidence of weight gain, chemical imbalances, depression and other mental difficulties, and even heart attacks.
- Don't skip meals. Eat regularly and maintain a balanced variety of foods.
- Don't eat on the run or while standing, driving, cleaning, working or watching TV. Eat in a relaxed manner, making each meal an event in itself. You will be more aware of what you eat and will be satisfied with less food.

- Schedule your meals at regular hours and do not snack in between, particularly at night.
- Don't skip breakfast.

Have Fun and Stay Fit

There are 3500 calories in each pound of fat. If you want to lose one pound in seven days, you have to burn up 500 calories a day in addition your normal caloric usage.
- It's obvious that you will spend more time at activities which you enjoy. Some people prefer activities which they can perform alone, while others like the benefits of group motivation.
- You may also want to vary your exercise sessions by alternating between three or four enjoyable activities.
- Exercise tones muscles and tissues while burning calories.

Calories Consumed during One Hour

Resting (Sleeping)	80
Sitting	100
Driving	120
Standing	140
Housework	180
Bicycling (moderate speed)	210
Walking	210
Golf, Mowing (push mower)	250
Rowing, Calisthenics	300
Volleyball, Square dancing	350
Tennis	420
Water skiing, Climbing a hill	490
Basketball, Football	500
Snow skiing, Squash, Handball	600
Running	900

Low-Calorie Frozen Dinners

The first frozen dinners (or "TV dinners") appeared in 1954, and consisted mostly of fat-rich foods. While producers eventually offered lower calorie dinners, sodium and fat contents remained high.

Frozen dinners are now advertised as healthy choices for the ever-growing market of health-conscious consumers. Their levels of fat, sodium and cholesterol follow the guidelines of the National Research Council and the National Cholesterol Education Program.

Today's low-calorie frozen dinners and entrees follow these guidelines:
- Less than 400 calories.
- Less than 10 grams of total fat.
- Less than 4 grams of saturated fat.
- Less than 30% of caloric content from fat.
- Less than 70 mg of cholesterol.
- Less than 900 mg of sodium.

Unfortunately for those who are truly health-conscious, these low-calorie frozen dinners have the following very serious drawbacks:
- They are generally deficient in some of the food groups, especially grains, vegetables and fruits.
- They are deficient in many vitamins and minerals.
- They are lacking in adequate fiber.
- Most frozen foods are highly processed and contain chemical additives. (See *Processed Foods* and *Food Additives*.)

Cellulite

Cellulite is made of fat, water and wastes that get trapped beneath the skin in specific areas of the body and produce gel-like bumps and bulges. When squeezed, these areas take on an "orange peel" appearance. They are usually found on the thighs, hips or upper arms, where circulation is often poor. Cellulite deposits are extremely difficult to get rid of. The causes of cellulite are many, but they all relate to our sedentary life-styles:
- The primary cause is an improper diet, especially one lacking in fiber.
- Insufficient water intake.
- Poor elimination.
- Too little exercise and physical activity.
- Tension and fatigue, which disrupt the normal body cycles of digestion and elimination.
- Female hormonal changes, particularly at puberty or menopause. Cellulite can also appear during pregnancy.

Fasting

A fast should not be undertaken for weight loss, but used only to cleanse the body and rest the gastro-intestinal system, to reestablish its proper balance. A few days' fast can help break up pockets of cellulite, as well as restore the proper functioning of the stomach and intestines.

No one who is on medication or who is not in perfect health should attempt any type of fast.

Instructions for Fasting
- Remember to drink plenty of water.
- A fast can last from one whole day (fruit juices only), which could be repeated once weekly, to a whole week (maybe once or twice a year).
- Rest as often and as long as necessary during the fast. Only very light exercise should be undertaken, such as stretching, yoga or walking.
- Break the fast slowly and gradually with light fare: whole fruits, light salads then broth, followed by lightly cooked vegetables, increasing the quantity of foods ingested over a couple of days before returning to a normal diet.
- Any dizziness, blurred vision or other unusual symptom is a sign to discontinue the fast immediately.
- It is not unusual to suffer from headaches during the first couple of days of fasting, as accumulated toxins are released into the bloodstream. This is especially true of habitual coffee and tea drinkers.

Weight Gain
Gaining weight may take even longer than losing weight. It is not as simple as eating more foods.

Any weight loss or weight gain program should first be discussed with your doctor. The causes for your low weight should be determined. The amount of weight that you wish to gain should be determined, taking into consideration your specific body build and life-style.

Construct your diet around the following guidelines:
- Exercise more often. Exercise builds muscle mass.
- Keep a food diary and increase your food intake slowly by choosing high nutrient-density, high-calorie foods.
- Eat nutritious snacks. You may wish to eat a bed-time snack.

Some Foods to Help You Gain Weight
- Milk-based drinks (shakes, malts).
- Yogurt.
- Cheese.
- Eggs.
- Meats, poultry, fish.
- Breads, cereals, pasta.
- Starchy vegetables.
- Soups, desserts and casseroles made with added dry milk powder.

Water

Our very cells originally emerged from the chemical sea that gave birth to all life on earth.
- Water is odorless, colorless and tasteless.
- Yet water is a nutrient required by all living creatures.
- Water constitutes the largest part of our bodies. Each cell in our bodies is mostly water.
- Blood is 90% water, and blood and sea water are strikingly similar in composition.
- We start our own lives as embryos, which are about 98% water. As babies, our water content decreases to about 75%. A typical adult human being is between 65% and 50% water, depending on body fat (the more fat, the less water).
- Water is the most essential nutrient to our survival. We would die within three to five days from lack of water. Water also carries minerals to the body.
- he body eliminates water through sweating, urine, and bowel movements throughout the day.
- Each day, the body needs to take in two quarts of water, some of which is obtained from the fruits and vegetables we eat.

Drinking Water

Unfortunately, most tap water is now "purified" by dozens of processes and chemical applications. And even though it remains odorless and colorless, it often acquires a bad taste, so many of us do not drink nearly as much water as we need each day. Instead we consume sugared drinks, sodas, coffee, tea, beer or other beverages. Many of these drinks actually rob the body of nutrients. The result is that

we do not get an adequate intake of water and the minerals which come with it, but instead we use some of our own internal supply of minerals to help digest these drinks.
- The body adjusts to the low fluid intake by sweating less, which decreases the normal elimination of toxins.
- Several conditions can result from inadequate intake of water: fatigue, constipation, headaches, urinary tract infections (particularly in women) and kidney stress.

How Safe is Tap Water?

Many chemical toxins find their way into our drinking water. In 1984, the water supplies of 954 cities were tested and 30% were found to be contaminated.
- Rivers and lakes are often the most polluted because of natural and industrial run-offs.
- Toxins have also been found in deep ground-water sources where they may form a slow-spreading "plume." One end of the underground reservoir or aquifer may be safe, while water taken from a different location or depth may show contamination.
- In some water samples, the EPA (Environmental Protection Agency) has been able to identify as many as 700 toxic compounds. These typically include pesticides, herbicides, metals and industrial run-offs.
- Many of these compounds are impossible to detect except through costly laboratory tests. Fortunately, growing public concern brought about the revision of the Safe Drinking Water Act in 1986. Today water companies are required to closely monitor the water they supply to their customers.
- Even good water can be contaminated as it travels to homes through old and decaying pipes. For instance, the two huge pipes that carry water from the Catskill Mountains to New York City were built in 1917 and 1937, and it has not been possible to shut them down since then to inspect them or repair them. Old pipes are much more likely to allow seepage of substances from the ground into the water.
- The EPA has also estimated that as much as one fourth of the water supplied to all Americans contains higher than recommended levels of lead. Lead is a well-known cause of nerve and brain damage, particularly in children, where even very low levels can lead to learning disabilities, hyperactivity and other behavioral problems.

- Even in new homes, copper tubing is often joined with lead solder.
- Plastic pipes are not completely safe. If they pass through very toxic areas, certain chemicals may seep through. Also, toxic compounds are added to the plastic to make it more resistant to heat, and other toxins are part of the cements and glues which are used to join the pipes.
- In rural areas, pesticides and herbicides are the major cause of contamination of underground wells. Agricultural chemicals, especially chlorinated hydrocarbons and organic phosphates, have been linked to birth defects, nerve damage, cancer and diverse symptoms of poisoning.
- Acid rain is a major threat to water safety in the northeast.
- In industrial and densely populated areas, toxic waste dumps or storage tanks, as well as petrochemical fallout and continuous run-off from city streets, create very serious threats to our drinking water.
- As a rule, infants and children are more susceptible than adults to any toxic compounds.

Wherever you choose to live, it makes sense to check water content with your local water quality department or health department. If you own land with your own wells, the water should be tested regularly for toxins.

City and Rural Water

Type of Water	Pros	Cons
City water	Little chance of bacteria. Mandatory regular testing for contaminants.	Chlorine content. Possible contamination from old lead water mains or pipes.
Rural water from a private well	No chlorine or fluoride treatment.	Possible contamination with bacteria, synthetic chemicals, others. Possible leaks from septic tanks and toxic waste dumps.

Bottled Water

Bottled water has become a commonplace item in supermarkets, convenience stores and drug stores. Today a gallon of pure water may cost as much as a gallon of gasoline for your car. Yet more and more people are purchasing bottled water or having it delivered to their homes and offices. But is bottled water absolutely safe? Not necessarily.

- Bottled water can be ground or surface water which has only been filtered or treated in some way to destroy bacteria.
- It could even be regular tap water that has been filtered and bottled. This is sometimes sold as "drinking water" in vending machines outside of supermarkets. Filtering does remove some pollutants, but the water may not be absolutely pure.
- In the recent past, substances such as heavy metals, pesticides and solvents have been found in some bottled waters.
- Some plastic containers can contaminate the water as well. Choose glass bottles whenever you can.
- You should refrigerate your water, even unopened, to prevent the growth of algae or bacteria.

Spring Water

Spring water must come from a natural spring, and is usually of superior purity as long as the aquifer (the underground water source) which supplies the spring has not been contaminated.

- In many states, water bottlers are not required to divulge their sources, but this does not mean that you should not ask.
- Ask which geological tests have been done to validate the purity of the water.
- At the present time, there are no regulations concerning the *name* of a bottled water, so the word "spring" can be part of the name of a bottled water, even if it is not real spring water.

Look for water that has the added words "pure spring water" or "artisan well water" clearly marked on the label, independent of the product name.

Mineral Water

Mineral water is also ground water, usually from natural springs. Minerals such as bicarbonates, chlorides, fluorides, calcium, magnesium, potassium and sulfates can be present in such waters.

In Europe, mineral water is used for drinking and bathing during "mineral cures," which are supposed to have specific health benefits.

Distilled Water

Distilled water (made by boiling water and then condensing the steam) is generally more pure and more expensive than other bottled water. Once used solely for filling steam irons or cleaning contact lenses, it is now used by more and more people for drinking and cooking.

Some "distilled water" sold in stores is really reverse osmosis water. This is quite close to distilled water, but is actually filtered through a very fine membrane.

Home Purification Systems

No home purification device now available can guarantee to remove all pollutants from our drinking water.

Before buying a home purification device, you should determine the specific contaminants in your water.

Specific Water Pollutants	Recommended Purification System	Drawbacks
Chlorine, some organic chemicals, some pesticides, bad taste or odor	Carbon filter	Will not filter out metals, bacteria or nitrates. Loses efficacy after a while.
Some organic chemicals, pesticides, heavy metals	Reverse osmosis	Uses large quantities of water, not 100% effective.
Minerals, nitrates, heavy metals, organic chemicals, bacteria	Distillation	Tasteless water, requires frequent maintenance and cleaning.

Water Softeners
Water softeners do not filter out chemicals and other contaminants.
- They replace certain minerals with sodium, and prevent the build-up of minerals inside pipes and other equipment (faucets, washing machines, etc.).
- They improve the cleaning action of soaps. However they may also increase the leaching of lead solder into the water, and add sodium.
- *Neutralizers* only reduce the acidity in the water and may also increase the level of sodium.

Flavor Variety in Drinking Water
- Add two tablespoons of lemon or lime juice for each gallon of spring or distilled water and refrigerate.
- In summer, four to six herbal tea bags can be steeped in a gallon of spring or distilled water exposed to sunlight for about an hour, then refrigerate. There are many wonderful choices of herbal teas which contain no caffeine and can be served unsweetened. Many of the herbs also contain some vitamins and minerals, and have other beneficial properties. (See *Herbal Medicine*.)

The Case Against Caffeine
- Caffeine, the active ingredient in coffee, is a powerful stimulant to the central nervous system. It is also found in tea, cocoa, and many soft drinks.
- Excess caffeine can cause or aggravate the following conditions: ulcers, heartburn, nervous stomach, high blood pressure, higher cholesterol levels, headaches, insomnia, irregular heartbeat, urinary infections, moist palms and nervousness.
- A reaction can be caused by as little as 250 mg of caffeine. There are 100 to 150 mg in one single cup of coffee. A single cup of black tea contains 65 to 75 mg of caffeine.
- Caffeine does not provide any nutrients. It also leaches many vitamins and minerals from the body.
- Weaning oneself from coffee may be difficult. Caffeine withdrawal has unpleasant side-effects, including headaches and irritability.

Other Water Uses

In addition to being a vitally important nutrient, water is also necessary to our cleanliness and hygiene. We use water to bathe ourselves, to wash our clothes and dishes, and to keep our homes clean. A hot bath can be ideal for easing tired muscles and reducing tension. A cold shower can be revitalizing and invigorating. Saunas and steam baths also have many health benefits.

Cleansing Baths

Usually we take a bath or shower to remove the dirt and grime accumulated on our skin during the day.
- A hot bath with mild soap will effectively remove germs, dirt and excess oil from our skin and pores.
- Avoid excessive scrubbing with harsh chemical soaps that can strip away too much of the skin's natural oils. Choose a mild pH balanced soap or one that is slightly acidic. (See *Skin Care*.)
- Cosmetic bubble baths and scented oil products are often harmful to the skin and can lead to urinary tract infections in women and children.
- Loofas are natural sponges made from dried gourds. They are efficient yet gentle scrubbers for the skin and help remove the outer layer of dead skin cells.
- Finish with a cool shower or splash.

Relaxing Baths
- A hot bath can be very relaxing, especially before bed. Be careful that it is not too hot.
- Do not eat for at least an hour before taking a hot bath.
- You can enhance your relaxing experience by adding soothing essential oils (extracted from plants) or dried medicinal herbs to your bath water.

Herbal Baths
- Herbs can be added to bath water for many different purposes. They may simply add scent, but they can also help relax, soothe or stimulate, according to their specific medicinal properties.
- To make an herbal bath, you can tie a handful of herbs in a washcloth with a twist-tie, rubber band or ribbon. Fill

the tub with hot water, drop in the herb bundle, and let it soak.
- While bathing, use the herb bundle to scrub yourself. Rinse and pat dry. You may wish to splash or shower with cool water afterwards.

Some Herbal Bath Remedies

Condition	Herbs to Use
oily skin	white willow bark, witch hazel and lemon grass
dry or itchy skin	oatmeal and/or almond meal, and a natural oil with or without scent
sore, aching muscles	half a cup of each of Epsom salts and witch hazel
tension and stress	chamomile flowers, linden flowers and lavender, also lavender oil or rose oil

Cold Showers and Baths

- Short cold showers or baths of half a minute to three minutes can be very beneficial.
- When used in conjunction with friction from a wash cloth or loofa sponge, these benefits can be increased still.

A quick, cold or cool shower depresses the physiological processes of the body. Perspiration stops, and heat loss through circulation to the skin is slowed. This triggers the central nervous system to react in order to prevent injury. The body counters the depressant with increased vitality and vigor. The tone of the heart and of the arterial walls is increased, peripheral blood vessels dilate, and general circulation is stimulated.

Benefits of a Cold Bath or Shower
- Increased blood circulation.
- Overall increased neuromuscular transmission.
- Increased respiration.
- Increased muscle tone and elasticity.
- Increased skin tone.
- Increased metabolism.
- Increased red and white blood cell count (which strengthens the immune system.)

Contraindications of a Cold Bath or Shower

You should avoid a cold bath or shower, if any of the following apply:
- You who are highly sensitive to cold.
- You feel cold, ill or generally unwell.
- You are very tired or chronically fatigued.
- You have poor kidney function or any degree of kidney disease.
- You have any degree of heart disease or condition related to blood pressure.
- You have any condition of the thyroid gland.

A Gift from Finland: The Sauna

The word "sauna" is a Finnish word that describes a certain type of bathhouse where cleansing of the body is done through intense perspiration. When "taking a sauna," a person sits or lies in a very hot room to induce sweating. The principles are the same as in the Turkish, Russian or Oriental steam bath, but with one major difference: a sauna is generally much drier, with a level of humidity not exceeding 10%.

Many ancient cultures built public bathing facilities. Remains of such structures exist in Egypt, Greece and Rome. In many of these bathing facilities, hot and cold baths were taken alternately, or hot baths were followed by exposure to cold air. Steam baths have also been used by Eskimos and Native Americans. Their structures are known as sweat lodges, and are used for both physiological and spiritual purifications.

- In steam rooms, the moisture in the air prevents a person from staying in for very long. The hot, damp air is very oppressive, and it is difficult to breathe. In a wet environment, temperatures of 110°F to 120°F are usually the maximum temperature that can be tolerated without burning sensations.
- The drier air in saunas is more comfortable, even at hotter temperatures. In a sauna, temperatures easily range from 170°F to 190°F, and can go over 200°F for experienced bathers. One may stay in for a full half-hour, though longer periods are not recommended.

Taking a Sauna
- The traditional way to take a sauna is to follow the heat treatment with an immediate plunge into cool water, in a pool where one can touch the bottom, or in a shower.
- This is followed by a period of rest, which allows the entire body to air dry. The sauna can then be repeated.
- Remove all jewelry, glasses, watches, etc. These could get dangerously hot.
- Always finish with a rest period, lying down and letting your body dry off and cool down naturally before putting on any clothing. Otherwise you may start sweating again in your clothes, and may get chilled, even in hot weather. Do not jump back into vigorous exercise or action.
- Begin with short periods in the sauna, and increase both time and heat as you become more accustomed to the experience.

A sauna bath must always be followed by a period of rest, allowing the body to cool off completely.

The Benefits of Saunas
- Moist air saunas or steam baths are excellent for the skin, as they increase the circulation to the skin, dissolve the outer layer of dead cells and excess oil, and clean the pores.
- Heat is a vasodilator, which means that it increases circulation throughout the body.
- The abrupt change in temperature caused by plunging into a cool bath or shower creates an immediate constriction of the blood vessels. This causes a rapid exchange of blood, which enhances the natural ability of the body to adjust to external temperature changes.
- A general feeling of well-being and relaxation is the principal aim of most sauna users. Saunas are known to soothe tired and aching muscles, reduce nervous tension, and refresh the mind. Taken in the evening, a sauna can help one sleep more soundly.

Precautions and Contraindications
- Do not use a sauna if you have dizzy spells, light-headedness, or high or low blood pressure. Consult your physician first.
- Do not take a sauna on a full stomach. Wait at least an hour after a light meal, and at least two hours after a full meal. Heat draws the blood towards the skin and away from the stomach, where it is needed to stimulate digestion.
- Do not drink a lot of fluid before a sauna for the same reason, and never drink any alcohol.
- Do not take a sauna immediately after vigorous exercise or physical exertion. It is best to be rested first.
- The U. S. Department of Health, Education and Welfare emphasizes the lack of adequate scientific evidence to back certain claims concerning saunas. Their valid recommendation is part of the labeling of sauna equipment built today in our country. It reads: "Warning – Elderly persons or those suffering from heart disease or high or low blood pressure should not use this device unless directed by a physician."
- Do not take a sauna or steam bath when ill or just recovering from an illness.

Skin

Skin is like the rest of our body: its health will determine its beauty. Our skin is the largest organ we have. It protects us from rain, sun and temperature extremes. It holds together and protects the other organs and tissues of the body.

The skin is made up of three layers:
- The *epidermis* is the outer layer. It protects the body from the environment, and from harmful bacteria.
- Just beneath the epidermis is the *dermis*, which gives the skin strength and elasticity. This layer contains the sweat and oil glands, hair follicles and blood vessels.
- Below the dermis is a layer of *subcutaneous tissue*, which insulates the body and stores energy in the form of fat.
- The skin, like all the other organs of the body, depends mostly on the nutrients brought to its cells by the blood. Excess consumption of fats, sugars, caffeine, alcohol and nicotine are all extremely detrimental to the health and appearance of the skin.

The pH Factor

The natural secretions of the skin's oil glands (the *sebum*) mix with sweat and other cellular secretions to produce a fluid cover on the skin. This fluid is somewhat acidic, and is sometimes called the *acid mantle*. It helps protect the skin against bacterial infections. Soap which is alkaline will destroy this acid barrier, at least temporarily. So will certain face creams and other products. It is important to cleanse the skin daily, but one should use a pH balanced product to help maintain the proper acid-alkaline balance.

Skin Care Products

In the last fifty years or so, major advances in the field of chemistry have caused great changes in the cosmetics industry. Thousands of products are now available for us to clean, soften, nourish and beautify our skin. Buying skin care products can be confusing. Fortunately, laws now require manufacturers to list all the ingredients contained in their products. Remember: Read the label and don't hesitate to inquire about ingredients which you do not recognize. Exercise your rights as a consumer.

Common Ingredients in Skin Care Products

Aloe vera	Has been shown to help heal burns and other skin injuries. Has a soothing effect. May lose these properties during processing.
Alum	An aluminum salt used in astringents.
Animal fats	Most closely resemble the natural oils of the skin. Lanolin (from sheep's wool) seems best. Mink, turtle and other expensive oils have not been shown to be of superior value to lanolin.
Citric acid	From citrus fruits, puffs the skin around the pores to make pores look smaller.
Collagen	Provides a protective film on the skin, but cannot repair the damaged collagen fibers in the skin.
Hyaluronic acid	A good moisturizer, found naturally in the skin.

Hydrolyzed animal protein	Protein supplement that can form a protective film on the skin.
Jojoba oil	Provides moisture and is easily absorbed by the skin, but expensive.
Lactic acid, or Sodium lactate	Found in yogurt, buttermilk. A moisturizer and rejuvenating agent. Can irritate skin if the concentration is too strong.
Mineral oils	Can actually thin out the skin's natural oils and increase dryness. May cause acne. Products that contain mineral oil should be avoided.
Parabens	Preservatives. Can sometimes cause increased pigmentation or acne in darker-skinned individuals.
Propylene glycol	Moisturizer. Can irritate skin and cause acne.
Silicon	Silicon derivatives (dimethicone, cyclomethicone) help prevent evaporation of the skin's moisture.
Sodium PCA	Moisturizer naturally found in the skin. Usually combined with urea or lactic acid for better absorption.
Urea	Helps hold water in the skin. A key ingredient in many moisturizers.
Vitamins	Vitamin A is beneficial and can be absorbed through the skin. Others (particularly vitamin E) cannot be absorbed through the skin.

Some Common Skin Problems

Most of us suffer from mild skin problems from time to time. While dry or oily skin can often be remedied, conditions such as acne and wrinkles may be very difficult to cure, though they can often be improved. Over-exposure to sunlight, however, can cause permanent damage to the skin, and can even lead to various types of skin cancer.

Skin Types

Almost everyone has problems with dry or oily skin from time to time, but for some people, these conditions can be chronic.

- Dry skin occurs when the oil glands do not produce enough oil to hold moisture in the skin, and too much water is then lost to evaporation. Dehydrated cells accumulate on the surface and give the skin a flaky appearance.
- Oily skin is caused by over-activity of the oil glands. This can be caused by many different factors. The skin's oil glands are sensitive to changes in the weather, slight hormonal changes, and certain foods. Genetics also plays a role in skin type.

A varied and complete diet, rich in vitamins and minerals, will ensure the best possible supply of nutrients to the skin. It is also best to drink plenty of water and fresh juices throughout the day.

- Normal skin can be washed with soap and water, though harsh or abrasive soaps should be avoided, particularly on the face and neck. The skin can then be moisturized with a cream or lotion with a low oil content. An occasional mild facial scrub or mask may be used.
- Dry skin can become dryer still, if washed with soap. Yet the flaky dead cells and dirt must be removed. Cleansing creams can leave a film which draws water out of the cells. The best products for cleansing dry skin, particularly on the face and neck, are the lotions and creams which are rinsed off completely with water. A superfatted soap can be used for the body. After cleansing, dry skin must be moisturized and protected from the sun, as it is especially sensitive to sun damage.
- Oily skin is somewhat easier to care for. For this type of skin, deep cleansing stimulates cell renewal. Oily skin should be washed with mild, non-drying agents that will not stimulate extra oil production. Oatmeal soaps are very good for the face and body. Oily skin does not usually need any moisturizing. An occasional paste mask of clay, oatmeal, or fuller's earth can be beneficial.

Cold Weather Skin Care

Cold weather dries our skin. This effect is worsened by indoor heating, which lowers the humidity. Frequent washing can aggravate dry skin by removing the skin's natural oils.

- In cold weather, try bathing only every other day. Bathe in warm, rather than hot water.

- Use a super-fatted soap.
- Moisturize your skin while you are still wet. Gently blot excess water with a towel, then apply moisturizer.
- Keep your home more humid by using a humidifier, or by putting pans of water on your heaters.

Acne

If you have acne, you most likely have oily skin, pimples, blackheads and enlarged pores. Severe acne can leave scars where it appears on the face, neck, shoulders and upper torso. Acne is caused by excess oil production from the skin's glands. Oil production can be affected by hormonal changes, cosmetics, diet, and genetic factors. It can be aggravated by weather changes, stress, and emotional factors.

- Acne is most common during adolescence, when hormone production is at its highest.
- A diet rich in fats (such as fried foods), spices, sugars (sodas), citrus products, shellfish and chocolate has been linked to acne, though tests remain inconclusive.

Methods and Products to Treat Acne

- It is important to avoid harsh soaps or abrasive cleansers that will irritate the skin.
- Oatmeal based products and clay masks are good for absorbing oil.
- Applying hot packs to the face is a good way to stimulate blood flow and dissolve excess oil.
- Some non-prescription acne lotions and anti-bacterial soaps may be effective.
- *Retin-A*, which was developed for severe acne, should only be used under a doctor's care. *Acutane*, an oral form of Retin-A, is prescribed only for the most severe cases, and has very serious side effects.

Beware of miracle products that promise overnight results. The skin is a very sensitive organ, and any irritation can worsen an acne condition. It is always best to consult your doctor.

Skin Allergies

Allergies are reactions to certain substances that have come into contact with the skin. The skin becomes inflamed, and if the contact remains, the condition may spread.

Swelling, redness, itching, and even blistering may appear within forty-eight hours of the contact.

There are many possible reactions to the various chemicals used in soaps, lotions, bath oils and other skin-care products. Natural, organic or hypo-allergenic products do not always guarantee that your skin will not react to one ingredient or another.

Skin can also be sensitive to certain fabrics, or a skin rash may develop due to a food allergy. (See *Clothing* and *Food Allergies*.) Several groups of products seem particularly likely to produce allergic reactions. They are:
- Chemicals that curl or straighten hair (permanents or relaxers) and hair colorants.
- Nail care products, especially hardeners and glues for artificial nails.
- Eye make-up.
- Some facial skin-care products, particularly those containing lanolin or preservatives.

Topical creams and antihistamine creams are the most common remedy for skin allergies. They are usually available at your local drugstore.

Skin allergies are best remedied by identifying the irritant and avoiding it completely.

Skin Wrinkles
- Our skin is connected to the fatty under structure by a woven network of collagen fibers. Around age fifty, these fibers lose elasticity and the skin begins to sag.
- Gravity, exposure to the sun, sleeping positions, smoking and habitual facial expressions create wrinkles.

To Limit and Delay Wrinkles:
- Cover your pillow with a satin pillow case, and change your sleeping position regularly.
- Practice relaxation exercises. Learn to quit frowning, squinting and wrinkling your nose.
- Quit smoking.
- Protect your skin from sun exposure with a strong sun screen.
- Eat a nutritious diet with plenty of fruits and vegetables. Drink plenty of fluids such as spring water and fruit juices.

- Maintain a good exercise program to stimulate blood circulation.
- Maintain your proper weight.

Some treatments are now available to reduce wrinkles, but they are usually expensive and may carry certain health risks:
- Liquid collagen can be injected into a wrinkle to make it appear smoother. Injections are expensive and must be repeated frequently. Deeper lines can be treated with a mixture of collagen and fat from the patient's body.
- Silicon injections work on the same principle as collagen, but there is increasing alarm about the possible dangers of silicone. Silicon has not been approved by the FDA for use in reducing wrinkles.
- Retin-A was first FDA approved and prescribed for the treatment of acne. Retin-A smoothes out the epidermis and may increase the formation of collagen in the dermis. There are still many questions, however, about the long-term use of Retin-A in the treatment of wrinkles.
- Chemical peels can be done with mild chemicals to remove the superficial outer layer of the skin and increase the formation of collagen. Stronger chemical peels can erase some of the fine lines. Deep peels, however, involve much stronger chemicals and carry more serious risks.
- Moisturizers cannot erase wrinkles. They can only help your skin retain moisture and temporarily improve appearance.

Sun and Skin

Exposure to the sun is very detrimental to the skin. It speeds up the aging process, can irritate acne-prone skin, and can worsen oily and dry skin problems.

Sun exposure is the major cause of the hundreds of thousands of skin cancers reported annually.

The sun radiates *ultraviolet rays* of two kinds:
- *UV-A rays* tan the skin by stimulating the melanocytes to produce more melanin, the dark pigment of the skin. The skin reacts this way to shield itself from the sun's

rays. The melanin granules must travel from the lower epidermis to the surface before you can see the effect of the tan.
- *UV-B rays* stimulate light-sensitive proteins in the skin. Cells start to reproduce more rapidly. There is swelling of the skin and redness. This accelerated process actually causes a tan to fade new cells move up to the surface and die and fall off faster than usual.

Prolonged exposure to the sun will cause intense redness and burning, followed by peeling of the dead cells and virtually no tan at all. Shorter exposures to sunlight allow a tan to develop more slowly and to ultimately last longer.

Unfortunately, it is not always enough to use a sunscreen to block out UV-B rays. Many doctors think that UV-A rays can also damage the skin and stimulate the growth of cancerous cells. The incidence of skin cancer has risen dramatically since the beginning of this century, when tanning was not fashionable. Today skin cancer affects nearly half a million individuals a year, including many teenagers.
- It is imperative that anyone who will be exposed to sunlight for any length of time use some protection on their skin. Hats, umbrellas and long-sleeved shirts are best. You can also get the maximum strength sunscreen available and use it on all skin areas that remain exposed.
- Tanning beds also emit ultraviolet light, and can cause skin damage including skin cancer.

> Certain common drugs can aggravate sunburn or rashes due to exposure to sunlight. Ask your doctor if you take any medication and plan to be outdoors in sunlight.

Sunscreens
- Sunscreens are rated by their *sun protection factor (SPF)*. It is recommended that you use products that have an SPF of at least fifteen. Reapply liberally after swimming or sweating.
- A higher SPF is required for children, people with very fair skin, or anyone remaining in the sun for an extended

period of time. They should also wear clothes and sun hats.
- Use a waterproof sunscreen if you spend much time in the water or in a very humid climate.
- SPF numbers indicate protection against UV-B rays only, and not UV-A rays. Skin cancer may be caused by light that sunscreen does not stop, so do not believe you can stay in the sun longer just because you use sunscreen.
- The amount of sunscreen contained in make-up is usually not enough to afford any real protection against UV rays.
- Only opaque substances such as *zinc oxide* or *titanium dioxide* can block out sunlight.

First Aid for Sunburn
- A cool bath with oatmeal will soothe the skin.
- The juice or gel of the aloe vera plant has been shown to soothe burned skin and to prevent infection.
- Do not use vitamin E oil. It is not readily absorbed by the skin, and can cause allergic reactions.
- Also avoid any other type of oil or butter, as it will only serve to hold heat in the skin, increasing pain and delaying healing.

Hair

The longest human hair ever measured was twenty-six feet long. An average head of hair contains 100,000 strands. The average hair loss is 100 hairs per day.

Each strand of hair on our head is made up of three parts:
- The *medulla* is at the center. Little is known about its function.
- Surrounding the medulla is the *cortex,* which contains the pigment that determines the color of the hair.
- The *cuticle* covers the cortex. It is composed of overlapping cells of *keratin*, which protect the hair shaft from the environment, and hold moisture in the hair.
- Each hair grows out of a *follicle* in the scalp.
- Each hair follicle has oil glands alongside it, and the oil runs into the follicles to coat the hair. This oil helps smooth out the cuticle and make the hair shiny. If too

much oil is produced by the glands, the hair becomes oily and limp. Oily hair attracts dust and dirt faster.

Hair Care

- Harsh shampoos that are too alkaline can damage the hair. Use shampoos which are slightly acidic or pH balanced, with moisturizers and proteins. Baby shampoos may be too mild to clean a full head of adult hair.
- Thorough brushing can help stimulate the scalp and circulation, as well as spread the natural oil onto the hair. Use a brush with round-ended bristles (natural bristles are the best) set in a rubber base. Too vigorous or too frequent brushing can cause an excess of oil to be released. Hair should be brushed gently and steadily.
- Learn to massage your scalp with your fingertips (not nails) until it feels warm and tingly. Massage your scalp for three minutes, twice weekly, to stimulate blood circulation and hair growth.
- Hair coloring and permanents can disrupt the cuticle, allowing moisture to escape. The hair then loses its elasticity, and can break easily.
- Excessive exposure to the sun or heat from dryers and rollers can also damage the cuticle.
- Sprays, setting lotions and mousses can make the hair sticky and dull.

Hair Conditioners

- Cream rinses are good for hair that tangles easily, but tend to make oily hair look limp. They are somewhat alkaline, and should be rinsed out thoroughly.
- Instant conditioners cannot rebuild hair, but they can make it look fuller and shinier. They can also help the hair retain moisture.
- Deep conditioners are available for damaged or treated hair. They can restore some moisture and protect the hair shaft.

Common Ingredients in Hair Care Products

Aloe vera	May be helpful. Usually in small amounts in shampoos.
Balsam	A resin that makes hair look fuller and thicker. Works well in combination with proteins.

Honey	Water soluble, it is rinsed away with shampoo.
Jojoba oil	Effective moisturizer. May be present in very small amounts.
Lemon juice	Particularly good for oily hair. Adds strength and shine.
Malt	A protein, mostly used in men's shampoos.
Milk	Used for its protein content.
Oils and waxes	Can help smooth the cuticle and make the hair shinier. Can make hair sticky and attract dirt.
Panthenol (Vitamin B5)	Excellent for strengthening hair and helping it grow. Sometimes mixed with other conditioners under the name Pantyl.
Polymers	Form a film over each strand of hair that can add bulk. Not harmful, but may make the hair feel sticky.
Proteins	Most hair can absorb some protein. May help repair the cuticle, make the hair look thicker. Egg protein is not readily absorbed.
Vitamins A, B, D and E	The hair cannot readily absorb these vitamins. Vitamin E mostly used in shampoos as a preservative.

Nails

There are many possible problems with the nails. The shape and appearance of the nails themselves can be a useful diagnostic tool for many conditions.

- Sometimes the nail will separate itself from the nail bed. This can be due to an injury, poor circulation in the fingers, or the result of an allergic reaction to chemicals in nail-care products (in particular formaldehyde and some glues for artificial nails).
- Cracked and brittle nails can result from chemicals such as polish removers and dish washing liquids. This problem can be remedied by using a good moisturizing hand cream or lotion and wearing rubber gloves for household tasks. The keratin of the nails needs moisture to remain healthy.

- Shredding nails, brown or greenish-brown nails, pitted nails, and thickened nails all generally stem from fungal infections.
- Spoon nails, yellowed nails, ridges in the nails and clubbed nails generally result from poor circulation. Some nutrient deficiencies and illnesses can also affect the appearance of the nails.

Nail Care

Just as for the skin, there are multitudes of nail care products and systems. One should be conscious of possible allergic reactions.
- Sometimes an allergic reaction to these products will not affect the nail area itself, but another part of the body such as the face, eye, or ear areas, which we are likely to touch often.
- While shaping the nails, be careful to avoid the cuticle, which should never be cut.
- Closely snip off any hangnail (a small piece of skin next to the nail).
- Because the keratin in the nail plate needs moisture, refrain from using polish remover (which is very drying) more than once a week.
- Soak dry nails in a solution of warm water and moisturizer for twenty minutes.
- Beware of artificial nails and nail tips. The glue products that are used to attach them can damage the nails, sometimes permanently. Also, foreign organisms such as bacteria can grow between the real and the artificial nail.
- Press-on nails, which are only worn for a few hours at a time, are much safer than other types of artificial nails.

Teeth and Gums

Tooth loss affects nutrition, speech and appearance. Cavities and gum and bone diseases can all be avoided. Even if you have suffered from dental problems, it is never too late to start caring for and preserving your teeth and gums.

Our teeth can last us a lifetime, if we care for them properly.

The teeth are not bones. In fact, they are much harder than bones. Originally teeth might have evolved from specialized fish scales. At one time in some ancient specie, they may have all had the same pointed shape, but evolution adapted different teeth to different tasks.

An adult normally has thirty-two teeth ideally suited to cut, tear and mash all foods as they travel from the front to the back of the mouth.

- Each tooth is covered with white *enamel* over a layer of *dentin* or ivory. Dentin is a very hard, inorganic substance.
- Inside the tooth is the *pulp* which contains blood vessels, nerves and cells that cause an increase in enamel as we age. The pulp is the living part of the tooth.
- The root of the tooth is formed of dentin covered with *cementum*, which is softer than the enamel. This surrounds the *root canal,* through which the blood vessels bring oxygen and nutrients.

Cavities

- There are hundreds of bacteria living in the mouth, but only those associated with the fermentation of sugar and refined carbohydrates cause tooth decay.
- These bacteria form an acid which destroys the enamel of the teeth, and mixes with saliva and food to form a sticky *plaque* which collects where the gum meets the tooth.
- If plaque is not removed and cavities are not treated, the infection can grow and eventually attack the bone itself.
- The back teeth have natural pits and crevices in their surfaces. Toothbrushes cannot always reach inside of these pits, so cavities often form there.
- Cavities can also form between teeth, or on the root of the tooth if the gum has receded. This condition is known as *periodontal disease.*
- Because the cementum on the root is softer than the enamel, cavities can grow rapidly there infecting the root canal and the pulp of the tooth. At this point the tooth must be extracted or receive a "root canal" treatment.
- Infected pulp within a tooth can lead to infection in the jawbone.

Caring for Your Teeth
- The first step in caring for your teeth is to eliminate all added sugar from your diet. (See *Food Additives*.)
- Sugar raises the acid level in the mouth, and this level stays high for about an hour. Regular snacking on sweets is extremely detrimental to your teeth. If you must eat sugared foods, you should brush your teeth afterwards, or at least rinse your mouth very thoroughly with water.
- Flossing is probably the single most important step in tooth care, and should be done at least once a day. It is essential to healthy teeth, and toothpicks cannot replace flossing. In fact, toothpicks can sometimes cause injury. Water irrigating devices also cannot replace flossing. Your dentist should show you how to floss properly.
- Brushing is also important, and to brush right, you need the right tools:
- The best toothbrush is one with soft polished nylon bristles. Stiffer bristles can damage the teeth and gums. Hold your toothbrush at a 45° angle and brush in a small circular motion, starting where the teeth meet the gums. Brush all tooth surfaces, paying particular attention to the insides and behind the last molars. Gently brush your tongue to remove bacteria.
- Toothpaste with fluoride may help strengthen the enamel and bone, especially in adults who have some root surfaces exposed. Avoid tooth whiteners and brighteners: they are abrasive and can damage the roots.
- Fluoride rinses can be a beneficial addition to regular brushing and flossing, but mouthwashes have little value for the teeth.
- Visit your dental hygienist or dentist every six months.

Periodontal disease starts between teeth, where the brush cannot reach, and it is the main cause of tooth loss in adults. Floss every day!

Dentists
Most of your dental needs can be handled by a family or general dentist. A visit to the dentist's office will usually start with a dental hygienist removing the plaque and calculus from your teeth. The hygienist is trained to

examine your gums and teeth for decay and other problems. Dental x-rays are now a common diagnostic procedure. In addition to your regular visits to the dentist or dental hygienist, you should contact your dentist immediately for any of the following symptoms:
- Pain is the most common sign of decay in the tooth or gum.
- Pain when chewing may be caused by infection in the jaw.
- Pain in the soft tissues of the mouth can be caused by bacteria, viruses, ill-fitting dentures, fungi or other problems.
- Sensitivity to cold or sweet foods can signal the presence of cavities.
- Sensitivity to hot foods usually indicates problems in the pulp of the root.
- There are different kinds of sores which can infect the mouth, and must be promptly treated.
- Most bleeding from the mouth, especially after brushing, is caused by periodontal disease. Watch out for signs of periodontal disease, including redness and inflammation of the gums.

Knock Out!

If a permanent tooth gets knocked out, place the tooth in milk and go to a dentist's office immediately.

Is Fluoride as Good as They Say?

It certainly seems to be: There has been a dramatic decline in the rate of tooth decay among U.S. children. This is generally attributed to the addition of fluoride to the drinking water of many municipalities. However, there has also been some concern that an increase in fluoride levels may cause skeletal damage (*osteosarcoma*).

At present, most studies indicate that the recommended levels of fluoridation in residential drinking water do not pose a risk, and in certain cases may actually provide some protection against osteosarcoma.

Clothing

Clothes, being worn directly on the body, form a very intimate kind of environment. This environment can be a source of comfort to us, or it can be detrimental to our well-being.
- We wear clothes to protect our skin, which is the largest organ of the body. Clothes shield us from cold and heat, rain and wind. They protect us from injury to our skin as we go through the day's activities.
- We also wear clothes for modesty – to hide our bodies from the sight of others – and to enhance our appearance. Therefore, the way each of us dresses should be appropriate to our lifestyle and personality.

If we know about the kinds of fabrics available to us, we can make educated choices about many of our clothes. There are also very sound tips on colors, textures, styles and forms which can help us harmonize our clothing with our life-style.

Synthetic Fibers

Synthetic fibers became available to the public after the development of the petrochemical industry in the 1940's. The intent was to create fabrics that would imitate natural fibers such as linen, silk, cotton and wool, at a fraction of the cost. Many of these synthetic fibers have not lived up to original expectations.
- Many chemicals and dyes used in the manufacture of synthetic fibers are carcinogenic, mutagenic, teratogenic or allergenic. (See *Toxins*.) At present, there are no guidelines to regulate the use of chemicals in wearing apparel.
- These chemicals can affect us in many ways, by absorption through the skin or by ingestion or inhalation of microscopic particles of the cloth. For instance, *vinyl chloride*, which has been proven to cause a form of liver cancer, is used in the production of certain fibers, as well as in synthetic leather and rain gear.

Nylon
- Created by Du Pont de Nemours and Co. in 1938 to imitate silk, the manufacture of nylon includes such

products as petroleum, coal, natural gas and water, all of which are now known to be in limited supply.
- Nylon is not porous and does not allow the free passage of air.
- It retains moisture and is not a good conductor.
- It can be very uncomfortable in warm weather.
- Formaldehyde, which is very allergenic, is added to nylon for dying and flame-proofing.

Polyester
- First produced by Du Pont in 1951, polyester is made from petrochemicals.
- Polyester absorbs oil from the skin and is difficult to clean.
- It does not absorb moisture well or conduct temperature, so it is too hot in summer and too cold in winter.
- Polyester can melt upon contact with an open flame.
- The dyes used in polyesters are known to be allergenic and corrosive.

Acrylics
- Developed by Du Pont in the 1930's, acrylics are also derived from petrochemicals. They include Orlon, Acrilan, Creslan, Zefran and Dynel.
- The fibers are weaker than natural fibers and generally do not allow for air circulation or the absorption of moisture from the body.
- Creslan and Zefran can blend well with natural fibers, but they are not recommended for people who are susceptible to allergies or have sensitive skin.
- Dynel is the least absorbent of synthetic fibers and becomes very hot and uncomfortable in warm weather. Dynel is used extensively in the manufacture of wigs. It contains vinyl chloride, which can be absorbed through the scalp.

Spandex
- Spandex was developed by Du Pont in 1940. It is also sold under the name Lycra. These elastic fibers are used mostly in swimsuits, dance wear and exercise clothes.
- Spandex does not conduct temperature well, so it is uncomfortable in warm weather.

- Look for dance and exercise wear that is made of blends of up to 80% cotton to 20% Spandex, which is more comfortable.
- Spandex should not be worn too tightly or for any length of time.

Olefins
- Olefins are also known as *polypropylene* fibers. These are non-absorbent fibers closely resembling wax.
- Olefins are good for cold weather because they wick away perspiration from the skin, but totally unsuitable for warm weather.

Rayon
- Although rayon is classified as a synthetic fiber, it is made from reconstituted plant fibers. It was invented in the nineteenth century as a substitute for silk.
- Rayon is not as strong as wool, cotton, silk or linen, but it is less expensive than these natural fabrics, and it is quite absorbent.

Natural Fibers

Natural fibers come from plants, animal hair and skin, and, in the case of silk, from the cocoon of the silk worm. For regular clothing needs, natural fibers are always preferable to synthetics.

Cotton
- Several varieties of the cotton plant are grown in warm climates. The most common fabrics made from cotton are terry, muslin, corduroy, canvas, denim, broadcloth, percale and oxford.
- Cotton fabrics are highly absorbent and permit evaporation of body moisture.
- Cotton can be mercerized for added strength and Sanforized to prevent shrinkage, which is one drawback of cotton. Another is its tendency to mildew if kept wet.
- Cotton is one of the most comfortable and versatile fabrics for all types of clothing.

Linen
- Linenis made from the stem of the flax plant. It was widely used in ancient Egypt, and remains quite

popular in modern times. Flax is harder to grow than cotton, and linen is therefore more expensive than cotton.
- Linen is very durable and comfortable in warm weather, and is frequently used in cotton blends.
- Linen dries quickly and is more resistant to stains than cotton. It also shrinks less and can be washed in very hot water. However, it also require more ironing.

Silk
- Silk comes from the thin thread produced by the silkworm in the process of spinning its cocoon. Silkworms must be kept in clean straw beds and fed the leaves of mulberry trees. The cocoons must be loosened by hot and cold water baths.
- Silk fabric is extremely comfortable and very attractive. It is very durable, warm in winter, and quite suitable for summer wear.
- Silk does not shrink much, but must usually be dry-cleaned or carefully hand-washed.
- Raw silk retains some of its sticky gum and has less luster than silk that has been boiled clean.

Wool
- Our ancestors who resided in cold climates used the skins of animals for protection and warmth. Later, shearing and spinning techniques were invented to produce wool from the fleece of native sheep.
- Wool does not conduct temperature well, therefore it can insulate a person from heat or cold. It is ideal for people who live in regions of extreme temperatures such as deserts, where the heat of the day is followed by cold nights.
- Wool is water-proof because of the natural oils which it retains, and is also somewhat flame-retardant. However, it does retain soil and odors, and needs frequent, careful washing with mild soaps.
- It can shrink if wet or overheated.
- Camel hair, angora and cashmere from goat hairs, alpaca and llama hairs have properties similar to wool.

Clothes made from natural fibers are always preferable to synthetics. They are stronger, more comfortable and more healthful.

The Comfort of Clothes

If the type of fabric we choose is important, so is the style and cut of our clothes. Even when social situations require us to wear articles of clothing such as ties, suits and high heels, we can still follow certain guidelines to make ourselves more comfortable and healthy.

- Girdles, tight pants, belts and skirts can restrict circulation and digestion. They can also slowly distort musculature by applying constant pressure on the abdomen, lower back and stomach areas.
- Stockings should not be too tight, particularly at the top of the leg, where they can impede the return of venous blood to the heart.
- The continuous wearing of high heels is a main cause of poor posture and subsequent back problems. (See *Shoes*.)
- Brassieres should not bind the chest or cut into the shoulders or sides.
- Choose shirts with collars one fourth size larger than your usual size. You should be able to fit two fingers inside the collar and one finger inside the cuff.
- Whenever possible, choose clothes that hang from the shoulders or hips, without tight fastening or binding at the neck, chest, or waist. Some examples are A-line dresses, drawstring pants, and wrap-around skirts.
- Comfortably cut clothes can be made to look more dressy by choosing more expensive fabrics such as linen or silk.
- Choose natural fibers, or blends that are mostly natural fibers over synthetic fibers.
- Wear loose clothes in warm weather, as the body tends to expand when the temperature rises.
- Sizing tips: Allow two fingers of spare room in any waistband. Lift both arms to the sides and twist. Raise each leg to the side. You should also be able to squat comfortably.

If you are free to move and breathe in your clothes, then your body is free to function efficiently and effortlessly. Your clothes should complement your inner health and beauty.

Shoes

We wear shoes mostly for protection from the elements and from the hard surfaces of our city environment. When our ancestors walked barefoot, they developed strong feet with tough pads (calluses) on their soles. The ligaments and muscles of the foot support the arch and the twenty-six bones that form each foot. Each foot is designed to adequately support the weight of the body and to enable locomotion.

Foot ailments can cause problems in the ankle, knee, hip and back.

Most problems with the feet are the direct result of ill-fitting shoes, walking or running on hard surfaces without proper cushioning, and too little exercise for the feet and toes. Few shoes are really designed to absorb shocks, cushion feet or enhance their natural movements. Most shoes are created with more thought to fashion than to health.
- Improperly fitted shoes can seriously damage the feet.
- Children, especially, need shoes that fit them well and do not restrict foot movement.
- Tight shoes can hamper circulation, and can create swelling, varicose veins and other conditions.
- Pointed shoes that press the toes together can cause soft corns between the toes, or hard corns which develop over the joints. Hard corns can grow into the joints and cause *bursitis*.
- *Bunions*, which are enlargements within the joint of the big toes, are also caused by improperly fitted or tight shoes.
- High heels are at the root of many problems: displaced weight onto the big toe can contribute to the formation of bunions, and calluses can develop on the balls of the feet. Very high heels (over two inches) put a lot of pressure on the toes and stretch the tendons of the foot abnormally. They can cause irreparable damage, particularly in combination with pointed toes. High heels also cause the wearer to push the pelvis forward, causing bad posture and chronic backache.

The Right Fit

In the United States, 88% of women wear shoes that are too small or too narrow.

- The soles of shoes should be flexible so that a shoe can bend without crushing the toes.
- In summer, sandals are best, as the feet can remain cool and air can circulate between the toes.
- During colder weather, leather or canvas shoes and boots are best, as these natural materials breathe and can stretch to fit better.
- Cotton or wool socks are much better than any nylon or other synthetic fiber hosiery.
- When buying shoes, try on both the left and right shoes and walk around in them. They should feel comfortable right away, with enough room for the toes, and no pinching, cutting or rubbing anywhere.
- Our feet are often two different sizes. Buy for the longer foot and use an insole in the other shoe if needed.
- Try on shoes before buying, even if you know your size, as shoes are often manufactured overseas and sized differently.
- Shop for shoes later in the day when your feet are tired and swollen. If new shoes feel good and comfortable then, they will fit even better on other occasions.

Older people and diabetics should pay special attention to their feet, as their circulation is often somewhat impaired.

The Environment

Our body's survival clearly depends on the elements in the world around us. Without air, the body sustains brain damage within five minutes; without water, death will come within days; without food we can only live a few weeks. Therefore the quality of the air we breathe, the water we drink, and the food we eat is of great importance. Together they form our environment, and the rapidity of deterioration of our environment has become an all-important issue in recent years. But we are hardly passive consumers of the environment: just as we have the capacity to pollute, deface or destroy our environment, we have the ability to conserve, restore and save it.

Toxins

A *toxic compound* is one that can cause an illness. The presence of a toxin in the environment is described as *contamination*, and contamination of the environment by one or several pollutants is measured in terms of its *concentration*. When a contaminant passes from the environment into the body, through inhaling, swallowing or absorption through the skin, there is *exposure* to the contaminant.

Classification of Toxins
- *Carcinogens* have the ability to cause cancer.
- *Mutagens* can cause genetic changes in a cell. Mutations occur naturally in the cells (in fact, one of the processes of evolution) but naturally occurring mutations are very rare. A mutated cell can continue to grow and divide. The mutation may then be passed on to offspring, and the next generation or even one after that.
- *Teratogens* are substances that can cause birth defects. Teratogenic literally means "monster causing."

Many mutagens are teratogenic as well, and there are obvious ties between carcinogens and mutagens.

The healthier we keep ourselves, the better chance we have to avoid being adversely affected by the environment. Good nutrition, regular exercise and a healthy life-style ensure the body's natural ability to fight off many potentially harmful substances.

Exposure to Toxins

We can be exposed to toxins almost everywhere we go, at work or at home, in cities or on the farm. While many toxic substances are the by-products of modern industry, some also occur naturally.

Toxins in the Workplace

Recurrent exposure to toxins is most common among industrial and chemical workers, plastic workers, pesticide sprayers, painters, medical technicians, textile workers and petrochemical workers.

How can we identify all the toxins on the job?
- So far, about thirty specific substances and industrial processes have been identified which cause cancer in humans. The federal government's National Toxicology Program has prepared a list of these carcinogens, along with examples of occupations providing a risk of exposure.
- Farmers and other agricultural workers are in danger of exposure to pesticides, herbicides and a host of other chemical products.
- There are more than 700,000 chemicals in industrial and agricultural use today.
- Of these, only about 500 have been tested for safe levels of exposure.
- If you suspect that you come in contact with any toxic products at work, you should obtain all available data regarding the product, and make sure that all necessary precautions are being taken to avoid exposure.

Natural Contaminants
- *Asbestos*, a natural compound, was extensively mined and processed in the last century, and used in thousands of products. Millions of tons were produced and eventually discarded in landfills and other places. Today, asbestos is an ever-present contaminant, found in air, water, and even some foods. Also found in the lungs of almost everyone who lives in a large city, this is a proven carcinogen.
- *Sulfur dioxide, nitrogen dioxide, carbon monoxide* and other pollutants are released by power plants, factories and motor vehicles. All of these substances have been directly related to serious health problems.

Synthetic Contaminants
Synthetic substances are another area of concern. Thousands of compounds have been engineered and released into the environment. Among these, several types are known to be especially harmful:
- *PCB's* are a group of very toxic compounds that were widely manufactured for use as electrical insulation. PCB residues have been found beneath the North Pole, at sea, and within most people's bodies.

- Other chemicals were manufactured to use as herbicides, pesticides and fertilizers. These have been so widely used, in such large quantities, that they are now present almost everywhere in the environment, including aquifers and surface water (See *Water.*), as well as in our food.

Nuclear Waste

Many of the toxins which now contaminate our environment were produced during the rapid industrialization of the Western world. With recent increases in the use of atomic energy, we are now encountering the huge problem of nuclear waste disposal. *Plutonium*, the radioactive waste of the nuclear reactors, is one of the most toxic substances known to man. The problem of permanent disposal of such waste has yet to be resolved in a satisfactory manner.

Examples of Toxins in Industry

Job Categories	Possible Chemical Exposure	Possible Results of Exposure
Petrochemicals, Insecticide production or application	Arsenic	Lung cancer, Lymphomas
Industries, Mining, Shipyards	Asbestos	Asbestosis, Lung cancer
Chemical industries	Benzene	Leukemia, Blood disorders
Coal mines	Coal dust	Black lung disease
Textiles	Cotton dust	Brown lung disease, Emphysema
Metallurgy, Battery manufacturing	Lead	Anemia, Nerve damage, Kidney disease, Birth defects
Medical technicians, Nuclear industries, Uranium mining	Radiation	Cancers, Leukemia, Genetic damage
Plastics industries	Vinyl chloride	Cancer of liver or brain

Sources of Toxins in the Home

Many of the same toxins that can affect us at work or in our city streets can also occur in the home to threaten our health and well-being. We usually spend more than half of our time at home, so it is important that we understand how external contaminants can invade our homes, to recognize sources of toxins which can exist inside our homes, and learn how to minimize these dangers.

- In the last couple of decades, the building and furnishing industries have increased their use of chemicals, especially plastics and polymers.
- At the same time, thousands of new household products have emerged, many of them toxic.
- We now build more energy-efficient housing with less natural infiltration of air, so that the increase of harmful products in the home coincides with a decrease in the circulation of fresh air to ventilate fumes.
- Unvented gas and kerosene heaters are the worst offenders in the home. Not only can they cause house fires, but they release *carbon monoxide*, a very toxic odorless and colorless gas.
- Chimneys in need of repair can also be a source of carbon monoxide, *carbon dioxide*, and other contaminants.
- A gas range releases carbon monoxide, carbon dioxide, and *nitrogen dioxide*.
- Coal stoves produce *sulfur dioxide* (SO_2).
- Nitrogen dioxide and *nitric oxide* (NO_2 and NO) cause coughing and burning in the throat, nose and eyes. They are the by-products of combustion, and components of smog.
- *Ozone* is another polluting gas. It is very unstable and decomposes readily into oxygen, but it can be released in the home by certain small appliance motors such as those in sewing machines, power tools, ion generators and photocopiers.
- Even in very small amounts, ozone can be extremely irritating to sensitive people.
- Install proper venting for all stoves, furnaces, hot water heaters and appliances. Have all chimneys cleaned, inspected and repaired.

Tobacco Smoke
- Tobacco smoke is dangerous not only to the smoker: it's harmful to others who inhale it from the air.
- Tobacco smoke adheres to carpets, drapes and all other furnishings.
- Children are especially susceptible to the dangers of tobacco smoke.
- If a person must smoke in the house, smoking should be restricted to one well-ventilated area that is off limits to children.
- Smokers are particularly at risk from carbon monoxide poisoning, because their blood already contains some carbon monoxide absorbed from tobacco smoke.

Formaldehyde
- *Formaldehyde* (HCHO) is well known as a home pollutant because of the widespread use of urea formaldehyde foam insulation (UFFI) in the 1970's.
- Formaldehyde can cause headaches, dizziness and depression, and can also aggravate asthma, colds, flu and allergy symptoms. It may be a carcinogen.
- A ban on UFFI was later rescinded, and formaldehyde is now used in thousands of products. It can be found in paints, adhesives, carpets, certain fabric treatments and dyes, cosmetics, shampoos, and many other common household items.
- Choose carefully for formaldehyde-free products. When buying a home, determine the type of insulation and building materials used.

Organic Compounds
- *Organochlorines* are compounds of organic chemicals (carbon and hydrogen) and chlorine. They are found in many goods and substances including pesticides, liquid solvents, cleaning fluids, paints, waxes, plastics, PVCs (polyvinyl chloride) and PCBs (used extensively in electricity insulators.
- Organochlorines can also form spontaneously when chlorinated water mixes with organic compounds. They are all very toxic carcinogens.
- All products containing organochlorines must be labeled "hazardous" in the United States. You can recognize these compounds on all labels because they contain the two syllables "chloro."

- *Volatile Organic Compounds* readily evaporate at room temperature. They come from petroleum oil and gas, and are generally used as solvents (benzene, ether, mineral spirits, alcohol, propane, butane, etc.). They are extremely toxic, and most are asphyxiant.

> Avoid the use of volatile organic compounds and organochlorines whenever possible. Ventilate with plenty of fresh air when using. Keep products tightly closed in a safe place, preferably outside of the home (in a garage or shed). Keep locked at all times, away from children and pets, and away from any heat source or flame. If kept indoors, keep in a locked and ventilated area.

Phenols are organic compounds made from petroleum or tar. Pure phenol (carbolic acid) is used extensively for disinfecting. These compounds are also found in household products, preservatives, plastic resins and tobacco smoke. Phenols can be highly toxic but usually are not recognized as such. They have a strong odor and should be avoided as much as possible.

Radon

- *Radon* is a odorless, colorless gas which occurs naturally in certain rocks and soils.
- Radon itself is fairly harmless, but it can decay into radioactive products that attach themselves to dust particles. The dust is then inhaled, and the radioactive particles release alpha radiation into the tissues.
- It can enter a home through cracks, drain openings in basements, or foundations.
- It can also contaminate deep wells.
- If radon enters the home through the water supply, a high concentration of the gas can permeate the air of the bathroom while someone is showering or bathing.
- In some areas that are rich in radon, local building materials such as stones, cement, concrete and gypsum can also be contaminated with radon.
- A map of areas which may have high radon levels can be obtained from the U.S. Environmental Protection Agency (EPA). If necessary, foundations and basements can be sealed and vented.

Other Air Pollutants

Added to the chemical stew that circulates throughout your house are common house dust, animal dander, and other biological pollutants.
- Viruses and bacteria are commonly carried by air currents, which is the most frequent method of contagion of colds and flu. However, they can only live a short time in the air, especially if the humidity level is below 60%.
- Mold, mildew, rust and mushrooms are all fungi. They grow best in damp, warm, dark places, like the grout between the tiles of your shower. They show up as stains, and often give the house a musty odor. Borax can be used safely to remove existing fungi and prevent future growth.
- Pollen, animal dander (hair and skin particles), dust and mites (tiny spider-like animals) are carried in the air of our homes. They are all powerful allergens to sensitive individuals.

Symptoms of Indoor Air Pollution

Be alert to any of the following signs, which may indicate dangerous levels of contaminants in the home or indoor workplace:
- Headaches, runny nose, colds, coughs and sore throats that won't go away.
- Upset stomach or intestines, lethargy, fatigue, dizziness or sudden depression.
- Compare your symptoms with other household members who spend less or more time in the house.
- Compare severity of symptoms when the house is being aired out, when the heat is on and when it is off, and at different humidity levels.
- Make note of all new furnishings, carpets, drapes, appliances and other objects. Compare installation dates with onset of symptoms.

Temperature and Humidity

Temperature and humidity have direct effects on our health and comfort.
- Heat and humidity promote the growth of bacteria and fungi, as well as increase the outgassing of toxins from furnishings and other objects.

- Extreme temperatures can irritate the lungs and respiratory tract.
- Colds, flu, asthma and allergies are aggravated by fluctuations in temperature and humidity.

Controlling Temperature and Humidity in the Home

- Insulation of floors, walls and ceilings is important in keeping the home comfortable throughout the year.
- Kitchens, bathrooms and laundry rooms should be ventilated to reduce humidity.
- If the relative humidity reaches 90% outside, inadequate ventilation may cause the humidity to reach 100% in the kitchen or bathroom. At this level, bacteria and fungi thrive.
- Optimum relative humidity ranges between 40% and 60%. This range allows effortless breathing and sufficient moisture for the skin, while deterring the growth of bacteria and fungi.
- Remember: plenty of ventilation, with air drawn away from the street side, will help minimize humidity and in-home air pollution.
- Fans that draw air out are ideal for kitchens, bathrooms and laundry rooms.
- Dehumidifiers must be cleaned and drained daily.
- Beware of humidifiers and dehumidifiers which can harbor bacteria and even promote their growth, particularly if water pans or reservoirs are used. Micro-organisms in air-conditioning systems caused several fatal cases of Legionnaires' Disease.

CHAPTER 2
BODY-MIND

Health is never concerned with the body alone. Health is concerned with the body and the mind. Optimal health is the result of both physical and mental components.

Overview of Chapter

The human brain is the most complex computer ever known. It consists of more than 100 billion cells. The brain communicates directly with the *immune system*.

There are many reports of very sick people who have had remarkable recoveries which were attributed, at least in part, to their positive mental attitudes.
- Our emotions have a direct effect on our immune system. Joy, happiness and serenity can improve and support its functioning. Stress, grief and pain can lower the functioning of the immune system.
- The mind can exert a strong influence on the immune system, and an individual can learn to increase his or her ability to fight disease.

Health and the Mind

Health and disease are equally rooted in the mind, in thoughts that nourish well-being or sickness: focus on health and you are much more likely to be healthy.

In societies that believe in magic, a sorcerer or witch doctor can only cause the illness and death of a person if this person knows that a spell has been cast against him. The belief itself can cause illness and even death: the individual becomes more and more anxious and fearful. Eventually his own thoughts make him sick, supporting the belief that the spell is effective, and thus increasing his fear. Our thoughts and feelings can just as surely make us well and promote physical health, strength and joy in living.

Thousands of diseases and types of illness have been identified. Due to the rapid advances of modern medicine, many symptoms of ill health are now easily treated and cured. In fact some contagious diseases have been eradicated altogether through vaccinations. Yet some illnesses are still with us, and they are responsible for millions of deaths each year. We are all frightened by such diseases, many of which are degenerative and incurable.

Norman Cousins tells of a football game in Monterey Park, California where several people got food poisoning. It was thought that the soft drink dispensing machines were the reason people were getting sick. A loud speaker at the game then announced that people were getting sick and requested that no one use soft drink machines. Suddenly pandemonium broke out and many people in the stands began fainting and vomiting. Even people who had not drunk from the machines were getting sick. Hundreds of ambulances drove people to nearby hospitals.

Soon it was discovered and announced that the soft drink dispensing machines were not giving people food poisoning after all, and most people made immediate recoveries. Norman Cousins attributes the people's sudden illness and recovery to the power of the mind.

When the mind is at ease, the body is healthy.

In this chapter, we will examine some of the most common diseases which plague our society: cancer, heart disease, diabetes and AIDS. We will look at some other very widespread conditions that are often chronic: backaches, headaches, the common cold, and allergies. The widespread problem of chronic stress, and the effects of cigarette smoking, alcohol, and recreational drug use will also be considered.

This chapter also covers some of the many ways in which we can improve the functioning and well-being of the body and the mind. This includes such topics as exercise, massage, biofeedback, modern and traditional medicine, and doctors. The effects of light, color and sound are discussed.

We will consider several issues in which the workings of body and mind appear to be inseparable: sleep and dreams, sexuality, menopause, and longevity.

But first we must understand how our bodies fight off the germs, bacteria and viruses which cause infection.

The Immune System

The immune system is complex, and works closely with other systems in the body:
- Before birth, primitive white blood cells called *lymphocytes* are formed in the bone marrow of the arms, legs, backbone and pelvis.
- After birth some of these cells mature within the bone marrow to become *B cells*. B cells discharge antibodies specifically manufactured to fight different invaders.
- Other lymphocytes migrate to a gland behind the breast bone called the *thymus* where they mature into *T cells*. T cells can kill other cells on contact.

- The *lymph system* has its own set of vessels and works in conjunction with the blood circulatory system. It absorbs fluids and waste materials from the surrounding tissues and transports them to the neck, where it connects directly with blood vessels.
- The lymph system also collects the white blood cells and produces its own white blood cells in the *lymph nodes*.
- Lymph nodes are strings of bean-shaped nodules found in the armpits, groin, abdomen and neck. They serve as a storage place for B cells, T cells and scavenger cells known as *macrophages*.
- When the body fights an infection, the lymph nodes are often swollen.
- When an *antigen* (a germ) enters the body, the immune system immediately recognizes it as a foreign object.

Parts of the Immune System

The parts of the immune system work together to destroy the foreign substance:
- Each cell is programmed to make one specific antibody.
- During an encounter with an antigen, some B and T cells become memory banks which store the blueprint for the specific antigen so it is immediately recognized in the future. When we say that we have acquired immunity to a specific antigen we are referring to this process.
- The immune system is so effective that it can kill a perfectly healthy transplanted kidney, which it views as foreign, in less than ten days.
- Unfortunately, the immune system is capable of becoming sick or malfunctioning. Occasionally the body may wrongly identify one of its own parts as foreign and the immune system attacks it: this condition is called an *auto immune disease*.
- Allergies occur when the immune system mobilizes against a harmless substance.
- If some component is missing in the immune system and its ability is therefore impaired, it is said that there is an immune deficiency disease. *AIDS*, Acquired Immune Deficiency Syndrome, is the best known of these.
- An immune deficiency disease can be the result of an inherited condition, infection by a virus, or the side effect of certain drugs.
- Aging, malnutrition and stress can also weaken or damage the immune system. After sexual maturity the thymus

gland slowly shrinks in size and movement of white cells from the marrow to the thymus decreases.
- When this happens the number of B cells and T cells may remain the same but their ability to combat antigens is lessened.

Stress and the Immune System
- Chronic stress has been found to interfere with the immune system by reducing the effectiveness of white blood cells in fighting disease.
- Diabetes, heart disease, cirrhosis of the liver, asthma, colds and flu, herpes, allergies and cancer are all known to be aggravated to some degree by stress. (See *Stress*.)

Vitamins and the Immune System
An adequate intake of vitamins and minerals is essential for optimal functioning of the immune system. For instance:
- To function efficiently, T cells need vitamin A and vitamin B6.
- Vitamin B12 is needed for proper functioning of T cells and other white blood cells.
- Vitamin C is important to the strength of the immune system in general.
- Some amino-acids and minerals (iron, zinc, selenium, magnesium and iodine) can enhance immunity.

For a healthy immune system, eat a varied and nutritious diet with lots of whole grains, fresh fruits and vegetables.

Exercise and the Immune System
- Contraction of muscles during exercise helps the lymph fluid to circulate throughout the body, which increases the efficiency of the immune system.
- Walk, run, bicycle, swim, or enjoy some other activity each day that will help you work up a sweat. A good exercise program will help keep your weight normal and enhance your immune system.
- But don't overdo it! Exercising to exhaustion causes stress and temporarily impairs immunity.

The Mind and the Immune System

People willing to take responsibility and act for their own best interest will avoid most illness in their lives. Unfortunately most people are not willing to make the necessary changes in their lifestyle.

You may be surprised to consider that there are benefits to every illness. The diseases we give ourselves help us maintain a belief system about ourselves and the world that we do not want to change. We subconsciously allow ourselves physical injury in order to protect ourselves from change and various other psychological fears. Our immune system becomes suppressed and a germ is allowed to grow into an ailment.

The vast majority of people will not accept this truth, and in fact become angry when told of the responsibility they have in their own illness. They are more comfortable in continuing to believe that they are the victims of a disease that is not, in any way, their fault.

These same people may know about the placebo effect, through which sugar pills are known to heal people. The placebo effect is actually a self–fulfilling prophecy: we expect a cure to happen and behave in ways that increase the probability that it will. Still, most people believe that this approach only works on others, and their own illness is a real disease that would not respond to sugar pills.

Recovery of health will come from understanding the link between our psychological and emotional states and stress in our lives during the year prior to the appearance of the illness. When we find the link we will also find the belief system about ourselves and the world that we do not want to change. Examination and modification of this belief system is our healing.

We can not always control the external circumstances of our life, but we can control our reactions to them. Taking responsibility for our actions and reactions is necessary to our well-being and the health of our immune system.

Cancer

Cancer is a disease which can often be prevented.

Cancer is the most dreaded disease today, next to AIDS. Cancer is now the second leading cause of death in the U.S. Almost half a million Americans die of cancer each year.

Tumor Growth

Most cancers are believed to develop in two separate steps:
- An *initiating agent* such as tobacco smoke or radiation causes some damage to a cell.
- A *promoting agent* then stimulates the development of the cancer. For instance alcohol itself does not cause cancer, but it is known to promote cancer of the mouth, throat or liver that has been started by cigarette smoking.

The most recent research indicates that a cancer tumor starts from a single cell in which the mutation of a growth gene causes the cell to start dividing endlessly. Cancer cells do not grow faster than other cells, but they lack the automatic mechanism called *contact inhibition* which stops a cell's growth as soon as contact is made with an adjacent cell. Cancerous cells keep growing, robbing other cells of essential nutrients. Tumors form and healthy cells begin to die.

Because cancer begins with the body's own cells, the immune system does not always react towards it as it would towards a foreign invader such as bacteria. There is however, some evidence that a strong and healthy immune system can contribute to the remission of cancer and certainly to its prevention.

Causes of Cancer

35% of all cancers are due to poor diet (especially one low in fiber and high in fats).
30% are due to tobacco smoke.
23% are due to excessive exposure to sunlight.
5% are due to viruses.
4% are due to exposure to carcinogens in the work place.
2% are due to pollution in the environment.
1% are due to food additives.

We now know that many chemicals are carcinogenic. Although many of these chemicals pollute our environment, we can often control certain aspects of our environment, and use precautions when in contact with known harmful products. Some substances, though not directly carcinogenic, may combine with other elements in the body to form carcinogenic compounds. This is true of some food additives. (See *Food Additives*.)

Cancer and Nutrition

Many cancers can be prevented by improving our diets.

- Adequate intake of fiber, vitamins and minerals from fresh fruits and vegetables is absolutely essential in the prevention of cancer. (See *Nutrition*.)
- High-fat diets are directly linked to cancer of the breast, colon and prostate gland.
- Japanese women have a much lower incidence of breast cancer than American women, and they also get less of their caloric intake from fat.
- Colon cancer is prevalent in societies where fat is obtained primarily from meats, dairy products or sweets. In cultures with diets rich in fiber, colon cancer is almost non-existent.
- Vitamin C and fresh fruits and vegetables help prevent cancer of the stomach.
- Vitamin A seems to have a good effect on certain types of cancer, such as cancer of the lungs and larynx.

Cancer and Exercise

Exercise programs which relieve tension and stress can be of great help in preventing cancer.

When used in conjunction with relaxation techniques such as meditation and visualization, exercise has been shown in some cases to inhibit the growth of cancerous tumors and to speed recovery.

Cancer Prevention through a Healthier Lifestyle

The following guidelines can help reduce your risk of cancer:
- Don't smoke, sniff, or chew tobacco.

- Avoid cigarette smoke in your environment (passive smoking).
- Get regular cancer screenings.
- Perform regular self-exams of breasts or testicles and skin.
- Restrict your exposure to sunlight, and wear protective clothing and sunscreen.
- Eliminate or restrict your consumption of alcohol.
- Eat a low-fat, high-fiber diet.
- Eat whole grains and high-fiber cereals.
- Eat foods that are high in vitamin C.
- Eat a wide variety of fresh fruits and vegetables.
- Steam, bake or broil foods. Do not fry or grill.
- Avoid foods that contain nitrites and other additives.
- Exercise regularly.
- Maintain your optimum weight.
- Learn and practice stress management techniques.
- Check for radon in your home if it occurs in your area.
- Wear protective clothing and follow all safety precautions when working with any chemical or hazardous material.

Early Warning Signs of Cancer

The earlier the condition is detected and treatment started, the greater the chance of recovery. This applies because cancer spreads throughout the body (*metastases*). A cancer started in one organ may invade other organs if left untreated.

Early detection of most kinds of cancer dramatically increases the chances of full remission.

Colon cancer can be treated successfully if detected early. Testicular and prostate exams are easily done at the doctor's office. Women can learn to do self-examinations of the breasts in a few minutes during a regular check-up with their doctor. A simple and painless *pap-smear* taken once a year in the doctor's office can detect pre-cancerous cells in the cervix.

Be alert for any of the following signs and bring them to the attention of your physician immediately:
- Any change in the size, color or shape or a mole or wart.
- A lump or thickening at any location.
- Any sore that does not heal.
- Persistent coughing or hoarseness.

- Persistent bleeding or discharge.
- Any change in bladder or bowel functions.

> We should all learn to do self-examinations on a regular basis. A few minutes once a month is all it takes to check for abnormal lumps or changes in the breasts, testicles, skin or mouth.

The Battle Against Cancer

The three main methods of treatment for cancer are surgery, radiation and chemotherapy.

- Surgery is usually used in easily accessible areas, when the cancer has not yet spread to other areas, or when a diseased organ can be removed without great risk to the patient. Today the amount of surgery is often reduced in favor of treatment with radiation and chemotherapy.
- Radioactive compounds can be injected to treat areas that cannot be treated with surgery, such as the lymph system. Very narrow beams of radiation can be focused on precise locations to shrink or even destroy a tumor. Side effects include nausea, fatigue and possible scarring.
- Chemotherapy utilizes powerful chemicals that must be carefully measured and administered because of the many and sometimes severe side effects, which usually include nausea, hair loss and overwhelming fatigue. Chemotherapy is used extensively, either alone or in conjunction with surgery and radiation treatments.

New Hope for Cancer Treatment

Today researchers are focusing on treatments using biological agents that are naturally produced by the body. These agents have no direct effect on cancerous tumors, but may be able to trigger or enhance the response of one's own immune system.

Monoclonal Antibodies

Live human cells carrying antigens are injected into mice, causing the mice to produce specialized lymphocytes in their spleens. These lymphocytes can be removed, mixed with a special B cell and cloned. The clones can be made to serve several purposes, including carrying radiation or a chemical treatment directly to the tumor source.

Interferon
- Interferon is a protein which interferes with a virus's ability to reproduce itself.
- However the body only produces interferon after a few healthy cells have already been killed by a viral infection.
- A high body temperature (over 103° F) can trigger cells to produce interferon.
- A high dosage of vitamin C may also enhance the production of interferon.
- Continued stress can slow the production of interferon by the cells.
- Interferon-alpha treatment causes a decrease in tumor size in 15% to 20% of patients with cancer of the kidneys or skin (melanoma). It has also been effective in some types of leukemia.
- The uses of Interferon-beta and Interferon-gamma are now being investigated.

Interleukins
- These agents are also of several types: Interleukin 1 through 9.
- Interleukin 2 appears to increase the activity of lymphocytes, making them more able to detect and destroy tumor cells.
- Other interleukins are also being investigated.

CSF's (Colony Stimulating Factors)
- CSF's play a major role in enhancing the activity of certain white blood cells.
- Since white blood cells are often destroyed by chemotherapy, the use of CSF's can allow the use of stronger doses of chemotherapy without increasing the risk of infection.

TNF's (Tumor Necrosis Factor)
- TNF's are a group of naturally occurring proteins that have proven effective against certain tumors in animals.

Beware of Miracle Cures
Beware of all claims about new and miraculous cancer treatments. While limited successes have been achieved with Interleukin 2 and Interferon, cancer may not always be caused by a failure of the immune system. The working of these

biological agents is not yet fully understood, and the long-term effects in the immune system are not yet known.

Heart Disease

There may be some hereditary factors involved in heart disease, but evidence shows that heart disease is overwhelmingly the result of an unhealthy lifestyle.

Heart disease is the number one killer of Americans today. It outnumbers lives lost to cancer by two to one and accidental deaths by ten to one. Heart disease kills as many people each year as do all other illnesses combined.

The heart is divided into four chambers and functions as a pump. The two chambers on the right side are filled with venous blood (used blood) that drains back through the veins carrying waste products and carbon dioxide from the body's cells. The heart pumps this blood to the lungs, where it is oxygenated and returned to the left side of the heart. It is then pumped back into the arteries and throughout the circulatory system to nourish the body's cells.

Blood Pressure

The kidneys and the nervous system work with the heart to maintain the correct blood pressure:
- Blood pressure rises as the heart pumps more blood into the circulatory system.
- The nervous system compensates for any change in blood pressure, no matter how subtle.
- If the blood pressure drops, the heart begins to beat faster.
- A drop in pressure also causes the kidneys to release substances into the blood which cause the arteries to contract. The kidneys also begin retaining sodium in the body.
- The increase in sodium causes an increase in the amount of fluids in the circulatory system. This makes the blood pressure rise.

High Blood Pressure or Hypertension
- Hypertension is a painless condition without visible symptoms. You can have high blood pressure without knowing it.
- High blood pressure puts a very serious strain on one's body. The heart has to work much harder, but may still be unable to expel the full amount of oxygenated blood with each contraction.
- If the kidneys receive less blood from the heart, they may interpret this as low blood pressure. The kidneys react by raising the blood pressure even more.
- A *stroke* occurs when high blood pressure causes a blood vessel in the brain to burst.

The Causes of Hypertension
- Heredity.
- Poor diet, especially too much salt.
- Cigarette smoking.
- Obesity.
- Habitual stress.

Stroke
A stroke occurs in the brain if the blood flow is suddenly blocked in the cerebral vessels or if a vessel ruptures. Blood clots can detach from the walls of arteries in the neck and travel to the brain where they can cause a blockage. A stroke can cause permanent paralysis, brain damage, or even death, so emphasis should be placed on prevention.

Lower Your Risk of Stroke
- Check your blood pressure regularly.
- Exercise regularly.
- Quit smoking.
- Avoid fatty foods that build plaque in the arteries.

Arteriosclerosis: Hardening of the Arteries
Arteriosclerosis is another dangerous condition in which deposits called *plaque* form inside the walls of the arteries.

These deposits block the free passage of blood. This condition is seen more frequently in people who:
- smoke.
- have high blood pressure.
- have a high level of cholesterol.
- do not exercise enough.

The heart must work harder to pump the blood past the plaque deposits in the arteries. A person with arteriosclerosis may suffer severe chest pains from participating in a strenuous activity such a climbing several flights or stairs or running a few blocks.

As arteriosclerosis gets worse, the chest pains come more often, are brought on by less effort, and last longer. This painful condition is known as *angina pectoris*.

Heart Attack

A heart attack, or *myocardial infarction*, occurs when an

> - Profuse sweating.
> - Paleness.
> - Dizziness or light-headedness.
> - Chest pains or tightness around the chest.
> - Pain that spreads from the chest to the shoulders, neck, back, jaws or arms.

artery is completely blocked and a certain area of the heart is cut off from its blood supply. This is a very severe condition, which frequently results in death. Even if the patient is saved, there may be permanent damage to the heart such as scar tissue and some loss of function.

At the first sign of a heart attack, prompt medical attention can usually assure full recovery. Unfortunately many people deny the symptoms and waste precious minutes.

Heart Attack Signs and Symptoms

Anyone who recovers from a heart attack must be treated and monitored for the many complications which can occur at a later date.

By understanding our risks and following sensible nutrition and exercise plans, we can help our hearts remain strong and healthy.

Cholesterol, high blood pressure and smoking seem to have the most detrimental effects on our hearts.

Treatments for Cardiovascular Disease

Heart Wrap
This procedure involves using a back muscle that is attached to the shoulder blade, teaching it to contract rhythmically with the help of an electrical device similar to a pacemaker, and then wrapping it around the heart and attaching it to the rib cage. In this fashion the muscle helps pump the heart. This technique has proven effective in cases of congestive heart failure and could eliminate the need for a heart transplants in the future.

Angioplasty: a Balloon in the Heart
When only a small section of a coronary artery becomes blocked, the use of angioplasty is sometimes very effective. A wire is inserted into an artery in the arm or groin and threaded through the artery until it reaches the blocked area. A small balloon at the end of the wire is then inflated, stretching the blocked area and dislodging the plaque.

The patient can remain awake during the procedure, which is done under local anesthesia. There are far fewer risks than with major open-heart surgery, and time spent in the hospital is greatly reduced. Unfortunately, it is not an appropriate course of treatment for every case.

The Rotoblator
With this new device, a small rotating blade is threaded along the path of an artery. When it reaches the blocked area, the blade is activated to chop away at the offending plaque. This technique is very new and still considered experimental.

Laser Surgery
Laser surgery is being investigated and holds great promise in the surgical treatment of heart ailments.

Coronary Artery Bypass
Coronary bypasses have become almost routine procedures in all cardiac centers. A long strip of vein is removed from the patient's leg and grafted onto the diseased

artery so that when the heart beats, the blood is pumped through the grafted vein and bypasses the blockage. This process can be repeated on all six of the cardiac arteries, however it cannot be used if the blockage is too extensive. Also, the grafted veins themselves may become diseased.

Preventing Heart Disease
- Maintain a positive attitude about your life, as will be discussed in the following chapters.
- Believe that you can make a difference, and take responsibility for your cardiovascular health.
- Exercise. Start a program of daily activities that you enjoy. Supplement with vigorous cardiovascular exercise every other day, after you've had a medical check-up for this specific purpose. (See *Exercise*.)
- Examine your diet and reduce your intake of saturated fats and cholesterol as much as possible.
- Maintain a healthy, balanced and nutritious diet.
- Lose weight if you need to and learn to maintain a healthy weight without dieting, but rather through exercise and proper nutrition.
- Learn to set aside relaxation periods during the day, and practice stress management techniques. (See *Stress* and *Meditation*.)
- Have regular medical check-ups.
- Know the first signs of a heart attack.
- Know your family's history of heart disease.
- Know the signs of overexertion.
- Take a stress test.
- Monitor your blood pressure and your cholesterol levels.
- Quit smoking.
- Do not make abrupt changes in your lifestyle.
- Learn to enjoy your life and to make time for healthy leisure activities.

Organ Transplants

The Good News
- Organ transplants are becoming more numerous and more successful.
- There are three times as many medical centers performing transplants as there were ten years ago. And medical

centers perform three times as many organ transplants today as they did then.
- Kidney transplants are the most frequently performed, followed by liver, heart, pancreas, and combined heart and lung transplants.
- The institutions which perform the largest number of transplants usually have the highest success rates.
- Transplant recipients now live longer and better than ever before.

The Bad News
- There are not enough organs donated to satisfy the demand.
- The ever-increasing cost of an organ transplant also limits the number of transplants that can be performed.

Diabetes

Diabetes was already recognized and treated in early Greece and ancient India. Today it affects approximately 11 million people in America.

There are two types of diabetes: insulin-dependent and non-insulin-dependent.

Type I: Insulin-Dependent

This is a condition in which the *pancreas*, a gland located just behind the stomach, loses its ability to make enough insulin.
- *Insulin* is necessary for the glucose (sugar) to be released from the foods we eat, in order to energize the cells of the body.
- In a healthy individual, the pancreas continually releases a small amount of insulin.
- When we eat, a greater amount is released all at once.
- When no insulin is produced, the store of glucose from the liver (called *glycogen*) cannot be utilized, and the glucose from foods cannot be released either.
- The glucose builds up in the blood, causing *high blood sugar* to spill into the urine. The body's cells actually begin to starve.
- When the pancreas has completely lost its ability to make insulin, the patient must compensate with injections of insulin two to four times a day.

An open-loop pump is now available that delivers insulin throughout the day, and that can be activated to deliver extra insulin at meal times. Research is also being conducted in the field of transplants and artificial pancreases for insulin-dependent diabetics.

Type II: Non-Insulin-Dependent

For many other diabetics, the pancreas still produces some insulin, but the body is resistant to it. The incidence of this form of diabetes is rising dramatically throughout the Western world.

In many parts of Africa where people eat mostly unrefined foods without much sugar, diabetes is very rare.

Who's at Risk?

Those at the highest risk of becoming diabetic are people over forty who are overweight, and those who have diabetes in their family.

Although the disease is often hereditary, with as many as one fourth of all Americans having family histories of diabetes, it is known that insulin-dependent diabetics can have non-diabetic children. The increase in non-insulin-dependent diabetes in the Western world is thought to be mostly due to obesity and sedentary life styles.

Precautions

Because the diabetic condition affects all the cells, it can have serious detrimental effects on many parts of the body. Even when the diabetes is successfully managed, certain precautions must be taken:
- Any illness, even a cold or flu, can become serious for a diabetic.
- If illness causes loss of appetite, a diabetic should drink some light soup or broth in small quantities throughout the day, and alternate with soft foods.
- A diabetic's tissues heal more slowly, and he or she may have less feeling in the extremities.
- Extra care should be taken with the feet, including careful washing, drying, daily massaging and wearing comfortable shoes of natural materials. (See *Shoes*.) Running shoes with open weave material can be particularly comfortable.

- Gums and teeth should also receive extra care. (See *Teeth*.)
- Hair and skin should be cared for to prevent excess dryness.
- Diabetes can cause damage to the blood vessels. This in turn can damage one's eyesight and kidneys. Almost 5,000 people lose their sight to diabetes each year, and as many as 4,000 will lose kidney function.
- Smoking can exacerbate the problems associated with diabetes, and must be avoided.
- Use extreme caution when taking over-the-counter medicines: read the labels or ask your pharmacist for included sugars or sugar-alcohol. Some medicines have warnings for diabetics.
- A diabetic woman should have her diabetes firmly under control before becoming pregnant, and she will require extra care during pregnancy. Diabetes sometimes develops spontaneously in pregnant women. This condition is known as *gestational diabetes*. It is a warning sign that the woman may later develop diabetes.

Taking Control of Diabetes

- A diabetic person must learn all the types and names of different sugars and how they affect the body. Everyone needs some glucose in their blood, but a diabetic can develop *hyperglycemia* or *hypoglycemia* (too much or too little blood sugar).
- Adjustments must be made to the diet under medical supervision, usually increasing the amount of fiber while decreasing the amount of sugars.
- Extra fiber in the diet helps minimize the fluctuations in blood glucose levels, and sometimes actually lowers the required amount of outside insulin.
- Fiber slows the absorption of glucose, and the extra bulk in high-fiber foods also helps control the appetite. (See *Nutrition*.)
- Diabetics should eat at least three times a day, avoiding large meals which cause a higher rise in blood-sugar levels. Meals should never be skipped.
- All types of candies, chewing gum, cakes, pies, cookies, sweetened condensed milk, fruits in syrup, jams, jellies, syrups and sugared soft drinks should be avoided. (See *Sugar*.)
- Snacking on raw vegetables provides extra fiber and is a good alternative to sweets.

- Eat apples, prunes and other fruits rich in pectin.
- Substitute fruits high in vitamin C (oranges, grapefruits, cantaloupes, mangoes) for sweet desserts. Vitamin C can prevent diabetic nerve damage and blindness.
- Increase the amount of chromium in the diet by eating fresh raw fruits, vegetables and whole grain products. Or take a chromium supplement of up to 200 micrograms daily.
- Use olive oil in place of other oils. It is known to improve cardiovascular health, and may help lower blood-sugar levels.
- Consult a professional dietitian with experience in the management of diabetes.
- Although alcohol can be consumed in moderation, it alters the blood-sugar level, and must be avoided at the times of greatest insulin action.
- Follow a medically supervised exercise program. Exercise can lower the blood-sugar level. Exercise times must be carefully balanced with eating times. Because diabetics often have a harder time exercising, the choice of an enjoyable activity is of great importance. Any new exercise program should be started slowly and monitored carefully.

> Every diabetic should wear a medic alert bracelet or tag at all times.

Diabetes can now be successfully managed. There has been tremendous progress in the techniques people use to monitor their own levels of blood glucose and adjust their intake of insulin. This has led to greater flexibility and freedom. Today a diabetic can lead a normal life and take vacations and trips, providing he or she is confident in the ability to monitor blood glucose levels and can carry all the required supplies at all times.

Cold and Flu

You can avoid the common cold with a little common sense.

Catching the Bug

- Every one of us catches an average of two colds a year. Children under age four average eight colds per year; their natural defenses against colds are not yet perfected.
- Colds are the leading cause of absences from work and school.
- Smokers are not more prone to catching colds and flu, but their symptoms may be worse because of prior damage to their lungs from the cigarette smoke.
- Colds and flu are caused by viruses. These extremely small organisms invade living cells, where they release their genetic blueprint to produce more of the virus.
- Cold viruses are divided into two main groups: the *Rhino Virus*, which usually causes colds and flu in the fall and winter, and the *Corona Virus*, which is prevalent in the summer.
- Cold viruses are transmitted primarily through hand contacts. This includes touching an object such as a door knob, and then touching the face prior to washing the hands.
- Flu viruses are extremely small, and can remain airborne for long periods of time. A flu is therefore much more contagious than a cold. Flu viruses can travel very rapidly throughout a community and even result in a global epidemic called a *pandemic.*

When a Cold Strikes

Every now and then, a cold germ gets through the body's natural defenses and settles in the upper respiratory tract. There the germ kills off some of the cells from the mucous membranes and triggers a strong reaction from the immune system.

- More mucus is produced, causing a runny nose.
- Blood fills the nasal passages and sinuses, and the nose feels swollen and congested.
- The swelling of the membranes can cause a headache and pain in the nose and under the eyes.
- The body attempts to rid itself of the extra mucus by sneezing.
- Sometimes there is a fever, particularly in children, as the immune system attempts to kill the germs.
- It is possible for the *larynx* (voice-box) to get infected too, causing hoarseness.

- The tear ducts of the eyes can become infected, producing itchiness and watery eyes.

Influenza

The flu produces symptoms similar to a cold, but much more severe:
- A fever is almost always present, in children and adults alike. To fight infection, the body's temperature is raised above normal range. This helps to destroy invading viruses and bacteria. This fever also activates production of infection-fighting antibodies from the immune system.
- The flu usually affects more of the respiratory tract.
- It causes more coughing and muscle aches.
- It may take up to three weeks to fully recover from the flu, whereas a cold is usually over within a week.

Prevention is the Best Remedy

At this time, there is no cure for the common cold or the flu, but most colds and flu can be prevented:
- Wash your hands often.
- Remain healthy through a nutritious diet and plenty of exercise.
- Stay warm.
- Avoid stress.
- Take vitamins A and C to boost your immune system.
- Humidify your environment. Cold and flu viruses thrive in a hot, dry environment.

If You do Get a Cold or Flu:
- Get plenty of rest.
- Drink lots of fluids to break up the excess mucus. Water, fruit juices, broth or herbal teas work best.
- Eat spicy foods to increase secretion of fluids.
- Inhale steam from a vaporizer or a pot of boiling water.
- Gently irrigate the nose with a mild saline solution.
- Drink hot herbal teas with lemon juice to soothe the throat.
- For flu, use aspirin, acetaminophen or ibuprofen to relieve pain and fever.

> Caution: Do not give aspirin to children as it may cause *Reye's Syndrome*, a serious and sometimes fatal illness of the liver and brain. It is recommended to use a children's brand of acetaminophen instead (such as Children's Tylenol or Panadol).

Medications that are sold over the counter can alleviate some of the symptoms of a cold or flu, but many have side effects, especially in children. The work of Dr. Linus Pauling seems to indicate that plenty of vitamin C does fortify the body's natural resistance to colds. However, very large doses of vitamin C are useless, as the excess vitamin is excreted with the urine. (See *Vitamins*.)

If, after proper care and time (a week for a cold, two weeks for flu), you are still sick or getting worse, particularly with increased coughing or painful breathing, you could be suffering from bronchitis or pneumonia. Check with your doctor immediately.

When to Call the Doctor
- If you or your child has an earache. Children are particularly susceptible to ear infections.
- If a fever is present for longer than three days.
- If you have a prolonged cough (more than a few days).
- If breathing becomes painful.

Who Gets a Flu Shot?

Every year, scientists evaluate the current strains of flu in action throughout the world, and come up with specific flu vaccines. Vaccinations should be considered by the elderly or any person at risk because of any existing illness.

Additionally there are some anti-viral drugs available by prescription, but they are only effective against some types of flu, and need to be taken continuously during an epidemic, for up to twelve weeks.

Asthma

Nearly one in ten Americans suffer from asthma.

- Asthma is a condition in which an allergic reaction causes the bronchial tubes to constrict, severely impairing breathing.
- During an asthma attack, the sufferer becomes unable to exhale.
- The person wheezes and gasps, often assuming a tense posture with shoulders raised.
- The panic which the sufferer experiences further interferes with breathing, and compounds the symptoms.

Treatment and Prevention

- Medication is available for asthma sufferers in pre-measured dose inhalers, which work very quickly to restore normal breathing.
- Drinking a hot beverage such as tea or coffee helps to end an attack, or at least to decrease its intensity. The caffeine in tea and coffee can also shorten the duration of the attack.
- Even after the attack has subsided, it is helpful to continue to drink warm liquids.
- Avoid cold liquids, which irritate the bronchial tubes.
- Have the asthma sufferer lie down with his head slightly lower than his torso, and gently pound the upper back with cupped hands. This may dislodge mucus and re-establish breathing. This procedure is very effective with children.
- Children and adults can learn relaxation techniques to use at the first sign of wheezing and tightness in the chest.
- Biofeedback has been used successfully to relieve asthma. (See *Biofeedback*.)
- Babies and pregnant women are particularly at risk, and should be treated by their doctor as soon as an attack starts.

For chronic asthma sufferers, some precautions can help decrease the incidence of attacks:
- Learn to relax.
- Learn breathing techniques. Yoga often helps. (See *Yoga*.)
- Drink lots of liquids during the day. Avoid ice-cold drinks.

Back Pain

At least ninety percent of the population will experience some type of back pain in the course of their lifetimes. It is the number one cause of visits to doctors' offices, and it causes more absences from work than any other condition except colds and flu. Yet the overwhelming majority of back pains could be prevented through exercise and correct posture.

What's in a Back?

- The main structural element of the human back is the *spine*, a long and sinuous column of twenty-four interlocking *vertebrae*, which are separated by fluid-filled, fibrous *discs*.
- The discs themselves are held together and in place by ligaments and muscles.
- The discs have a spongy texture which allows them to absorb shocks from jumps and falls, and to compress when a person bends over.
- The spine protects the *spinal cord* and the nerves that run through it. The spine is involved in almost every movement of the body, from reaching for the phone to running, jumping or twisting around.
- Three sets of long muscles support the torso and the spine: The *back extensors* follow the length of the spine. The *abdominal*, the *obliques* and the *dorsal muscles* form a girdle around the torso. The *quadriceps* bulge along the top of the thighs and help support the pelvis.

Causes of Backaches

Severity of back pain is not always proportional to the extent of the injury. Certain serious conditions can cause only a nagging pain, while simple muscle spasms can cause excruciating pain.

Back pain associated with symptoms involving the bladder, sexual organs, fever, vomiting, numbness or tingling in an arm or leg should be examined by a medical expert.

The period of greatest risk for back injury and pain is between the ages of thirty and fifty-five, when the discs lose some of their fluid and shrink. The loss of flexibility and the friction between vertebrae can cause recurring pain. After the age of sixty, the spine tends to become more rigid, and the likelihood of back pain diminishes.

Nearly all back pain is felt as muscle tension and spasms. Some common causes of back pain are:
- poor posture, with large curves such as sway back.
- weak muscles in the back and abdomen.
- obesity.
- improper bending and lifting.
- osteoporosis, especially in older women.
- stressful emotional situations which promote muscle tension.

Preventing and Treating Back Pain

An active life-style that encourages both flexibility and muscle strength is the best insurance against back trouble. Strengthening the back and abdominal muscles promotes a healthy and pain-free back.

Exercising for a Healthy Back

Regular exercise is the single most important thing for a healthy back. Exercising only on weekends is not enough, and may actually cause harm by putting stress and strain on weak back muscles.
- If you suffer from back pain or other medical conditions, your exercise program should be evaluated by a qualified health professional.
- Stretching exercises are especially important to keep a straight and healthy spine, particularly if they are designed to bring other benefits to the body as well. For instance, certain forms of yoga help firm up muscles, and also help to facilitate digestion and elimination. (See *Yoga* and *Tai Chi.*)
- Stretching exercises should never cause any pain beyond the normal feelings associated with stretching of tight muscles, joints, and ligaments.
- Swimming is the perfect sport for back pain sufferers. It uses all the spine muscles and requires no lifting of weights. However avoid diving or swimming entirely on the stomach.
- Bicycling and hiking are also great exercises.

- Jogging a few miles is good, providing it does not jar the back. Avoid marathons.
- Many forms of exercise do not build back strength or flexibility. Hard contact sports such as football or basketball can lead to back injuries. Golf is also risky because of the repetitive, sudden twisting involved in swinging the golf club on only one side of the body.
- Exercise also helps you to maintain your proper weight. Excess weight, particularly in the abdomen, tends to weaken the muscles that form a girdle around the area, and to pull on the already vulnerable lumbar region.

Lifting

When we bend forward to pick up an object and use the lower back to lift, instead of using the legs, we can strain the long dorsal muscles that run parallel to the spine. This can cause pain, bring the vertebrae out of line and create further difficulties. The National Safety Council recommends six steps to follow to assure proper lifting of any object:

Lifting Tips
- Place your feet about twelve inches apart, pointing forward, with one foot forward of the other. This gives you greater balance and allows you to adjust forward or backward without any twisting or leaning.
- Your back should remain straight and very slightly inclined.
- Your chin should remain tucked in, as this keeps your spine properly aligned.
- Grasp the object firmly with both hands and assure yourself of a steady grip before lifting.
- Bend at the knees to lower yourself towards the object.
- Your arms and elbows need to stay as close to your body as possible to keep the center of gravity nearer to you.
- Keep your body weight directly over your feet. This will also give greater balance and more strength for lifting.

Posture

Bad posture causes distortions of the spine, which can cramp the organs and impair their proper functioning. We cannot breathe deeply when our lungs are not able to expand fully. Digestion and elimination can also be impaired by bad posture.

Precautions can be taken to avoid developing bad posture, or to help restore the proper alignment of the spine:
- Examine all furniture to see if it supports the back and promotes good posture, particularly chairs in the work place, and beds and mattresses at home. Mattresses should be firm.
- Check your car seat. Add a small pillow behind your lower back if necessary.
- When sitting, the knees should be slightly higher than the hips and the lower back should be firmly supported. This can be accomplished with a footstool, by shortening the back legs of furniture, and by using little firm pillows in the small of the back.
- Rocking chairs can be soothing to the spine.
- Good posture should be maintained even while sleeping. Sleeping on your side is best. Pull your knees up towards your chest in a fetal position. This rounds and stretches the spine and helps relieve accumulated tension. You can put a small pillow between your knees for comfort.
- If you sleep on your back, put a pillow under your knees.
- The one position you must avoid is sleeping on your stomach. This increases the hollows in both the back and neck.
- Do not sleep on a hard mattress. It will not allow the spine to relax enough. Choose a medium or soft mattress. Box springs frequently sag and this is bad for the straightness of the back, so put at least one–half inch thick plywood between the box springs and the mattress.
- The right pillow should not be so big as to elevate the head above the torso. It should support the neck but allow for a natural position of the head.

Feet and Posture

It is important to mention here the crucial part played by the feet, which support our entire weight and allow us to stand, walk and run. The foot has a built-in arch in the sole which absorbs shocks. If, through weakness or extreme stress, the arch flattens out, a person is said to have *flat feet*. Flat feet are not able to absorb the constant jarring from walking, and the successive waves of shock are transmitted up the spine to the skull. This can lead to a variety of painful conditions. Wear comfortable shoes with good arch support. You may also want to use innersole cushions in your shoes. Do not wear high heels. (See *Shoes*.)

First Aid for Backaches

Learn to recognize the first signs of back fatigue and make time for rest, lying down. Most attacks of back pain are first felt as fatigue, mild aches or twinges.
- The minute the attack begins, get into a crouching position with feet flat on the floor, and stay there for a couple of minutes. This may stretch the back and avert the attack.
- Next lie down, if possible on the back, keeping the knees bent.
- If the pain persists, bed rest and an analgesic (aspirin or aspirin substitute) are usually recommended.
- Ice packs the first day will protect the spine from further injury, but do not leave ice in one area for more than ten minutes. After twenty-four hours switch to heat applications. Be careful not to turn the heat up too high.
- Massage may ease the pain.
- The pain should subside within a couple of days. Complete recovery generally occurs within ten days to six weeks.
- Pain is occasionally caused by a disc that has ruptured or is bulging out between two vertebrae and pinching the adjacent nerve. Discs do not really slip, but they can partially collapse or sustain a tear in the outer tissue.
- The lumbar region is the most vulnerable to disc problems because it carries the most weight, has the largest curve, and is the most likely to be injured through bending, lifting, or twisting.
- Back and neck braces might help limit movement but they also further reduce muscle strength and flexibility. If used, they should be removed as soon as possible.
- Acupuncture has been reported to be successful in some cases.
- For acute cases, drugs such as pain killers or muscle relaxers can be prescribed. Like many drugs, however, they often treat the symptoms rather than the underlying causes of back pain.

Surgery is reserved for the most severe back problems, as the spinal column is very delicate, and back surgery always involves serious risks. About 280,000 Americans do have back surgery each year to remove bulging disks that have been associated with back pain. However, over half of these surgeries may be unnecessary.

A 1994 study conducted by Dr. Michael Modic and reported in the New England Journal of Medicine found that 64% of healthy people with no back pain still had at least one disk that bulged abnormally.

The Semi-Supine Position

One can lie down in a semi-supine position, to allow gravity to encourage the proper alignment of the spine.
- Lie down on the floor or a firm surface (not a bed) and support your head without bending it forward. Try putting some books or a hard cushion under it.
- Raise your knees by bringing your feet halfway towards your buttocks. Your feet should be about two feet apart, with knees touching each other for support, or supported with large pillows.
- Stretch your arms along the sides of your body and relax. Imagine the weight of each body part sinking into the floor, and imagine your back and particularly your spine stretching more and more, while making contact with the floor.
- In this position, you can also learn to relax the dorsal muscles, the shoulders, the torso and arms, the pelvis and legs.
- Even the weight of the head should be allowed to rest completely on its support.
- This passive exercise should be done every day for at least fifteen minutes to relieve aches and tension in the spine. It is best to do this at the end of the day.

Chiropractic: The Touch that Heals

Once considered by many practitioners of traditional medicine to be quackery, chiropractic is now the third most frequently used health care profession in the U.S., after internal medicine and dentistry. Over two dozen hospitals have one or more chiropractors on their staff. Five percent of all Americans use chiropractic care once a year or more.

Chiropractic medicine is based on the theory that any misalignment of the spinal column interferes with the proper functioning of the nervous system, which in turn prevents the body from being totally healthy. Many chiropractors believe that they can help manage or even cure diseases and conditions other than back ailments. This belief is still being debated. However:

- It is certain that chiropractic care can be quite successful in treating back pain that is not caused by a tumor or fracture.
- Realignment of the spine can help prevent bad posture and subsequent back problems.
- A good spinal alignment contributes to a general feeling of well-being.

Choosing Chiropractic Care

It is necessary to exercise caution when choosing chiropractic care, as when seeking any other form of health care:

- Back x-rays should not be done on a routine basis. There should be a specific and valid reason to warrant one's exposure to any x-ray radiation.
- The approximate length of treatment should be determined before beginning therapy, and there should be some steady improvement seen during the course of the treatment.
- Ask questions and make sure you understand the specifics of the course of treatment.
- Chiropractors must be licensed to practice. Ask your chiropractor about his or her professional education and experience.
- Chiropractic services are often covered by workers' compensation plans and some insurance companies.

Headaches

It has been shown that humans suffered from headaches at least as early as 10,000 years ago. Ancient Egyptian texts about headaches have been found from as far back as the third century BC, and Indian texts date from 1500 BC. Throughout the ages, the treatment of headaches has been varied and extremely creative, ranging from the ancient use of herbal medicine to outlandish quackery.

Types and Causes of Headaches

- Tension and aching in the muscles that contract around the brain mass and its membrane cause tension headaches.
- Migraines and cluster headaches are brought on by the constriction or dilation of the blood vessels supplying the brain.

- Chemical irritation of the nerve endings due to any of a variety of substances can also cause headaches.
- Sinus headaches are caused by fluids and bacteria in the sinus cavity.

Tension Headaches
- Tension is the most common cause of headaches. Tension headaches usually start at the base of the skull, then wrap around the sides to the temples or sometimes to the eyes.
- They usually affect both sides of the head, and feel as if the head is being squeezed by a band.
- Stress and poor posture can create tension headaches.
- Eye strain, squinting or straining the eyes, and repetitive eye movements can create tension headaches.
- These headaches are habitual to the people who develop them. Some have suffered from them for many years.
- Tension headaches can be prevented by making the necessary adjustments in lifestyle, posture, or the physical environment (proper lighting, for example, or a better chair), and learning to relax.
- Tension headaches are also common in people who suffer from depression.

All tension headaches can be prevented.

During a tension headache, the major arteries of the scalp are constricted, so that the blood supply to the muscles, which are already in a state of tension, is diminished.
- Aspirin, a heating pad, a soothing massage or even an alcoholic drink (which helps dilate the arteries) can relieve such a headache.
- Other treatments can include prescribed tranquilizers, muscle relaxers, or anti-depressants.
- To cure chronic tension headaches, however, the cause of the tension should be eliminated.
- Relaxation techniques, exercises and other self-help methods often work well on tension headaches. (See *Stress*.)
- Good posture is essential to the prevention of tension headaches.
- For those whose tension headaches are brought on by suppressed anxieties or personal conflicts, therapy may be beneficial.

Dilation of the Arteries

Dilation of the arteries causes the tiny nerve fibers that surround the arteries to pulse with each heart beat, resulting in a throbbing headache.
- Such a headache can be brought on by nitrites used in cured meats, or by MSG, an additive commonly used in Chinese foods. (See *Food Additives*.)
- Alcoholic drinks can also dilate the arteries, especially red wines, which contain tyramine and histamine.

Migraines

The word *migraine* is French, and originates from the Greek *hemicrania*, which means "half of the head." Migraines usually affect only one side of the head.

During a migraine, the main arteries of the head dilate, while the smaller vessels which irrigate the cerebral cortex are constricted. Most migraine sufferers have very sensitive blood vessels, and there is some evidence that many of them may be unusually tense and meticulous people.
- Women generally suffer from migraines twice as often as men.
- The pain is often preceded by visual disturbances such as flashing lights or streaks, and tactile disturbances ranging from tingling to weakness or numbness in localized areas.
- A migraine may also be preceded by loss of balance, and nausea which may be so severe it induces vomiting.
- Migraines affect a person at recurring intervals, which are particular to the individual.
- Sudden changes in lifestyle and emotional upheavals appear to trigger migraines. They may also be caused by changes in atmospheric pressure.
- Alcohol will make this type of headache worse.
- Fried foods, chocolate and some spices may cause migraines, although research on the subject is currently inconclusive.
- Hormonal changes are also being studied, as many women are more likely to suffer migraines at the onset of menstruation.
- Migraines often start in childhood or early adulthood. They may be hereditary.
- The pain can sometimes be alleviated by pressing directly on the carotid artery in the neck on the affected side to diminish the flow of blood to the area.
- Lying quietly in the dark also helps.

- Habitual migraine sufferers should learn to plan their activities in regular patterns whenever possible. For instance, rising at the same time every morning has been known to stop attacks of "weekend migraines."
- Certain drugs can be used to alleviate the pain of migraines, however, they all have serious side effects.

Cluster Headaches

This type of headache is so named because the person sees clusters of bright lights at the onset of the headache. It is similar to a migraine, often causing nausea and pain which is localized in one half of the head. It may start with intense pain behind one eye only, lasting for up to an hour.
- Treatment of cluster headaches is usually similar to that of migraines.
- Cluster headaches afflict more men than women.

Pain and Pain Management

Acute pain is the kind of pain caused by an injury, such as smashing a finger or a sudden heart attack. As the wound or affliction is treated or heals, the pain diminishes.

When pain persists and gets worse in spite of medication or treatment, then it becomes a condition in itself: *chronic pain*.

Nearly 40 million Americans suffer from chronic pain due to illness, injury or stress.

Pain Relievers

In 1973, specialized sites were discovered in the brain that receive pain-relieving chemicals. Drugs such as *morphine, heroin, Demerol, Darvon, Percodan, Dilaudid* and other *opium derivatives* relieve pain by attaching themselves to these sites on brain cells. It was further discovered that the brain itself can produce its own opiate-like substances known as *endorphins, enkephalins* and *dynorhins*.
- People who take artificial analgesics for pain control soon build physical dependence and resistance to them, increasing the amount needed to relieve pain.

- It is now believed that the body's production of endorphins and enkephalins can be stimulated. Their biggest advantage is that they produce no side effects.
- Some oriental therapies such as *acupuncture* encourage the production of these natural pain relievers.
- Changes in diet and increased exercise may also be beneficial in reducing chronic pain. A low-calorie diet, high in amino acids, can sometimes stimulate the production of endorphins. The diet should be rich in fresh fruits and vegetables, and low in fats, salt and sugars. Refined or processed foods, additives, caffeine and alcohol should be totally eliminated from the diet.
- It is also possible that a person's attitude toward his or her illness and treatment can have an effect on the degree of pain endured.

Pain Clinics

Today, people who suffer chronic pain can be helped at pain clinics, using some of the following techniques:
- Step-by-step relaxation, similar to that used for stress management. (See *Stress*.)
- *Acupressure* or *Acupuncture*: is a form of treatment in which thin needles are inserted in specific points throughout the body. Acupressure substitutes fingertip pressure for needles. Scientists are not exactly sure how these methods work, but they are now regularly used for many forms of treatment and even for anesthesia.
- Learning to focus on the pain through exploration and verbalization: By learning to speak of the pain, one can gain insight and even some control.
- Biofeedback training: Biofeedback teaches people to exert some control over functions which are generally believed to be involuntary. Biofeedback has been used successfully to teach people to control the acidity of their stomachs, to regain some muscle control after nerve damage, and to lessen the feeling of pain. (See *Biofeedback*.)

> If you or someone you know suffers from chronic pain, help is available through pain clinics. Any one of the above techniques can be easily learned, and can bring some degree of relief.

Stress

Reaction to stress is what enables each of us to meet the many challenges of daily life. We need stress to add flavor, challenge and opportunity to our life: without any kind of stress, life would be dull and we would have little chance to grow as human beings.

Stress was defined in 1956 by Hans Seyle as "the nonspecific response of the body to any demand made upon it." Seyle also spoke of stress as "the wear and tear within the body."

Stress is divided into two types:
- *Acute stress* is sudden and brief, as when we are rudely accosted by a stranger in the street.
- *Chronic stress* continues over a long period of time, as happens if we have a very demanding job or live in a high-crime neighborhood.

Chronic stress has been closely related to physical illnesses such as high blood pressure, ulcers and heart disease.

The Fight or Flight Response

When we perceive an event or condition around us that causes stress, our systems go into a "fight or flight" reaction. This is what all animals do when confronted with potential danger.

However, there are two major differences in the response of human beings to stress:
- First, we perceive stress on many different levels: mental, physical, emotional, and even spiritual. From what we know, animals seem to experience stress only on the physical level. Animals *do* fight or flee. Our choices are rarely that simple.
- In many cases, society does not define any acceptable way for us to relieve our stress. When an animal encounters a stressful situation and then accomplishes one or the other of its options, the stress is relieved and the animal relaxes. Its mind and body systems return to normal functioning. Because human beings are able to imagine and to think about the future, we do not have such simple means of relieving stress, and we are therefore unable to relax and readjust to normal functioning. For example, we know that

we cannot deal with an unreasonable boss by running away and hiding whenever he approaches, and nor can we physically attack him.

Stress often comes more from the perception of a situation than from the actual events.

How Stress Influences Body Functions

As soon as we perceive a situation as stressful, certain changes take place in the central nervous system:
- The *hypothalamus* and the *pituitary glands* stimulate specific *endocrine glands*.
- Discharges into the blood from these glands further influence the activity of the hypothalamus.
- The *adrenal glands*, which are located above the kidneys, release *adrenaline* and *corticoids*. Elevated levels of corticoids in the bloodstream promote inflammations, as happens in stress-induced allergic reactions. The continued presence of corticoids in the bloodstream can eventually lead to high blood pressure, kidney trouble and arteriosclerosis.
- The increased amount of *hydrochloric acid* in the stomach can create problems in the digestive tract.
- Even though the stress factor may be purely psychological, the results are physical, and very variable between different individuals.

Who's at Risk?

Harmful levels of stress are commonly seen among medical workers, teachers, air traffic controllers, police officers and middle managers.

The work place is often the greatest source of stress in our lives, with time pressures, peer pressures and achievement pressures.

Professionals may have to work in an extremely competitive environment, and may require many extra hours of labor to meet deadlines, while blue collar workers frequently suffer from boredom, lack of competition and recognition, and economic difficulties.

It is not only the workload which determines the amount of stress one is subjected to at work. For instance, top-level executives generally seem less affected by stress than middle-level executives. Stress often stems from frustration, lack of authority to make decisions and implement changes, and feelings of stagnation and even boredom. Those at the top are less likely to encounter these stress factors.

While work is usually the primary cause of stress for most people, there are many other causes as well:
- Environmental conditions such as pollution, noise, improper lighting and overcrowding inflict stress on our bodies and our minds. (See *Environment*.)
- Major social changes such as the civil rights movement and women's liberation can create stress for most members of society in many different ways.
- Instant global communications make it difficult for us to withdraw from the problems of the world: war, famine, epidemics and natural disasters are broadcast into our homes every day.
- We are also faced with economic recessions, unemployment, homelessness, inflation and crime here at home.

Assessing Your Level of Stress

When we think of stress, we generally think of our worries and fears. But stress is not caused only by negative events. Falling in love and getting married can be stressful events. Getting a new job, beginning college or becoming a parent can also cause a great deal of stress. We must recognize all the sources of stress in our lives so that we can find ways to reduce, alleviate or manage the stress.

The Holmes and Rahe Chart

The Holmes and Rahe Chart was drafted after the discovery of a strong correlation between certain changes in life and the occurrence of illnesses and accidents. Dr. Holmes and Dr. Rahe at the University of Washington School of Medicine were able to predict which people would get ill depending on their score from the following chart. Also, the greater the change, the more severe the illness or accident tends to be.
- Using this chart, check the recent changes in your life. Total the number of points.

- A score of over 300 corresponds to a 49% chance of illness or accident during the next year.
- A score of under 200 corresponds to only a 9% chance that you will experience the onset of some illness in the next year.

The Holmes and Rahe Stress Chart

Death of a spouse	100
Divorce	73
Separation	65
Jail term	63
Death of close family member	63
Personal injury or illness	53
Marriage	50
Losing one's job	47
Marital reconciliation	45
Retirement	45
Family member's illness	44
Pregnancy	40
Sexual difficulties	39
Business adjustment	39
Changes in financial status	38
Death of close friend	37
Change in line of work	36
Change in number of marital arguments	35
Loan or mortgage of over $10,000	31
Foreclosure on loan or mortgage	30
Change in work responsibility	29
Trouble with in-laws	29
Outstanding personal achievements	28
Changes in spouse's work	26
Starting or ending school	26
Change in living conditions	25
Change in personal habits	24
Trouble with boss	23
Change in work hours or conditions	20
Change in residence	20
Change of school	20
Change of recreation	19
Change in church activities	19
Change in social activities	18
Mortgage or loan under $10,000	17

Change in sleeping habits	16
Change in number of family get-togethers	15
Change in eating habits	15
Vacation	13
Christmas	12

Performing Under Stress

An individual's performance will suffer if the level of stress is very low (not enough challenge) or if the level of stress is becomes excessive.

Stressed Out

There are many symptoms of stress:
- Anxiety or nervous disorders.
- Depression.
- Headaches, back pain, high blood pressure, and digestive system imbalances, all of which can be psychosomatic disorders (involving the relationship of the mind and body).
- Alcohol and drug abuse.

When stress becomes too high, an individual may experience "burn-out." The person becomes too fatigued, depressed, and irritable to function. A person suffering from burn-out may feel totally drained and exhausted, or constantly hounded by others. He or she may feel overwhelmed and abandoned, and will generally be unable to see any solutions other than escape or defeat. Burn-out is more frequent in the helping professions such as teaching, nursing, social work and police work.

Stress Management

The following facts are important to understanding stress management:
- Stress comes mostly from our perception of a course of events.
- Chronic stress invariably leads to health problems.
- Healthy individuals show a higher tolerance for stress.

The first step in managing stress is to assess the causes and levels of stress by doing a thorough and realistic examination of your life and its problem areas.

You can do the following to relieve stress:

- Learn meditation or biofeedback techniques. These two topics are discussed immediately after this section.
- Exercise regularly. Physical activity helps reduce tension, and creates sensations of well-being and harmony.
- Learn to verbalize and share your problems with others. Even if they cannot offer solutions, talking may help you define the problem more clearly. Expressing ourselves also releases tension.
- Know when to quit. You cannot resolve every problem you encounter, and you cannot accomplish everything in one day. Keep your goals flexible and do not set unnecessary deadlines.
- Good nutrition and plenty of rest are essential to managing stress.
- Schedule time each day for relaxation and for fun.
- Notice opportunities for both pleasure and relaxation in your daily life, such as sharing a lunch break with a friend, taking a short walk, getting involved in a special project at work, or just sitting down and reading a magazine you enjoy. As you learn to recognize the stress-reducing activities that work for you, find ways to incorporate them throughout your daily and weekly schedule.
- A good solution to stress that is triggered by fear is to confront the fear directly and see it for what it really is. Even the fear of death is unnecessary since it will eventually happen to all of us. Death is perfectly safe and is a natural result of life. If even death need not be feared, why fear the lesser things in life?

Stress in itself is not bad, if we learn to cope with it and to make time for relaxation. It is only when stressful situations continue over weeks or months that they become harmful.

Physical Exercise to Lower Stress

- People who remain active and exercise regularly are better able to cope with stress.
- Exercise promotes to distribution and assimilation of nutrients throughout the body.
- Hormones are released which actually lift the emotions and help decrease the levels of mood-depressing substances commonly found in the bloodstream.
- Other substances are released within the muscles which induce a sense of well-being and relaxation. (See *Exercise*.)

- Exercise boosts the efficiency of the immune system, which helps the body resist stress-related illnesses.
- Physical exertion is a great way to release tension.

Step-by-Step Whole Body Relaxation

This technique is extremely easy to learn:
- Have someone read these instructions to you slowly, or tape-record the instructions yourself.
- Lie down on a firm surface (not a bed), away from noisy areas or possible interruptions.
- Close your eyes and adjust your body into a comfortable position. This may be with your knees drawn up slightly and a pillow tucked under them.
- Now, starting with your feet, your friend or your tape-recorder will name each body part in turn and instruct you to feel each specific part become relaxed, heavy and limp. For instance: "Your (My) feet are now totally relaxed, heavy and limp." etc.
- Allow yourself to feel this relaxation in your feet.
- Then move on to "Your calves are also relaxed. They feel limp and heavy." "Your knees are becoming relaxed, heavy and limp."
- All body parts should be named in turn: thighs, pelvis, buttocks, waist, torso, back, shoulders, neck, arms, hands, head. Don't forget the jaw, chin, cheeks and eyes. Feel your body sink into the floor with heaviness.
- This relaxation technique takes only a few minutes and can bring very enjoyable sensations of warmth and heaviness.
- You may feel tingling, particularly in your toes and fingers.
- Soon you will not need the taped instructions, as your body will learn to relax automatically as soon as you lie down.
- You can then substitute soft classical or new-age music for the instructions.
- Enjoy this relaxed state for a few minutes, then slowly sit up and stretch yourself before getting up and returning to your activities.
- Repeat this relaxation technique for a few moments as needed during the day, or at least once each day for fifteen to twenty minutes.

Meditation

Anyone can learn to meditate.

Meditation is not very different from sitting quietly and allowing your mind to wander, except that meditation is a focused, not a passives state of mind.
- Meditation techniques allow your mind to rest while you maintain alertness and awareness.
- People who meditate regularly report an increase in their energy levels and a decrease in their need for sleep.
- Meditation can be very effective in lowering stress.
- Meditation is believed to play an important part in helping heal the body and mind by creating a vibration that harmonizes with the other natural vibrations of the body and mind. For instance, one's organs are believed to function or pulse at specific vibrations for optimum health. A slower brain wave can harmonize with this pulse or help readjust it if the organ is not functioning properly.
- Meditation is often used in conjunction with the stretching exercises of yoga and other Oriental disciplines. (See *Yoga.*)
- Some Eastern religions use daily meditations to attain spiritual enlightenment (See *Mind-Spirit* and *Spiritual Meditations.*), but meditation techniques in themselves are only a tool to focus the mind's activity. There is nothing mysterious or abnormal about the meditative state.

Step-by-Step Breath Meditation

- Sit on the floor or on a cushion, with your legs crossed. If this is uncomfortable, you can sit on a straight-backed chair with your feet flat on the floor or on a couple of books. There should be no pressure on the thighs where they meet the edge of the chair.
- Remove your shoes, belt and any other restrictive clothing, so you are comfortable and can breathe easily from your abdomen.
- Sit very straight, yet relaxed. Imagine that you are suspended by a cord through the top of your head. Visualize your spine hanging down from this cord.
- Relax your face and particularly your jaw.
- Next, relax your shoulders and arms, and let your hands rest in your lap. Do not clasp your hands. Let your palms face upward, fingers slightly bent.
- Once you have comfortably adjusted your posture, allow your breath to relax by letting your stomach expand naturally with each inhalation and contract with each exhalation.
- Focus on your breath by counting "one" silently as you inhale your first breath, then count "one" again as you exhale.
- Count "two" as you again inhale and exhale again.
- Continue in this fashion, counting your inhalations and exhalations.
- If you catch yourself thinking of other things, gently bring your attention back to your breathing and pick up where you think you left off.
- Do not let yourself be discouraged, no matter how often your attention wanders.
- You may feel some tingling sensations in your body as areas of tension begin to relax.
- Keep your meditation sessions short at first. Five minutes a day is good for the first few days, then increase to ten minutes for a couple of weeks, then gradually build up to fifteen or twenty minutes once or twice daily.
- As you become a regular meditator, you will be able to stop counting, and will simply observe your breath: in and out, in and out. You will be able to keep your attention focused on your breathing, while passing thoughts are effortlessly moved to the background.

Eliminate Pain

Close your eyes and begin abdominal breathing (as explained above). Allow yourself to fully feel your pain. Open up to the pain. Notice how intense it feels. The pain may come in waves or move around. Continue abdominal breathing while you follow the pain with your whole being. Do not push the pain away but watch it.

Continue your abdominal breathing, and with the in breath feel warm love enter your body and flow towards the source of your pain. Imagine that the in breath brings white light to the source of your pain and that the out breath is slightly gray as carries the pain away.

Recall a memory or create a fantasy in your mind of being deeply loved. Let this love surround your pain. Instead of fighting the pain just allow yourself to relax and encompass the pain with that loving feeling.

Biofeedback

Biofeedback technique is based on the fact that every single movement we make causes some electrical change, however small, in the cells of our muscles. These tiny electrical charges can be picked up by small discs called electrodes that are wired to an *electromyograph*, or EMG. The electrodes from a biofeedback machine are attached to different parts of the head and body in order to record the activities of the nervous system. The information is then made available to the person through a light or sound alarm.

One can therefore receive instant feedback about the tiniest changes in any part of the body. By paying close attention to the signals from the machine, the person can quickly learn to control his or her own nervous activity. Eventually, one can learn to affect body temperature, blood pressure, heart beat, muscle tension and other body functions.

Biofeedback works in somewhat like the thermostat in an air-conditioning system. As soon as the temperature in the room has reached the set temperature, the thermostat is triggered to initiate an automatic shut-off of the system. Many machines and mechanical systems work automatically through such *feedback loops*.

Many of our biological systems are also controlled by feedback loops:

- If we have not eaten in several hours, the sight of food makes us hungry, so we eat, and we no longer feel hungry.
- Levels of hormones and other secretions are constantly adjusted depending on variations in our blood chemistry.

It has generally been assumed in the West that we could only control our voluntary functions. However, experiments have now confirmed that even *autonomic functions* (those which depend on the involuntary autonomic nervous system), can be modified by control from the mind in a biofeedback loop. This theory has always been practiced in the East, where yogis have been known to slow their heart beat, breath, blood circulation and other involuntary functions.

Biofeedback has been used to teach people to control chronic pain, headaches, migraines, high blood pressure, muscle spasms, chronic stress and even cancerous growths, as well as to rehabilitate paralyzed limbs from accidents or strokes, and to teach deaf children to speak.

Biofeedback to Relieve Stress

Let us examine how biofeedback is able to relieve stress:
- The brain produces different types of waves.
- Alpha waves are generated in a relaxed state, such as during meditation.
- Beta waves are associated with more concentrated, active thought.
- Delta waves are indicative of sleep.
- Theta waves are associated with anxiety or creativity.
- Using a biofeedback loop, a person can learn to enter and remain in an alpha (relaxed) state for longer periods of time.
- The person becomes aware of the thoughts, movements and breathing patterns which induce relaxation.
- Eventually, most people can learn to relax themselves automatically, without the biofeedback apparatus.

There are certain risks and recommendations concerning the use of biofeedback. Some scientists believe that the doctor-patient relationship may really be the cause of the patient's improvements. The patient's condition may improve simply because of the physician's caring, encouraging attention, and the patient may be unable to maintain good results on his or her own. This is a valid concern, and there is no doubt that a supportive environment and a good doctor-patient relationship can aid the healing process.

On the other hand, there are many documented cases of paraplegics and stroke victims who have made lasting improvements with the use of biofeedback training, even though some of these cases were originally regarded as hopeless.

Portable biofeedback equipment is now available for people who need to continue working on their own, after the supervised training period. Use caution in purchasing such equipment, as some models may not perform correctly.

Massage

Massage, the art of using touch for healing purposes, has probably been in use since the emergence of the human race.

If we bump our shin, we automatically rub the bruised area. Similarly, we massage our tense necks or foreheads after a long work day, and rub our feet when they are sore and aching.

Today many different types of massage and licensed massage practitioners are available in almost every town and city in America.

East and West

Some general distinctions can be made between the Western and Eastern forms of massage.
- Western techniques aim at creating certain physiological changes and inducing deep relaxation.
- Oriental massage techniques are more concerned with re-balancing the body's flow of energy and reestablishing open channels of energy flow. This energy is named *Chi* in China and *Ki* in Japan.
- Shiatsu and other Oriental body manipulations are more of an art than Western massage, and are more difficult to learn.

Choosing a Masseur

Choosing the right type of massage depends on your personal needs. You should be very careful, however, in choosing a massage professional.
- Make sure the masseur is licensed to practice, and willing to fully explain the methods he or she employs.
- You should feel that you trust and are completely at ease with the masseur. Only when you are completely at ease can you reap all the benefits of a massage.
- The masseur should be in good health and at peace at the time of the massage, and able to devote his or her full attention to you.

The Benefits of Massage

Regardless of the type of massage you select, you can expect the following benefits:
- Massage relaxes: The massage experience often allows one to drift between sleep and alertness, creating a state similar to meditation. This is very restful for the mind and body, and regular massages can often be part of a stress management program. (See *Stress* and *Stress Management*.)
- Because massage increases circulation, digestion and elimination, it helps nourish the tissues and remove toxins from the tissues and joints for excretion. This in turn promotes healing and restoration of energy.
- On an emotional level, the masseur's caring and gentle touch can revitalize a person who's feeling drained or fatigued. People who are employed in "giving" professions such as medicine, teaching, or homemaking benefit greatly from an hour of healing attention.
- Many people also report greater alertness and ability to concentrate after a massage because of the period of deep relaxation of the mind: small problems fall into perspective and important ideas or problems can be brought into focus.

Different Types of Massage

Swedish Massage

This technique uses rather brisk and vigorous strokes to increase circulation and muscle tone. It is a well-known form of massage and many of its strokes are incorporated into most of the other forms of massage. It is the usual form of massage for athletes.

Esalen Massage

Esalen massage uses most of the strokes of the Swedish massage, but moves more slowly and in a more relaxing way. In addition to improved circulation, digestion, elimination and muscle tone, Esalen produces a very relaxed state similar to meditation. This is a very good all-purpose massage for improving health and relieving stress.

Rolfing

This is a deep tissue massage that must be done in a series of ten sessions. It realigns the structure of the body and rectifies posture. It can relieve neck and back pain.

Polarity Therapy

This treatment uses massage in conjunction with exercise, changes in diet, and changes in the patient's attitude toward life. The massage focuses on the flows of energy throughout the body, from positive areas to negative areas. Pressure is applied to certain points to release blocked energy and reestablish the proper balance and flow. This method often produces deep relaxation.

Reflexology

This is usually a foot or hand massage. Certain points on the feet and hands are said to correspond to areas and organs of the body. By applying pressure to these points on the hands and feet, the corresponding areas are affected and can be restored to health.

Shiatsu (Acupressure)

In this method, pressure is applied to certain points along meridians which connect the systems of the body. This massage is designed to release tension patterns and blocked energy, and to induce healing from within. The word *shiatsu* in Japanese means "finger pressure."

Exercise

We all need some form of exercise every day of our lives.

Let's face it: our lifestyle has become much too sedentary. We drive everywhere, we work at desks, we spend our relaxation time sitting or lying down watching TV, reading or listening to music. Few of us still haul our water from the well or river, or cultivate gardens, or walk to work or school. Instead of hunting, we drive to the supermarket.

Yet the human body is engineered for a great variety of movements and exertions. In fact, it thrives on exercise.

The Benefits of Exercise

Regular exercising has many benefits:
- Exercise helps maintain a healthy weight.
- Improved flexibility and strength helps prevent back pain.
- Exercise probably helps prevent heart disease.
- It helps create a positive mental attitude.
- It increases the person's activity level and improves sleep. It may even give one a more active and satisfying sex life.
- Exercise actually helps reduce fatigue, even though it may be vigorous.
- People who exercise regularly have been shown to feel less depression and less recurring anxiety.
- They are better able to handle daily stresses without unnecessary tension, and seem to enjoy challenges.
- Exercise helps keep the immune system in good working order.

Any exercise program should include activities which cause our heart and lungs to work harder for a period of time, while strengthening our muscles and improving our flexibility.

Elements of Fitness

Muscle Strength
- Muscle strength is necessary to accomplish many daily tasks without strain or injury.
- It helps give support the spine and prevent recurring backaches.
- Muscle strength can be improved through weight training, calisthenics, isometrics and isokinetics.

Muscular Endurance
- Endurance is helpful to safely accomplish many daily tasks that require sustained activity.
- Muscle strength and endurance are necessary to maintain good posture throughout the day.
- Endurance can be improved through weight training, calisthenics and aerobics.

Flexibility
- Flexibility helps us avoid pulled or strained tendons and ligaments and other injuries, by giving us better balance and a greater range of movements.
- Flexibility of the spine helps to prevent backaches.
- Most people differ in areas of flexibility, but nearly everyone needs to increase their flexibility in the back, neck, chest and the backs of the thighs.
- Good overall flexibility is obtained through slow and sustained stretching movements. The practices of yoga and Tai Chi are excellent methods to improve flexibility.

Cardiovascular Endurance
- This is also known as aerobic fitness or power, and is considered the most important element of fitness.
- It enables the heart to continuously deliver oxygen and nutrients to the cells of the body, which allows for high and sustained levels of activity without undue stress on the body.
- Many activities and sports can develop cardiovascular fitness, especially fast walking, jogging, running, bicycling, rope-skipping, swimming and aerobic dancing.

Before Starting any Exercise Program

The following precautions are necessary to insure your safety while exercising:
- Have a complete medical check-up, including a cardiovascular examination and examination of the muscles and joints.
- Cholesterol and triglyceride levels should be evaluated.
- The blood pressure should be measured, and an *electrocardiogram* (EKG) may be performed in order to determine the kind and level of exercises to be undertaken.
- Strength and endurance tests may be used to determine the beginning level of one's exercise program.
- Most of these tests can be given by a physical therapist or a professional exercise trainer.

Warm-up and Cool-down

To warm up before exercises raises the body's temperature in order to prevent injuries which could otherwise result from cold and stiff muscles and ligaments.

Warm-ups are essential to prevent injuries, especially in cold weather.

- You can warm up with a hot shower or steam bath.
- You can do a general warm-up with non-specific body movements such as slow calisthenics, or with stretching exercises.
- You can also warm up the particular muscles which you intend to use the most.
- You can practice the movements you will be using in your particular sport in slow motion.
- If you are involved in cardiovascular exercise, you can warm up your heart by starting slowly for a few minutes and easing into the more strenuous part of the work-out.
- For people who suffer from migraine headaches, a careful and lengthy warm-up can help prevent a migraine after exercising.

A cool-down period is a warm-up in reverse. You allow your body to cool down gradually before returning to normal activity. This can be done with stretching exercises, walking, or slow motion movements of your particular sport.

Types of Exercise

There are thousands of different sports, exercises, and fitness programs. You can exercise alone, at home or outside, or you can join a fitness club or take up a team sport. We will look at a few of the more common types of exercise:

Aerobic Exercise

Aerobics includes any form of exercise which increases the oxygen supply and the rate of metabolism of the body.

During such exercises, the heart beats faster, breathing becomes deeper and the blood vessels expand to carry more oxygen to the large muscles that are being used.

The benefits of aerobic exercise include:
- Increased strength and endurance of the heart.
- Improved processing of air by lungs.
- Improved tone of the blood vessels.
- Increase in total blood volume.
- Reduced levels of cholesterol.
- Improved digestion and utilization of nutrients.
- Improved elimination.
- Weight maintenance.
- Increased energy and general well-being.
- Improved mental and emotional balance.

Aerobic exercise must be continual, must maintain a certain rhythm and must involve the whole body. Determining whether your aerobic exercise program is of the right intensity for you can be done by taking your pulse or heart rate. You can feel your pulse under one wrist with the second and third finger of your other hand.
- The pulse must be taken immediately after exercising, as it will drop off rapidly.
- Count the number of heart beats in a fifteen second period and multiply by four to obtain your heart rate.
- Compare to the following table.

Age	Exercise Target Heart Rate
20	140 – 170 beats per minute
30	130 – 160 beats per minute
40	125 – 150 beats per minute
50	115 – 140 beats per minute
60	105 – 130 beats per minute

- The more intensity you put into the exercises, the shorter the period required to reach your target heart rate.
- Better results will be obtained with much less risk of injury by starting with low-intensity activities, and gradually intensifying your workout.
- Exercising daily is best, but cardiovascular fitness can be achieved with regular aerobic exercise from three to five times weekly.
- Remember that you must increase your fitness capacity slowly and progressively.

A good aerobic program will enable the individual's skeletal muscles to perform more work with less effort on the heart, which lowers one's risk of sudden heart problems.

The following are all good aerobic exercises:
- Brisk walking is great for beginners, is safe, and requires no equipment.
- Jogging and running are also good, but require quality running shoes to absorb shocks and prevent injuries to the feet and ankles. Running on dirt or grass produces less shock than running on concrete surfaces.
- Cycling, rope-skipping and skating are good aerobic activities.
- Swimming is particularly healthful since its movements encourage stretching, the water resistance builds strength, and the water supports the body's weight and helps prevent back strain.

Calisthenics
- Calisthenics have been popular since the 1930's in many fitness plans, physical education classes and military and other training programs. Most of these exercises can aggravate certain conditions or cause injuries if they are performed incorrectly. For instance, leg lifts can aggravate a sway-back, and toe touches done with a bounce can cause injury to the joints of the lumbar spine.

- It is necessary to learn the proper form for these exercises from a qualified instructor, and to put great emphasis on the proper form at all times.
- Calisthenics can improve cardiovascular fitness if they are performed in a continuous and fast-moving sequence. For instance, running in place between exercises would increase the heart rate.
- There are calisthenics exercises specific to almost every muscle group in the body. These exercises do not require any special equipment.

Isometrics

Isometrics produce muscle contractions without movement. For instance, pushing one's hands against each other in front of one's chest produces contractions of the upper chest muscles (*pectorals*).
- Isometrics are not as effective as calisthenics for overall fitness.
- They can be particularly helpful for a person with posture problems that other forms of exercise would worsen.
- Isometrics do not promote cardiovascular fitness, and must be supplemented with a program of aerobic activities.

Isotonics

Exercises which produce muscle contractions with movement are called isotonics. Calisthenics, aerobics and weight training belong to this category of exercises.

Weight training has become very popular. Done under the right supervision, weight training can:
- Increase muscle strength and endurance with little chance of injury, particularly if the proper breathing is used during the exercises.
- Develop one's physique to improve appearance.

But weight training has the following disadvantages:
- It does not improve cardiovascular fitness.
- It can add unsightly bulk if performed incorrectly.
- It can aggravate certain heart conditions.
- It does not improve flexibility, balance or coordination, and may actually lessen them.

Weight training should only be used in conjunction with a program of other exercises to develop cardiovascular fitness and flexibility.

> Weight training should not be undertaken by people with heart problems or high blood pressure.

Isokinetics
Isokinetics are a combination of isometrics and isotonics performed with special equipment which controls the amount of resistance exerted against a whole range of specific movements.
- Isokinetics can increase strength and endurance with little risk of injury.
- It requires a special machine, and its benefits have not been proven to surpass isometrics or isotonics.
- It does not contribute to cardiovascular fitness.

Dance
- Dance of any form – folk dancing, square dancing, ballroom dancing – can be a wonderful exercise.
- Dancing can be a fun leisure activity, especially for older people, as it usually includes positive social interaction.
- However, not all forms of dance are sufficiently aerobic to ensure cardiovascular fitness.

The Key to Staying Active and Fit
Apart from the organized forms of exercise and sports already mentioned, there are hundreds of popular activities that you can enjoy during your leisure time and which benefit your health.
- Golf (providing you don't use a cart), bird watching, nature walks, badminton or table tennis, gardening, or playing with children all help keep you active, alert and alive.
- Many of these activities are not great cardiovascular exercises, but their benefits are still important.
- Add some fast walking to other leisure activities whenever possible.

Remember the following Important Points:
- Consult a physician before beginning a strenuous exercise program.
- Cultivate positive attitudes towards yourself, your abilities and your choice of an active life-style.
- Perform some activity each and every day.

- Encourage others to join in your activities, and develop friendships with other active people.
- Choose some more vigorous activity to perform every other day for cardiovascular fitness.
- Learn to check your pulse regularly and become familiar with your target zone (heartbeats per minute). Pay attention to danger signals from your body such as dizziness, heavy breathing or sweating, chest pains, etc.
- Choose activities which you enjoy.
- In warm weather (over 80°F) cut down on your outdoor activities and drink lots of cool (not cold) water or juices, and protect your skin from sunlight.
- In cold weather, wear warm clothes that allow air circulation over the head, hands, neck and chest.
- Use the correct type of athletic shoes for each activity, to prevent injuries.
- Don't compare yourself to anyone else, or set unrealistic goals.
- Don't make abrupt changes in your exercise routine. Every change should be slow and progressive.
- Avoid hot baths, showers, whirlpools or saunas after strenuous exercise. They pull blood circulation away from the heart.
- Don't exercise vigorously when you are feeling ill.
- Eat foods that are high in complex carbohydrates for energy. Breads, grains, cereals, pasta and potatoes are ideal.
- Don't eat foods rich in proteins or fats (meat, eggs, dairy products) before exercising and don't eat a full meal within two hours prior to exercising.
- Don't become compulsive. A moderate activity each day is much safer and healthier than sudden overexertion between periods of inactivity.

Yoga

The rules of yoga were established by an Indian sage named Patanjali around 200 AD. He wrote that "the control of thoughts and emotions is linked to the control of the breath."

The word yoga itself means "to yoke," that is, to harness the body and mind. There are many forms of yoga. Some of these forms are primarily spiritual practices. However, the forms of yoga which concern us as valuable methods of exercising our bodies and minds are *Hatha yoga* and *Kundalini yoga*.

Kundalini yoga is more dynamic than other forms, but shows quick results in toning muscles and strengthening the nervous system. It is devised to raise the energy (Kundalini) upward through the spinal column. Others may prefer the quieter and more relaxed tempo of Hatha yoga.

A qualified yoga instructor should be able to explain the types of yoga and the benefits of each.

Each class should start and end with a relaxation period which can include silent meditation, chanting meditation or a breath exercise. (See *Meditation*.) This period is the equivalent of a warm-up or cool-down with other forms of exercise.

The Benefits of Yoga

- Yoga offers greater flexibility, balance, and strength of both body and mind. Yoga is a great form of exercise for almost everyone, particularly when practiced in conjunction with a cardiovascular fitness program.
- Yoga is easily taught to children and can be practiced into old age, when balance and flexibility can reduce the risk of injury.
- It is helpful to pregnant women, and can be practiced throughout pregnancy with some modifications of postures.
- People who encounter daily stress on the job can attain mental clarity and maintain high energy levels with regular yoga sessions.
- Arthritis sufferers can benefit greatly from *Iyengar yoga*, which teaches proper alignment of the joints. This helps heal arthritic joints and build strength in joints and bones.
- Yoga is perfect for people who are recovering from many types of injuries or illnesses including heart ailments.
- Asthmatics can benefit greatly from the practice of yoga, which trains them to breathe more deeply and to gain control of the stressful situations that often trigger asthma attacks.

Tai Chi

Tai Chi means "the supreme ultimate way of life." It is based on Chinese teachings thousands of years old and involves slow, flowing series of physical movements. It is a system that circulates an internal energy called "chi" through the practitioner's body.

Millions of Chinese perform this exercise every morning and receive great health benefits. Some of the benefits include the massage of internal organs, increased flexibility, better balance and more strength. However, even greater benefits come from the circulation of the "chi" energy. This circulation removes blocks that may cause disease. The Chinese have a view of disease as energy related, instead of the Western clinical approach. They believe that disturbances and blockages in energy are what allow the germs and bacteria to gain power. They believe that we are constantly exposed to many germs, and our bodies' energy conditions either fight off the germs or allow them to take hold and cause illness

Energy disturbances arise from poor nutrition, emotional pressures and other lifestyle causes. They can be corrected by a number of methods, including the movements of Tai Chi.

In addition to its health benefits, Tai Chi is also a meditation that calms the mind, and it can be used as an effective martial art as well.

Sleep

Sleep is an altered state of consciousness. It is almost as if when we fall asleep, we enter a completely different world.

- While asleep, the muscles of the body relax almost completely (a physical state that cannot be achieved while awake.)
- The blood pressure in the arteries drops, smaller vessels dilate, and there is a marked decrease in pulse rate, nervous activity and brain activity.
- During sleep the body produces many hormones. These help in digestion and assimilation of proteins, fats and glucose.
- Other hormones produced while we sleep stimulate bone growth in children, and bone and cell rejuvenation in adults.
- Sleep is an absolute necessity for every one of us, although the amount of sleep required can vary greatly between individuals.

- Lack of sleep can have very detrimental effects, ranging from mild fatigue and irritation to serious physical and mental disruptions.
- Severe sleep deprivation causes auditory and visual hallucinations and a feeling of pressure around the head. Yet a single night's sleep is usually sufficient to alleviate most of the effects of deprivation.
- Sleep deprivation is sometimes used to combat depression. However, once the individual returns to his or her normal sleep pattern, the depression may also return.

Our Sleep Rhythms

Around 1920, Dr. Hans Berger of Germany was the first to record the regular and relaxed brain waves known as *alpha waves*. It was discovered that during each sleep period we go from light sleep to deep sleep and back again. During a certain portion of the cycle, we also go into *REM* (Rapid Eye Movement). During REM dreaming usually occurs.

We generally have several periods of REM each night, although we may not remember any or all of our dreams. People who are deprived of their REM periods become very anxious and unable to concentrate. They may lose muscle coordination if REM deprivation continues.

During a full night's sleep we will usually go through four to five recurrent cycles of light to deep sleep, interspersed with periods of REM.

Different people have different needs regarding sleep:
- Some people do very well with less than six hours of sleep per day. Others need eight or nine hours or even more on a regular basis.
- The average seems to be within the range of eight to eight and a half hours.
- Short sleepers spend more of their sleeping time in deep sleep.
- As people get older, it is common for them to sleep less well. Yet many older people nap frequently during the day, so their total sleep time probably remains the same.
- There is an increase in the use of sleeping pills among the elderly.

Sleep Disorders

Almost all of us have difficulty falling asleep at times. But other, more serious problems affect some people's sleep.

Insomnia

Some people frequently have trouble falling asleep and staying asleep. This condition is known as insomnia.
Insomniacs tend to have longer REM periods and to dream more. They have shorter deep sleep periods, and remember waking up often during the night.

If you have trouble falling asleep and staying asleep, you can try the following:
- Determine the amount of sleep that you need. If six hours is all that you require to feel rested, do not try to sleep longer.
- Try to maintain a regular bed time.
- Do not take naps during the day.
- Check your family history. Heredity plays a role in sleep patterns.
- Do not use sleeping pills, as they interfere with REM sleep, are addictive, and lose their effectiveness rapidly.
- Determine that your bed and mattress are comfortable and offer enough support.
- Make sure your bedroom is quiet and dark enough, and that it is not too hot or stuffy. Some colors are also more relaxing to the senses. (See *Colors*.)
- Try drinking warm milk before retiring. Warming the milk releases *L-tryptophan*, an amino-acid found naturally in the body which helps induce asleep.
- You can drink chamomile tea, which is known for its relaxing properties.
- Do not drink coffee, black tea or any soft drink that may contain caffeine (a known stimulant.)
- Determine which foods are hard for you to digest. Avoid them in the evening, and also avoid late meals.
- A long and leisurely walk or other light exercise before going to bed can help.
- Determine whether you've been unusually moody, stressed or depressed. Mood changes can affect sleep patterns.
- Use a relaxation or meditation technique to help relax your muscles and your mind. (See *Stress Management* and *Meditation*.)

Sleep-walking

It has long been believed that people who walk in their sleep are acting out their dreams. Sleep-walking actually

begins during deep sleep, when it is rather rare for the person to be dreaming.
- If the sleep-walking episode is short, the person probably remains in deep sleep. Otherwise the brain waves resemble those of someone coming awake or just falling asleep.
- While some people only speak in their sleep or stand upright with their eyes open, others walk around rather rigidly, and accidents do occur.
- Sleep-walking is more prevalent among children, and seems to have a hereditary factor.

Snoring

Almost one third of all men and one fifth of all women snore. Snoring is caused by vibrations of the soft palate as air is inhaled through the mouth while an individual is lying on his or her back. Overweight people tend to snore more because of the extra fatty tissue in their throats. They also tend to sleep on their backs more often.
- Most loud snoring takes place during deep sleep.
- Some people snore only when suffering from a cold, sinusitis or allergies.
- Enlarged tonsils can sometimes cause children to snore.
- Snoring can usually be alleviated by preventing the person from sleeping on his or her back.

Sleep Apnea

Sleep apnea is a condition in which a person actually stops breathing for a short time, usually a few seconds, but sometimes up to a full minute. The upper airways become blocked temporarily, and the person grows restless without waking, then suddenly inhales again with a loud snore. This condition may be caused by excessive relaxation of the throat muscles. People with sleep apnea may also suffer from increased blood pressure and irregular heartbeats due to oxygen deprivation during sleep.

People who suffer from sleep apnea should not use sleeping pills or alcohol, which depress respiration. They should consult a physician for treatment.

The Case Against Sleeping Pills

Barbituric acid was discovered in Belgium in 1864. Since 1900, about fifty barbiturate compounds have been used for medicinal purposes, mostly as sleeping aids. For many years, barbiturates were widely regarded as safe and effective.

We now know that barbiturates pose a real danger of poisoning through accidental overdose. They are also addictive. Today the preferred sleep medications are *benzodiazepines*, with nearly 100 million prescriptions written each year in the U.S. Some of these drugs are known to us under the names of *Librium*, *Valium* and *Halcyon*.

- Benzodiazepines can be prescribed in smaller doses than barbiturates, and carry lower risks of serious poisoning or severe addiction. However, they can be just as dangerous if used in conjunction with other drugs or alcohol.
- Benzodiazepines also remain in the body for quite a while, with *half-lives* (the time it takes for a drug to lose half of its potency), of up to three days.
- However, it appears that barbiturates reduce REM sleep, while benzodiazepines interfere with deep sleep.
- Lately, there has been a lot of concern over severe side effects such as amnesia, anxiety, confusion, violent hostility and even psychotic behavior in some users of benzodiazepines.
- Sleep medications may help you fall asleep faster, lengthen your total sleeping time, and prevent you from waking up during the night.
- Although the mortality rates of long sleepers and short sleepers show no remarkable differences, the mortality rate of those using sleeping pills is almost double the rate of those who do not.

Dreams

Some people claim that they never dream. In fact, we all dream, but some of us do not remember our dreams. We dream every night, and our dreams help keep us in good mental health.

It was not until the beginning of the twentieth century that Sigmund Freud and Carl Jung detailed the important relationship between our dreams and waking life. Through the analysis of his patients' dreams, Jung demonstrated that dreams could help one store life's many experiences. Dreams also helped compensate for events or situations that the dreamer could not or should not change in waking life.

Interpreting Our Dreams

Dream interpretation books are not likely to help you in deciphering your own dreams. Most symbols and images in dreams are highly personal, and may hold very different meanings for different people.

One way to better understand our dreams and to obtain some direction from them is to keep a dream diary. Keep a notebook and pen right by your bed, and write down any dreams or pieces of dreams which you remember immediately upon waking. This is important because even a few seconds of wakefulness can mean the loss of important parts of a dream.

- We sometimes find many different ideas or problems condensed into a single dream image.
- An obvious symbol may be placed into a totally incongruous context. Most of the important meanings behind our dreams are thus disguised.
- Sometimes a dream is brought on by some physical discomfort such as aches and pains or an upset stomach.
- A dream can relate to and try to resolve some problem or worry which has occurred during the day or in the very recent past.
- Some dreams portray the opposite of what is really happening.
- Studies among children indicate that they dream mostly about the places with which they are most familiar, and about animals. As they grow up, their dreams increase in scope in accordance with the new developments in their lives.
- Dreams seldom allow for obvious explanations, so it is sometimes necessary to seek advice from a professional psychologist or psychiatrist familiar with dream analysis and free word associations.

Daydreams

Daydreams are not very different from true dreaming. By letting our thoughts wander, we can encounter remarkable associations of ideas. This process can be very beneficial to artists and other people in creative fields. Many people claim to have suddenly solved problems while daydreaming or immediately upon waking. We often recommend, when faced with a tough problem, to "sleep on it."

Nightmares and Night Terrors

Nightmares are frightening dreams from which we emerge with a start, but also with the awareness that we were only dreaming. Night terrors are more frightening, because we awaken from them with complete disorientation. Children in particular may suffer from night terrors and may not be able to calm themselves for a while.

While nightmares may be caused by psychological or emotional events, such as personal problems or the need to make a hard decision, they can frequently be the result of eating a heavy meal before bed, or sleeping in a hot and stuffy room.

Aging and Longevity

Aging is a natural process: from the time we are born, we begin to age.

Of all the mammals that inhabit the lands of Earth, humans live the longest, followed by the Asian elephant, with an average life span of sixty years. Our longevity results and follows from our ability to adapt to our environment and avoid many of its perils. Our capacity to survive as long as we do is based on our biological complexity and our social system. However, the unique structure of human society has also produced many factors which shorten life expectancy, such as air and water pollution, crime, overcrowding and chronic stress.

We do not all age at the same rate. Two people who have the same chronological age may have very different biological ages. Aging occurs at the cellular level, at the tissue level, and in each individual organ and organ system.

Research on aging is divided into four main areas: genetics, cellular aging, nutrition and environment. Among the factors that affect longevity, many can be controlled. While we cannot change our genetic make-up, we can alter our diet and change our life-style, we can use seat belts, quit smoking, and start a regular exercise program. Later in this section, we will examine some actions we can take to increase longevity.

Laboratory experiments show that cell function decreases at the rate of 1% per year over the age of thirty. This should give us a life expectancy of 120 years. As a matter of fact, the oldest person whose birth date could be verified lived to the age of 118.

The stereotype of the elderly person who is senile and unable to care for himself or herself is a gross misconception. Most senior citizens are healthy and full of vitality. They are able to take care of themselves, and have a wealth of experience to contribute to society.

Mental functions should remain unimpaired into old age unless affected by illness. The same is true of sexual functions: older people are fully capable of a satisfying sex life if they remain in general good health.

Old age does bring its share of difficulties. There are many changes that take place as we age and some can be quite stressful:

- Seniors must accept their decreasing physical capacities and explore new ways to remain active.
- Some physical losses and impairments are very gradual. Sight and hearing progressively deteriorate starting around age twenty to thirty, but we only notice these losses once they become acute enough for us to need eyeglasses or a hearing aid.
- Other changes and losses can be more abrupt, such as those brought on by a stroke or a sudden illness.
- Emotional losses resulting from the death of a spouse, a child, or friends, or from children moving away can take a physical toll.
- The way these changes, losses and stresses are handled by the individual greatly impacts his or her overall quality of life.

Yet for many people, old age also brings many rewards:
- There may be pride and satisfaction from a successful career.
- Many elderly people enjoy the company of their children and grandchildren.
- There is more free time to spend with family and friends or to pursue activities and hobbies.

In some cases, however, the burden of emotional losses combined with physical and mental difficulties may cause an older person to feel isolated and depressed. The way people cope with advancing age can make the difference between a life of sorrow and sickness or one of happiness and growth.

Older people need to recognize and understand the changes that are affecting their bodies. In countless instances, many continue to produce worthwhile achievements even in the face of great physical difficulties.

As people age, they become increasingly susceptible to diseases. Old age in itself does not cause the diseases to appear; the presence of illness, however, can speed up the process of aging. The immune system also loses some of its capacity to protect the body from disease, due in part to the deterioration of individual cells. The decrease in cell function is mostly linked to repeated stresses encountered during ones lifetime.

Disorders Associated with Aging

Menopause

Menopause is not a actually a disorder, but rather a natural occurrence in every woman's life. It is, however, associated with certain disorders such as sporadic elevations of the skin's temperature (*hot flashes*) and osteoporosis. (See *Menopause*.)

Osteoporosis

This is a condition in which the skeleton loses calcium and becomes fragile, causing the bones to fracture easily. Men and women both tend to lose bone mass beginning at the age of thirty-five, but women are more at risk. Adults should get 300 mg to 1,200 mg of calcium each day as protection against osteoporosis. This is roughly equivalent to one and a half quarts of milk.

Parkinson's Disease

Parkinson's disease is associated with *dopamine* deficiency in certain areas of the brain such as the brain stem, which controls motor and muscle coordination. It manifests itself in tremors, difficulties in coordination and a rolling gait.

Senility

Senility is recognized by such symptoms as inability to solve problems, loss of short-term memory, difficulties of speech, and general disorganization of the personality. There are several causes of senility including *Alzheimer's disease*, which accounts for more than 50% of all cases. There are several theories on the cause of Alzheimer's disease, including genetic predisposition, an auto-immune disorder in which antibodies attack neurons in the brain, and a slow virus. Excessive levels of aluminum have been found in the brains of senile people, particularly in areas of abnormal neuron tangles peculiar to sufferers of senility.

Other Disorders

Old age may bring with it a number of physiological problems, including depression, sleep disturbances, auto-immune disorders, and greater occurrence of degenerative diseases such as cancer and heart disease.

Increase Your Life Expectancy

The same factors which are important in maintaining good health throughout life, are also crucial to longevity. These factors are stress management, nutrition, and exercise.

Relax and Live Longer: Stress and Longevity

There is no doubt whatsoever that stress is a very important factor in determining one's chances of fulfilling his or her life expectancy. Poor adjustment in young adulthood is clearly linked to major health problems in middle age. These are a few of the factors which influence one's longevity:
- Life satisfaction (work, self-esteem, social life, etc.) reduces stress and may contribute to living longer.
- Physical functions (activity levels, physical self-esteem) play a large role in stress management and reduction.
- Poor judgment, taking excessive risks, self-neglect or abuse, tobacco, drug and alcohol abuse, all conspire to diminish one's present and future life.
- Married people tend to live longer than single, widowed or divorced individuals.
- Good health, positive religious convictions, feelings of well-being, physical and mental activity, creativity and productivity all enhance one's chances of long life.
- Women tend to live longer than men, and this is widely attributed to differences in life-styles. Women are generally more able to express feelings and emotions and ask for support in stressful situations.

Eat Well and Live Longer: Nutrition and Longevity

Even though nutrition is a complicated matter, a few simple dietary changes can increase an individual's chances of good health into old age.

- Caloric requirements decrease with age, even if the person has never been overweight.
- Maintaining ones ideal weight (or a little less) has been shown to increase longevity.
- A daily diet low in cholesterol and low in saturated fatty acids and high in fruits and vegetables is highly recommended.
- Avoid over-processed polyunsaturated oils.
- Many vitamin and mineral requirements increase with old age. Even with a nutritious diet, supplements may be necessary.
- Atrophy of the gastro-intestinal tract has been related to deficiencies of iron and vitamin B-complex.
- A lack of vitamin B12 can cause mental confusion, which can be mistaken for senility.
- Vitamin E is a potent anti-oxidant, which can prevent certain types of cellular damage such as those found in pre-cancerous conditions.
- There is a progressive loss of taste buds in elderly people, which can lead to over-compensation with sugar and salt. Both are related to hypertension.
- Excess sugar can also aggravate tooth decay and other conditions of the mouth.
- Lack of fiber is common among the elderly, who generally prefer soft foods. Constipation can become chronic, and laxatives often aggravate many other conditions, including depletion of vitamins. Regular consumption of mineral oil to treat constipation can deplete fat-soluble vitamins.
- Occasional fasting seems to promote good health and longevity as well. (See *Fasting*.)

Play and Live Longer: Exercise and Longevity

The American Cancer Society conducted a twenty-year study involving more than one million people. The results indicated that regular physical exercise can definitely add years to one's life by diminishing the risk of heart disease and other conditions.
- Physical endurance increases the performance of the blood vessels, which reduces strain on the heart.
- Exercising the large muscles helps the body maintain the proper bone mass.
- Exercise is helpful to lift mild depression, cure insomnia, and improve poor appetite, all health problems which frequently affect older persons.

Who Lives Longer?

There are centenarian communities throughout the world which can teach us a lot about longevity. Studies of these communities as well as Mormons, Amish and Seventh Day Adventist cultures all seem to experience a higher than average resistance to disease, can help us to identify the factors which are important to good health and long life.

One region of the Caucasius Mountains where many people live to be over 100 is populated by at least ten different ethnic groups. This demonstrates the minimal role played by genetics in longevity.

However, among all the centenarian communities, we find similar dietary practices and lifestyles. In such communities in Pakistan, Tibet and Central America, people live mostly off of agricultural products which they grow themselves.
- Vegetables and grains are supplemented with small amounts of protein and fats from animal sources (milk, cheese).
- Caloric intake in these communities averages less than 2000 calories per day, for the most part from unrefined carbohydrates. The average daily caloric intake in the U.S. is 3300 per day.
- They have neither refined sugar nor excess salt in their diets.

The people in these communities remain active throughout their lives, engaging in long distance walking, climbing, planting, harvesting, and hauling water and other goods. They remain totally integrated in and important to the community, never ceasing to be productive. Most of them also remain sexually active.

The least-documented factor contributing to these people's longevity is their physical environments. However, it seems that they all share mountain or hillside abodes, and live in areas with very little environmental pollution.

Your Life Expectancy

Insurance companies can calculate how many years an average person has left to live. These statistical standards reflect the population as a whole, and vary significantly from person to person. The readers of this book will probably live much longer that the statistical average because of their interest in their health and well-being.

Following is the statistical life expectancy table showing years (plus days) left to live, based on current age, for the average American.

Life Expectancy Table

	Time Remaining			Time Remaining	
Age	Male	Female	Age	Male	Female
10	66(307)	72(17)	52	27(54)	31(121)
11	65(314)	71(20)	53	26(112)	30(151)
12	64(316)	70(24)	54	25(181)	29(180)
13	63(329)	69(28)	55	24(256)	28(207)
14	62(341)	68(32)	56	23(334)	28(8)
15	61(359)	67(39)	57	23(96)	26(290)
16	60(364)	66(43)	58	22(126)	25(351)
17	60(6)	65(46)	59	21(188)	25(35)
18	59(8)	64(54)	60	20(292)	24(89)
19	58(10)	63(57)	61	20(28)	23(143)
20	57(37)	62(64)	62	19(123)	22(200)
21	56(41)	61(67)	63	18(207)	21(262)
22	55(50)	60(75)	64	17(327)	20(338)
23	54(53)	59(78)	65	17(61)	20(35)
24	53(84)	58(89)	66	16(167)	19(103)
25	52(90)	57(96)	67	15(273)	18(167)
26	51(84)	56(103)	68	15(32)	17(241)
27	50(100)	55(100)	69	14(147)	16(320)
28	49(106)	54(116)	70	13(270)	16(28)
29	48(112)	53(126)	71	13(39)	15(104)
30	47(138)	52(130)	72	12(160)	14(190)
31	46(212)	51(140)	73	11(303)	13(278)
32	45(182)	50(147)	74	11(92)	13(17)
33	44(187)	49(160)	75	10(67)	12(123)
34	43(190)	48(170)	76	10(35)	11(217)
35	42(206)	47(180)	77	9(106)	10(354)
36	41(209)	46(191)	78	8(4)	10(116)
37	40(264)	45(201)	79	8(177)	9(232)
38	39(270)	44(204)	80	7(171)	9(28)
39	38(291)	43(217)	81	7(180)	8(176)
40	37(320)	42(244)	82	7(17)	7(343)
41	36(358)	41(259)	83	6(204)	7(144)
42	36(6)	40(270)	84	6(58)	6(330)

43	35(14)	39(281)	85	5(267)	6(150)
44	34(28)	38(312)	86	5(123)	5(364)
45	33(106)	37(330)	87	4(347)	5(125)
46	32(124)	36(348)	88	4(173)	5(91)
47	31(162)	36(4)	89	4(75)	4(303)
48	30(201)	35(21)	90	3(307)	4(194)
49	29(241)	34(46)	91	3(156)	4(99)
50	28(313)	33(67)	92	3(92)	4(15)
51	25(364)	32(92)	93	3(2)	3(302)

Secrets to the Fountain of Youth

- Replace anger with acceptance. If you can't change a situation, do not remain angry, judgmental, and resentful. These emotions destroy your health.
- Stay sensitive to the needs of your body. Do not habitually override pain and other body signals. Take care of your body.
- Do not abuse your body with drugs, smoking or alcohol.
- Replace feelings of fear with feelings of love. Most people developed unreasonable fears when they were small children. These unnecessary fears send the wrong signals to our body, which upset the body chemistry.
- Relax and experience quiet time or meditation on a daily basis. This will bring peace and harmony into your life.
- Exercise regularly, and include both stretching and aerobic exercises.
- Overcome your need for approval from others and replace it with self approval. Seeking outside approval increases your anxiety and creates harmful body chemistry.
- Eat healthy with lots of vegetables, grains, and fruits, and very little fat.
- Breath correctly from your diaphragm and fill your lungs with oxygen.
- Discover your purpose in life and work towards fulfilling that purpose.
- Make happiness a priority and follow your bliss.

Menopause

Menopause was not openly discussed by many people until the 1960's or later. There are still many misconceptions about this condition. Some do not regard menopause as the normal occurrence that it is, but as a disorder related to aging.

Menopause is a series of gradual changes that usually begin when a woman reaches her late forties or early fifties. The period of change, called the *climacteric* or *climacterium*, may last up to ten or fifteen years.
- The ovaries of post-menopausal women continue to produce sex hormones, though they do atrophy and produce less of them.
- Eventually the ovaries cease to respond to the hormones sent from the brain.
- Ovulation becomes more irregular and less frequent, until menstruation ceases altogether and the process of menopause is complete.

There are some common symptoms associated with menopause:
- Some women experience "hot flashes," a sudden rush of heat in the upper chest, neck and face, sometimes accompanied by sweating or chills. They affect up to three fourths of menopausal women at one time or another.
- Emotional changes can also take place at this time. Some women suffer from bouts of nervousness, headaches, tension, anxiety or sleeplessness. These effects usually result from the lower levels of hormones produced by the body, but some symptoms may also be linked to the negative attitudes which society still has about menopause.

Sex and Menopause

There is no reason for women to stop being sexually active during or after menopause. Yet some suffer from limiting attitudes that associate sex with youth and child-bearing. In fact, many people remain sexually active in old age, experiencing even feel freer sexual desire since there are no more fears of unwanted pregnancies.

It is very important for women to continue to use a reliable method of birth control during menopause, as ovulation may still occur. Consult a doctor before discontinuing birth control.

Treatments

Estrogen supplements are sometimes prescribed to alleviate the symptoms of menopause. They should be used only when necessary, as they are not completely safe. Other

drugs such as tranquilizers may also be medically recommended
- The risks of *Estrogen Replacement Therapy* (ERT) include endometrial cancer, breast cancer, increased blood pressure and the formation of blood clots. ERT may also cause water retention and bloating, and vaginal spotting.
- During and after menopause some dryness of the vagina may develop due to the decrease in hormones. ERT may be prescribed, but other low and no-risk options such as some estrogen creams and regular lubricating creams, are often sufficient.
- Tranquilizers may be prescribed to women who are affected by emotional upheavals, however these women should first try some form of counseling or a women's support group, as their symptoms may be due to their own or others' attitudes, or lack of emotional support.

Osteoporosis and Menopause

Post-menopausal women are particularly vulnerable to osteoporosis, the loss of bone mass. Proper nutrition, including vitamin and mineral supplements, and a comprehensive exercise program are essential in post-menopausal women to prevent this ailment. During menopause, women require 1,200 mg of calcium daily. After menopause, the requirement rises to 1,500 mg daily.

Male Menopause

While men usually do not have a marked period of change in reproductive functioning, their testes gradually secrete lower amounts of hormones. Most men remain capable of reproduction throughout their lives, but by the age of sixty (about the time that women complete menopause) a man's hormone production will have dropped to pre-puberty levels.

Sexuality

Our sexuality entails much more than the anatomy and functions of our male and female sex organs. The sex hormones produced by our bodies affect our entire systems. Sex therapy is a growing field, as people recognize the importance of the psychological aspects of human sexuality.

Our sexual behavior affects society, and society itself regulates our sexuality.

Our Sexual Organs

In both males and females, the reproductive systems share basic structural similarities. The systems remain undifferentiated until the seventh week of gestation in the mother's womb. By the fourth month, however, the sex of the fetus is clearly visible. Both reproductive systems include:
- A set of similar organs that produce the *germ cells*: the testes in the male which produce sperms, and the ovaries in the female which produce the ova or eggs.
- Similar sets of ducts for the transport of the germ cells.
- Organs for the transfer and union of the germ cells: the penis in males and the vagina in females.
- Men and women produce many of the same sex hormones, but in very different proportions.
- In both sexes, puberty takes several years from onset to full sexual maturity.

Sexual Functions and Responses

Researchers have separated a standard sexual encounter into four different phases:
- A period of excitement or arousal.
- A plateau or period of sustained excitement.
- Orgasm or climax.
- Resolution, a period of relaxation and contentment.

Even though each one of us may respond in a different way to a given sexual situation, certain general patterns do exist:
- Women have a wider range of sexual responses than men. Some women will reach a plateau of sustained excitement after arousal, then will reach orgasm and achieve resolution in a pattern similar to men. However, some women can reach orgasm without the plateau phase, and some women may reach an orgasm during the plateau phase, allowing them to experience repeated orgasms before the period of resolution.
- Men experience a *refractory period* after orgasm, with a certain lapse of time before arousal can begin again.

Sexual Behavior

Humans exhibit an amazingly wide variety of sexual behaviors. The only predictable behaviors determined by sex researchers concern age:
- Males generally reach their sexual peak shortly after puberty and maintain their highest level of sexual activity until around thirty years of age.
- Females, on the other hand, seem to generally reach their sexual peak around age thirty, maintaining this level for about a decade.

People all over the world experiment with sexual positions and techniques. Many cultures have such representations throughout their art work such as Greek paintings on vases and pottery, Japanese paintings and woodcuts,. Some cultures even have ancient texts and illustrations dealing exclusively with sexual knowledge such as the Indian texts called the *Kama Sutra*.

Sex in Society

Ever since the writings of the eighteenth century French Romantics, people have believed that in more primitive times and cultures sex was care free, satisfying and unregulated. Truthfully there is no society in which sex is not regulated in some way. Every culture that has ever been studied has had some laws, customs and taboos regarding the sexual behavior of its people.

Many societal limitations extend throughout very different cultures. For instance, taboos against incestuous relations seem to exist in every known society. Although many forms of sexual behavior have been experimented with throughout the ages, the most widely accepted form of sexual activity is heterosexual intercourse between adults.

Some forms of sexual activity are often judged negatively, even to the extent of being outlawed and persecuted. Many activities are considered harmful at times, sometimes with little or no evidence. For instance:
- In many Western societies, boys are often warned of the supposed dangers of masturbation.
- During the Victorian era in England, only sex between married people was acceptable, and even then women were not encouraged to express themselves sexually.
- Today certain sex acts are against the law in some states of the United States.

Sexual Malfunctions

Just as sex can be a source of great pleasure, joy, emotional growth and personal enhancement, so it can also lead to great suffering and loss of self-esteem.

Both men and women occasionally experience a lack of sexual interest. This is not a sexual malfunction. It can be caused by stress, temporary illness, worries, tiredness, depression or a number of other factors.

Some real malfunctions are as follows:
- Men may experience impotence or the inability to achieve or maintain an erection.
- Another frequent malfunction in men is premature ejaculation.
- Occasionally, a man can maintain an erection but remain unable to ejaculate. Or his ejaculation may be retrograde, with the semen flowing backward into the bladder. A man may also sustain a painful erection independent of any sexual desire.
- In females there is no erection to lose, so women cannot be termed impotent, but some women experience *frigidity* or the inability to achieve an orgasm.
- In some instances a woman may suffer from *vagisnismus*, a condition in which spasms of the vaginal opening make intercourse painful.
- Impotence or frigidity affects almost everyone at some time.

For sexual problems of an emotional or psychological nature, help can be found from a number of sources, including individual counseling with a psychologist or sex therapist, group therapy, and organizations, telephone referral and information services for specific problems.

If the problem appears to be the result of physical causes, help is also available in various forms:
- Talk to a doctor about any medication you may be taking. Some medications affect sexual desire and performance.
- External vacuum devices are available which can help men achieve an erection within two to three minutes.
- An injection into the penis itself can give an erection that will last from twenty minutes to two hours.
- Because of this new injectable drug, prostheses are rarely used, and should only be implanted as a last resort.

Sexual Ecstasy

Set the Stage
- Decorate the room sensually. Candle light or soft lighting really helps set the mood. Red or purple or ultraviolet colored light is fun.
- Flowers, good smells, and sexy clothing are all great amenities.
- Sometimes arrange a special time for sex with your partner, rather than wait until everything else is done and it's time for bed.
- Experiment with different settings: a different room, outdoors, a hotel room, etc.

Foreplay
- Massage can be an important part of foreplay. (See *Massage*.)
- For most people, feelings of affection for their sexual partner are necessary to make the sexual act a pleasurable and fulfilling experience. If such affection is present, sexual activity between two people can help fill their needs for nurturing and closeness. It is in this sense that foreplay can serve more than the simple purpose of arousal.
- The *clitoris* is located at the top of the vagina just above the interconnection of the minor lips. Try stroking the clitoris with a lubricated finger. The pressure should at first be very light and soft. After full arousal, the movements can be firmer and faster.
- The *G spot* is an important point in females for vaginal orgasm. It is located just inside the vagina, at the top, and behind the ridge of the pubic bone. The male should use one or two fingers and curl them so the tip is hooked behind the pubic bone. Massage it using very firm pressure.

The Main Event
- People generally use only a few of sexual positions that they have found are comfortable and in which they can achieve a climax. There are many postures for sex and experimenting with different postures adds excitement. We can always return to the favored postures just prior to the climax.
- The speed of sex can be changed for added variety. Slow motion sex is very different than hot and quick sex.

- Sounds – moans and groans, cries and laughter – all add to the excitement. Make sounds that express your feelings.
- Experimenting with different positions, techniques and settings allows a couple to break the monotony that can set in to the sexual part of their relationship. More importantly, it requires partners to communicate their desires and feelings with each other.
- Extended sex occurs when the man moves only enough to keep an erection. This builds up the sexual excitement and leads to a more powerful climax.

The Climax
- The couple can repeatedly move close to the point of climax but then stop just before climax and wait until they can move again. This builds energy for a more powerful climax.
- Spreading the climax energy away from the genitals and to the rest of the body is a means of expanding the sensations. Rather than focusing only on the genitals, spread the pleasurable sensations by using your mind to move the pleasure into the rest of your body.

Afterwards
- Stay together, maybe fall asleep, hug, hold each other or have coffee or dessert.
- Oral sex is not only for foreplay, but also can be fun after sex.

There is no substitute for genuine caring, love and open communication between two individuals to enhance the quality of their sexual involvement.

Exercises for Women
For women who do not easily attain orgasm, but who otherwise feel a normal enjoyment of sexual activities, a simple set of exercises is sometimes sufficient. These are called *Kegel's exercises* after the physician who developed them.
- This exercise is particularly helpful to regain tone of the perineal muscles after childbirth.
- Many women have also reported increased sexual pleasure after learning to perform voluntary contractions.
- Men can also perform Kegel's exercises and have reported better erections and stronger orgasms.

> ### Kegel's Exercises
> The muscles which control the openings of the urethra and the vagina form a figure eight, so voluntary contractions of one will strengthen the entire muscle structure.
> - While sitting on the toilet, stop the flow of urine and hold for a few seconds.
> - Release then repeat, until you can feel the proper way to contract these muscles.
> - This should be done several times each day, in sets of ten contractions, each contraction being held for a count of ten. An entire set takes only a couple of minutes. Kegel's exercises can be practiced any time, anywhere.

Birth Control

The following chart estimates pregnancy protection based on usage for an entire year, and not just one encounter.

Type of Birth Control	Pregnancy Protection	Disease Protection	Information
Rhythm method	Varies 50-86%	None	18 safe days per menstrual cycle
Male condom	About 85%	Good	Use only once
Female condom	74-79% estimated	Good	Use only once
Spermicide used alone	70-80%	Some	Apply 1 hour or less before intercourse
Sponge	72-82%	None	Insert up to 6 hours before intercourse
Diaphragm & spermicide	82-94%	None	Insert up to 6 hours before intercourse
Cervical cap & spermicide	At least 82%	None	Insert up to 6 hours before intercourse
Pills	97-99%	None	Must be taken daily
Implant	99%	None	Lasts 5 years
Injection	99%	None	Lasts 3 months
IUD	95-96%	None	Physician must insert and remove
Sterilization	Over 99%	None	Surgery required

Sexually Transmitted Diseases

Most sexually transmitted diseases can easily be prevented with a condom.

Although some sexually transmitted diseases (STD's) can be treated with antibiotics, new strains of diseases are now emerging that are drug-resistant. Other STD's have no symptoms, such as *chlamydia*, or no cure, such as *genital herpes* and AIDS. In all cases, STD's are detrimental to reproductive health.

Protection involves:
- Abstinence from sexual intercourse.
- A mutually monogamous relationship with a known healthy partner.
- Using a condom. Condoms, however, are not fool-proof. They can tear or slip off.
- A condom with spermicide may lower the risk of infection from some STD's. However, the spermicidal chemicals can sometimes cause irritation of the tissues, which may increase the risk of infection.

Gonorrhea
Gonorrhea is an infectious disease which is transmitted through sexual contact.
- There is a two- to ten-day incubation period without symptoms.
- A genital discharge is the first symptom, followed by pain for men and women alike.
- Untreated gonorrhea can lead to sterility, blindness and arthritis.
- A pregnant woman can infect her baby's eyes during birth.

Gonorrhea is treated with antibiotics, although there is now a new and untreatable strain. Prevention is always the best approach.

Syphilis

Also an infectious disease, syphilis is highly contagious and can be fatal if left untreated. It is transmitted through sexual contact and its symptoms occur in three stages:
- Between ten to ninety days after infection, a small sore or *chancre* appears at the site of the infection. This sore oozes, and can infect other sexual partners. The sore will go away in about a week's time.
- The infection spreads throughout the body within two months. A rash may cover part or all of the body. There may be flu-like symptoms that will go away in time.
- The third stage of the disease may not develop until months or years later. Then there may be heart disease, brain damage, blindness and even death.
- Syphilis can be passed from a pregnant woman to her baby, causing blindness or deformities at birth.
- Syphilis is treatable with antibiotics.

Genital Herpes

This disease results from a sexually transmitted infection caused by the type two Herpes Simplex virus.
- The symptoms develop in two to ten days after contact with an infected partner.
- There may be pain in the buttocks, legs, or genital area, especially while urinating.
- There may be a vaginal discharge.
- Small blisters appear in genital areas. They eventually rupture, crust over and heal. Healing may take several weeks.
- The virus then retreats into the nervous system and remains dormant. The active phase of the disease is now over, but the virus never leaves the body.
- During the active phase, sexual contact must be avoided until all sores are completely healed.
- The symptoms can be treated, but at this time there is no cure for genital herpes.
- The severity and frequency of the active phases can vary. Stress and other factors can activate symptoms.
- A pregnant mother can pass on the disease to her baby during birth, and a cesarean section is almost always required for herpes-infected mothers.

AIDS

AIDS (*Acquired Immune Deficiency Syndrome.*) is caused by a virus which breaks down the body's defense against illness. The immune system, which would normally fight off infections, becomes impaired and unable to do its job. Consequently, common infections can be fatal to a person with AIDS.
- AIDS is caused by HIV, *Human Immunodeficiency Virus*.
- AIDS is a venereal disease; it is transmitted through sexual contact.
- The virus may remain in the body in a dormant state for months or even years. You cannot tell if people are infected with HIV by looking at them.
- Once the virus is activated, however, it eventually results in death from opportunistic infections.
- The AIDS virus itself does not kill the carrier; it only makes the body unable to defend itself against other disease.

Who's at Risk?

Almost all of the HIV-infected population of the U.S. can be classified in five groups:
- Sexually active homosexual or bisexual men.
- Men and women who use intravenous drugs.
- Men, women and children who have received infected blood through transfusions. However, transfusions are now much safer, as most blood supplies are tested for HIV. (Blood donors are not at risk.)
- The heterosexual partner of any infected person. It is important to note that heterosexual women, being the receptors of semen, are at greater risk than heterosexual men.
- Children born to infected mothers. A pregnant woman who is infected with HIV has a significant chance of infecting her unborn child.

A few health care workers and health care recipients have been infected, but this is unusual, especially since proper precautions have now become routine in most health care settings.

The rate of contagion has slowed among homosexuals because homosexual men are practicing safer sex more consistently since the discovery of the virus' means of transmission.

The AIDS virus has been found in blood, semen, vaginal secretions, tears and saliva. Yet AIDS cannot be contracted through contact with toilet seats, shower stalls, doorknobs, books or other objects, food, sneezes or coughs.

Women and AIDS

Among heterosexual women, the risk of HIV infection appears to be greater than previously thought. During any heterosexual encounter, a woman faces a higher chance of infection than a heterosexual man if she engages in vaginal sex without a condom.

- More body fluid usually passes from the man into the woman than vice versa.
- A woman may have a sore inside of the vagina of which she is unaware, or may develop a lesion or bruising of the vaginal wall during intercourse.
- A woman is also at greater risk during menstruation, when the uterus sheds its lining and offers the virus a passageway into the blood stream.
- The virus may also be able to penetrate certain mucous membranes, such as those in the vagina.
- The use of the spermicide *Nonoxynol-9*, which is available in pharmacies and is added to some brands of condoms, has sometimes been recommended. It is capable of killing the AIDS virus, but it can also cause irritation of the mucous membranes in some women, thereby increasing the risk of transmission of the virus.

As there is presently no cure or vaccine to combat the AIDS virus, it is essential for each one of us to know as much as we can about the virus, to understand how it works, and is transmitted, and most importantly, how to protect ourselves.

AIDS Prevention

To completely protect oneself from HIV infection, one must avoid any and all contact with the body fluids (blood, semen, vaginal secretions, saliva, urine, feces, vomit or mucous secretions) of an infected person.

High-Risk Behaviors

Some forms of behavior carry a much greater chance of contact with body fluids than others. These are high-risk behaviors, which should be avoided:

- Anal sex is a very high-risk behavior for men and women. The cellular lining of the rectum is very rich in blood capillaries and is easily damaged, allowing HIV transmission from semen. It is also possible for a man to be infected if blood from his partner's rectum enters the opening of his penis.
- The sharing of syringes for injecting drugs is high-risk behavior. Small amounts of blood almost always go up into the needle and syringe, and are then injected into the next person. If one must inject drugs, it is essential to use a new needle and syringe each and every time, or clean them both with a bleach solution. Simply sterilizing the tip of the needle over a flame, or with alcohol, is not enough to be effective.
- The greater the number of sexual partners one has, the greater the risk of infection with HIV. While it is possible to be infected in only one instance of unprotected sex, the more sexual partners one has, the greater the chance of encountering an HIV-infected individual.

Safer Sex

The only completely safe sex is no sex. A mutually monogamous relationship between partners who are not infected with HIV is also safe, provided that testing has been done properly. Otherwise, there are ways to practice *safer* sex:

- Use a latex condom each time the man's penis comes in contact with his partner's mouth, vagina or anus. Natural skin condoms may allow the virus to leak through. Condoms with the spermicide Nonoxynol-9 are best, as the spermicide kills HIV.
- Do not use oil-based lubricants that can irritate the tissues of the body as well as weaken and break latex condoms. Use only water-based lubricants.
- Avoid multiple sexual partners. The more partners you have, the greater the risk. Know your partner's sexual history. Open and honest communication is essential.
- Avoid anal intercourse. This is the most dangerous of all sexual practices for both partners. Condoms are much more likely to break due to increased friction.
- Do not have sex with an intravenous drug user.

- Do not share sexual objects that can carry the virus between partners.
- Oral sex can also be risky insofar as the AIDS virus has been found in semen, saliva and the vaginal secretions of women (especially near a woman's ovulation time.) Semen that is swallowed is probably neutralized by the stomach acids, but sores, bleeding gums or inflamed tissues in the mouth or throat can transport the virus into the bloodstream.
- Do not douche before sex, as it rids the vagina of its natural defenses against infection.

Remember: AIDS is fatal. There is no cure for AIDS at this time.

AIDS Testing

AIDS testing does not actually look for the virus itself, but for antibodies to the virus. Being diagnosed HIV positive means that the body is manufacturing antibodies to the AIDS virus, indicating that the person has been infected. However, a negative test does not necessarily mean that the person is not infected with HIV.

- It is possible for an infected person to have a delayed reaction to the virus, in which case the immune system may not produce antibodies to the virus for several weeks or months.
- Anyone who tests negative for HIV antibodies, but has engaged in any risky behavior, should be tested again a few months later.
- Once antibodies are present, the person may still go many more months or even years before developing any illness.
- Even if the infected person tests negative for antibody production, or tests positive but remains healthy for several years, they can still infect others.

Doctors

Most of us think being healthy means never needing to see a doctor. However we all need a doctor whom we know and trust, because regular check-ups and prompt attention to medical problems can be important factors in staying healthy for a lifetime.

Choosing a Physician

It is important to remember that we can choose our doctor, and we do not have to continue seeing any physician with whom we are not satisfied, for whatever reason.

A feeling of trust may be the single most important factor in choosing a doctor, though training, experience, competence and other elements should also be considered.

Medicine has become such a huge and highly technological field that it is hard to find a family doctor or general practitioner. Instead we are referred to different specialists. Even then we should feel comfortable enough to discuss our concerns and to ask questions until we are satisfied that we understand what's going on. After all, we are not made up of disconnected and interchangeable parts, but exist as a whole, body and mind.

One alternative to the family doctor is the medical group. A small group of two or three physicians who work together closely can provide the same kind of personal care as a single doctor. Teaching hospitals and many other institutions can also offer excellent care, and many teaching hospitals charge reduced fees for services based on the patient's income.

Remember that you can always request all the information pertaining to your case, including diagnosis, prognosis and treatment plans. You are also entitled to get a second opinion from a doctor of your choice.

A caring and competent physician should not resent anyone getting a second opinion or asking pertinent questions. After all, recovery from any illness involves the mental and emotional cooperation of the patient. A good physician should thoroughly explain the nature of the illness and the plans for treatment, including the purpose of any medication, dietary restrictions or requirements, special exercises or physical therapy, and any other treatments.

The Medical Check-up

Everyone should have a complete check-up each year. It should include the following:
- Review and update of your medical records.
- Review and evaluation of any medication you may be taking, including over-the-counter drugs.
- Review and evaluation of your life-style, including alcohol intake, cigarette smoking, exercise, general fitness, leisure activities, moods and emotional condition, stress factors, and diet.
- A complete physical check-up, including reflexes, heart and lungs, eyes, ears, nose and throat, blood pressure, weight, skin condition, etc.
- Breast and gynecological exams for women. All women should have a pap-smear annually.

Modern and Traditional Medicine

In modern medicine, the nature of an illness and the course of medical treatment are determined by a physical examination. The doctor–patient relationship historically has been considered in the west to be relatively insignificant as a factor in treatment.

In many "traditional" or "alternative" methods of healing, however, the relationship between the patient and the healer is considered to be the most important part of any successful treatment plan.

Whereas modern medicine focuses on the physical body, the traditional healer examines symptoms of the body, mind and spirit, and attempts to cure all three.

But the narrower focus of modern medicine is not all bad. The exacting scientific approach has accomplished wonders in health care:
- Medical science has eradicated many deadly and contagious diseases, including almost all of the dangerous childhood diseases.

- Organ transplants are now almost routine medical procedures.
- Microsurgery, laser surgery, and many other life-saving technologies have been developed.

Alternative Therapies

There are benefits to be gained from both the modern and traditional practices. According to medical scientists themselves, alternative therapies can be very useful in preventing or in helping to treat many illnesses. Most medical experts agree that these aspects of traditional medicine are very beneficial:
- The emphasis on prevention of diseases through a healthy lifestyle, including a nutritious diet and exercise.
- The emphasis on making each person more responsible for his or her own health.
- The emphasis on treating body, mind and spirit as a whole.

Most alternative therapies that are offered to the American public today have their roots in ancient scientific wisdom, such as Ayurvedic medicine from India, acupuncture and acupressure from China, and herbal medicine from most cultures throughout the world. For many minor or recurring ailments, we can consider proven alternative methods of treatment:
- Acupuncture often works well in chronic pain management.
- Biofeedback has been used successfully to treat chronic pain and high blood pressure.
- Hypnosis and relaxation techniques have helped asthma sufferers.
- Chiropractic is very effective for back pain that is not caused by any fracture or tumor.

Choosing Alternative Therapies

Some caution should be exercised when shopping for alternative therapies:
- Do not buy any "secret" therapy or ingredient. It is highly unlikely, considering the amount of medical research now being done, that someone could discover a truly effective treatment which no one else is aware of.
- Get an thorough explanation of your treatment. Find out exactly how long the treatment process will take, and

when you can expect to see some improvement in your condition.
- Some natural remedies and certain herbs can be toxic. Ask about side effects, and follow prescribed dosages exactly.
- Investigate your practitioner's background. Ask about certification or licensing requirements. The practitioner should be willing to provide references from teachers or other patients.

Herbal Medicine

At the root of herbal medicine is the belief that for every ailment that can afflict us, the all-pervading balance of the universe dictates that there must necessarily exist a remedy for this ailment, and that it can be found in nature.

During the past century, many people have discounted herbal or folk medicine as superstition. However, we should remember that plants have been used to alleviate illness throughout human history.
- In both India and China, an extensive knowledge and systematic study and use of herbs was developed over several thousand years. Over 1,000 medicinal herbs were used in India.
- Ancient Egyptians used the bark of the sycamore tree and the oil of the cedar tree for medicinal purposes.
- Cedar was also used in Mesopotamia, along with castor oil, mint, fig, mandrake, henbane, poppy and other plants.
- Recently in the U.S. Southwest, a Native American medicine woman prescribed a certain root for a woman's severe headaches, which were not responding to medications. The root, which had to be specially prepared by the patient herself, was found to contain ibuprofen, which is now the active ingredient in many pain relievers.
- In Louisiana, French settlers learned from the Native Americans to chew on the leaves of the willow tree. Those leaves contain *acetylsalicylic acid*, the active ingredient in aspirin.
- Various herbs have proved to be very efficient remedies for many minor illnesses. Other herbs function as pain relievers or tranquilizers, which help a patient rest or alleviate symptoms while an illness runs its course.
- In most cultures, herbal remedies have been used in conjunction with ceremonies, prayers and other forms of

spiritual rituals to give the patient faith in the treatment. This can be equated with the use of psychotherapy or counseling. We know that a positive outlook has a great influence on a patient's recovery.

Folklore to Modern Medicine

Almost all of modern pharmacy is derived from plants, either with actual plant extracts, or through chemical reproduction of active agents found in the plant. In many cases it has been possible to change or control the substances to diminish side effects, and to produce them in large quantities in the laboratory.

- The alkaloid *reserpine*, from the Chinese rawolfia plant, has been used to make a treatment for hypertension.
- *Ephedra* led to the manufacture of epinephrine for treating asthma.
- *Quinine* from the cinchona bark is used to cure malaria.
- *Digitalis* from the purple foxglove is synthesized to treat heart ailments.
- The use of spores from moldy bread to treat sores led to the discovery of penicillin.

A big advantage of many medicinal herbs over modern, laboratory-made drugs is their mildness: most herbs, if overused, will quickly and naturally be eliminated by the body. Chemical compounds, on the other hand, can burden the liver and remain present in cells for a long time.

Many books are readily available on herbal medicines and treatments, listing most common herbs and their uses. Select one that includes a detailed list of the toxic effects and side effects of some herbs. There are also reputable herbalists in many large American cities.

Ayurvedic Medicine

Translated literally, Ayurveda means the Science of Life. Ayurvedic medicine examines the position of the individual within the environment, and tries to determine the imbalance which is responsible for the illness.

Ayurveda requires a more intuitive and holistic approach than Western medicine, a vision which encompasses not only the physiology of the patient but also the psychological, environmental and spiritual factors.

The use of medicinal plants is only one part of a vast scientific system called Ayurveda.

- Ayurvedic medicine is quickly gaining credibility in the West, particularly for minor or recurring ailments which have not responded well to modern medicine.
- Emphasis is placed on determining and understanding the cause and course of the illness, rather than simply treating symptoms. This is important to prevent the illness from recurring.
- An Ayurvedic doctor may prescribe changes in diet, herbal remedies, massage or other forms of manipulation, and spiritual exercises.
- A massage therapist, chiropractor, health food store or macrobiotic center should be able to recommend a reputable Ayurvedic doctor or center.

Possible Mental Reasons for Physical Disease

Disease	Possible Reason
Arthritis	Allowing too many restrictions and rules to limit your actions.
Bladder problems	Unresolved guilt and self–blame.
High blood pressure	Not performing to a level of expectations that may be unrealistically difficult.
Cancer	Not forgiving and loving yourself enough.
Overweight	Unrealistic need to protect yourself from others.
Headaches	Indecision or restrictive thinking.
Heart problems	Over–competition with others. Reacting to responsibility as a tremendous aggravation.
Hemorrhoids	Holding back and not sharing your emotions with others.
Neck	Overly concerned with responsibility for others.
Prostate	Too much or too little sexual activity.

Drugs

Almost everyone will use some sort of drug at some time in his or her life. But just because a drug is available without a prescription, or a doctor says to take something, does not mean that it is always completely safe. There are many factors which affect the safety and effectiveness of any drug, such as allergies, drug interaction, alcohol consumption, age, weight, general health, and a number of other considerations.

Over-the-Counter Drugs (OTC)

Most households have a medicine cabinet stocked with a variety of over-the-counter drugs for use throughout the year. These drugs may be antihistamines for runny noses or hay fever, decongestants for colds, cough medicines, pain relievers, first-aid ointments or sprays, antacids, laxatives and sleep aids.

Such medications are called "over-the-counter" because they can be purchased without a prescription.
- Americans medicate themselves four times more often with over-the-counter drugs than with drugs prescribed by a physician.
- The Federal Food, Drug and Cosmetic Act, requires that habit-forming drugs or those drugs that are unsafe to use without a doctor's supervision to be dispensed only through prescription.
- Drugs considered safe to use by following the directions and warnings on the label are made available over the counter.

It is the responsibility of the consumer to read the label and follow the instructions exactly.

Required information on the label of any OTC drug includes:
- How much of the drug to take.
- When to take the drug and how often.
- How to apply, in the case of a cream or ointment.
- When to avoid using the drug, and possible adverse reactions.
- Warnings concerning children.

Special cautions applying to certain drugs must also be included:
- Drugs that can cause drowsiness must include a warning not to drive or operate machinery while taking the product.
- Drugs that can reach the placenta or fetus of a pregnant woman, or affect the baby of a nursing mother must also carry warnings not to use without first consulting a doctor.

- Many drugs carry a warning to consult a physician if symptoms persist over a certain period of time. This is to prevent over medication and allow a medical expert to determine if another, more serious condition is exists.
- A warning must be present if the drug does not mix well with alcohol. In many cases alcohol increases or alters the effect of certain drugs.
- It is always best not to drink alcohol while taking any medications.

Virtually all OTC drugs are now sold in tamper-resistant packages and carry a warning to check for signs of tampering before using. Always read the warning and check the seal, then check the product itself.

The FDA is constantly reviewing OTC products and adding new medications to the list. This gives us, the consumers, more control of their own health care, and make many products more accessible and less expensive. However, availability of OTC drugs does not give us license to medicate ourselves irresponsibly and indiscriminately.

Prescription Drugs

Many of us take prescription drugs without knowing very much about how they are made or how they work. We rely on the assurances of the manufacturers, our pharmacists and our physicians.
- In any given year, over two thirds of all American households use at least one prescription drug.
- Americans are living longer, and drug use often increases as people age and begin to suffer from chronic conditions.
- New drugs are discovered and manufactured daily.

Yet we often forget that whenever we take any drug, there are risks as well as benefits. Most drugs are concentrated, very specific, and very effective. There are several ways in which they can cause problems:
- Drugs can be taken in the wrong dosage or at the wrong time.
- If a drug is taken with another drug (over-the-counter or prescription), there can be negative effects from the interaction of the two.
- There can be interactions between certain drugs and certain foods.
- Drugs may interact badly with alcohol.

- Drugs are sometimes improperly prescribed, or not really needed.
- People sometimes take drugs that were prescribed for someone else, because they have similar symptoms.
- Sometimes a person stops taking a drug as soon as the symptoms fade away. This often happens with antibiotics. As a result the infection may recur, and be even harder to treat the second time.
- People also renew prescriptions when the medication is no longer necessary. This is often the case with tranquilizers, which can have serious side effects, (including addiction.)

Doctor-Patient Communication: Ask and Ask Again

To ensure that you fully understand the course of your prescribed treatment, you should ask your physician the following:
- The name of the drug prescribed.
- How the drug or treatment works and how long it should take.
- Exact dosage that you must take, and intervals between doses.
- Any side effects.
- You may wish to ask for other sources of information about your illness and treatment, particularly if a new or experimental drug is prescribed.

It is your duty to make sure that you fully understand the purpose and instructions for any drug prescribed for you. You have the right to demand a complete explanation from your physician or pharmacist about any drug.

Your doctor should ask you about the following:
- Drug allergies, including OTC and prescription drugs. Do not overlook anything.
- Any other allergies, such as foods, textiles, or household chemicals.
- Any other medications you are taking. This includes birth control medication and over-the-counter drugs such as aspirin, cold medicine, sleeping aids, laxatives, etc.
- Any other physician you may be seeing for any reason.
- Whether you are pregnant or trying to conceive.
- Whether you drink alcohol, smoke tobacco, or use any recreational drugs.
- Any special diet and its purpose.

Usually in a doctor's office, many of the above questions are routinely asked on a medical history sheet which the patient must fill out prior to the consultation. However, if you have forgotten to write down some item or you think any of these topics were not covered, by all means volunteer the information.

You must give full and accurate information, so your doctor can make a correct diagnosis and prescribe safe and effective treatment.

Drugs and Pregnancy

Any drug that a woman takes will likely cross the placenta and affect her unborn child.
- This includes over-the-counter drugs such as aspirin and cough medicine.
- The fetus may be most adversely affected shortly after conception, during the period of great cell division and organ formation.

> **Pregnant women, women who are trying to conceive and nursing mothers should avoid all medication.**

Of course there are times when the mother's condition must be treated because of its severity, or because it threatens the child as well. In such a case, doctor-patient cooperation is most important. The woman must fully understand the need, dosage instructions and possible side-effects of the drug.

Drugs and Children

> **Never give a child aspirin or any other adult drug.**

In addition to the regular concerns about taking any drug, there are some very important safety measures related specifically to children:
- Always use childproof caps and always reseal medications immediately.
- Put all medicines away in a locked and out-of-reach cabinet.
- Educate your children about the dangers of medications.

- Sweet and fruit-flavored pills, syrups and chewable vitamins are a great temptation for children. Treat them like any other drug.

Drugs and Alcohol

- Alcohol and drugs are both metabolized by the liver.
- If you drink alcohol and then take medication, it may take longer for the drug to be metabolized in your liver, so that the drug may then remain in your body longer than intended.
- The reverse may be true and the drug may leave the body at a faster rate.
- Alcohol is particularly dangerous in conjunction with drugs that depress the nervous system, because alcohol itself is a potent depressant.

If you usually drink, even if it is only one drink a day, you must mention it to your doctor and follow his or her instructions precisely.

How Some Drugs React with Alcohol

Drug Type	With Alcohol
Pain relievers with Acetaminophen	May make the liver more vulnerable to the effects of alcohol.
Pain relievers with Aspirin	Regular drinking with aspirin can cause bleeding of the stomach.
Pain relievers with Narcotics	Can increase the degree of sedation. Do not drive.
Anti-depressants	Can cause drowsiness, lack of coordination.
Antihistamines	Can slow reflexes, cause drowsiness. Do not drive.
Arthritis medication	Can cause stomach irritation, decrease coordination.
Barbiturates	Can be lethal. Watch out for cough medicines that contain alcohol.
Diabetes medications	Can trigger wild fluctuations in blood-sugar levels.
Antibiotics	Can decrease effectiveness.
Heart medications - Nitroglycerin	May cause dizziness.

Tranquilizers	May increase sedation, cause dizziness, drowsiness, and lack of coordination. Do not drive.
Sedatives and Sleeping pills	Increased sedation, lack of coordination.
Time-release capsules of all kinds	Alcohol may cause the capsule to dissolve too quickly.

Interactions between Drugs and Foods and Vitamins

Some foods and vitamins may have a negative effect on drugs, by inhibiting their effectiveness, while others may enhance the effectiveness of certain drugs.

Drug Interactions

Drug	These Substances *Inhibit* Drug Effectiveness
Anticoagulants	Liver, bacon, leafy green vegetables, vitamin C, vitamin K
Anticonvulsants	Liver, leafy green vegetables, folic acid
Anti-thyroid	Cabbage, cauliflower, Brussels sprouts, turnips, leafy green vegetables, soybeans
Barbiturates	Leafy green vegetables, whole grains, nuts, potatoes, beans, vitamin B6
Diabetes drugs	Sugar, alcohol
Digitalis	Foods high in fiber
Diuretics	MSG, salt, licorice
Levodopa	Liver, malt, skim milk, beans, wheat germ, oatmeal, vitamin B6
Tetracycline	Dairy products, acid foods

Drug	These Substances May *Enhance* Drug Effectiveness
Anticoagulants	Vitamin A, vitamin E
Birth control pills	Vitamin C

Generic Drugs and Brand-name Drugs

When a new drug is developed by a pharmaceutical company, the product is protected under a patent so that the company retains exclusive rights to market the drug for a certain period of time. When the patent runs out, other companies are able to produce cheaper generic versions of the same drug.

A brand-name drug and the equivalent generic drug always contain the same amount of the active ingredient.

However, the methods used to produce the drug, and the quality of fillers, coloring agents and binding agents can differ. Some pharmaceutical companies claim that most generic drugs are not as effective as their brand-name equivalents. However, many generic drugs are being manufactured by subsidiaries of the same companies who own the brand-name drug in the first place.
- The availability of generic drugs is growing rapidly, due to increased expirations of patents.
- Generic drugs are often as much as 50% cheaper.
- The U.S. military has been using generic drugs consistently since the 1950s.
- Whenever you receive a prescription from your doctor, ask whether the generic drug would be acceptable.

Smoking

The tobacco plant has been a part of American culture for a very long time, perhaps as long as 2000 years or more. As Europeans arrived on American shores, they learned from the Native Americans how to smoke tobacco, and little by little this new habit made its way back to Europe. Tobacco farming was the first successful cash crop of European settlers in the New World.

Nicotine, the active ingredient in tobacco, was named after the Frenchman Jean Nicot, who brought the seeds of the tobacco plant back to France.

In the nineteenth century, smoking a pipe became the popular form of tobacco use. Snuff and cigar smoking also increased in popularity. Cigarettes first appeared towards the end of the nineteenth century, probably from Spain.

Nicotine is very addictive..

In 1964, the Surgeon General's Office released an official report stating that cigarette smoke is the predominant cause of lung cancer. In 1970, it was announced that even second-hand smoke or passive smoking, which is unavoidable when sharing a room with a smoker, also constitutes a definite threat to health.

The Effects of Tobacco Smoke

Smoking is believed to be the primary cause of 400,000 deaths a year.

- A heavy smoker usually develops a chronic cough as the normal response of the body trying to rid itself of foreign materials.
- When the bronchial tubes get clogged, the risk of infection increases, and these airways lose their ability to expand naturally.
- *Bronchitis* occurs which may become a chronic condition.
- After years of smoking, the lungs themselves lose their ability to expand and contract.
- *Emphysema* makes each breath difficult and painful for the victim, who may survive for years with no hope of improvement. This is an incurable disease.
- Smoking can cause such destruction in the lungs that often abnormal cells start to grow and cancerous tumors develop.

Lung cancer is hard to treat and the survival rate is low.

- Every time a person smokes a cigarette, the heart must work harder to pump blood because of constriction of the blood vessels.
- Blood pressure rises.
- Carbon monoxide is absorbed into the blood, where it is thought to cause damage to the lining of the arteries.
- Carbon monoxide may also increase cholesterol deposits.
- The combination of constricted arteries and plaque build-up is very harmful to the cardiovascular system.
- When an artery becomes completely blocked, a heart attack is sure to follow.
- Strokes, caused by a lack of blood to the brain, are more likely to happen among smokers. (See *Heart Disease*.)

- The incidence of heart attack, stroke and the formation of blood clots is further increased among women who smoke and use birth-control pills.
- If a woman is pregnant, the decrease of oxygen in her bloodstream is very unhealthy for her unborn child.
- There is a much higher incidence of miscarriages, still-births and low birth weights among mothers who smoke, than among non-smokers.

Other Hazards

Some people are turning to other forms of tobacco use, such as smoking a pipe or cigar. These products contain the same harmful ingredients and have been linked to several forms of oral cancers and cancer of the larynx. It is true, however, that pipe and cigar smokers do not usually inhale the smoke, and may smoke less throughout the day.

Chewing tobacco and snuff are becoming increasingly popular among some young people. Both products are directly linked to oral cancers. They are not safe alternatives to smoking.

> **All tobacco products are harmful to the body and extremely addictive.**

Simply being in a room while someone else is smoking is harmful, because the same toxic chemicals that enter the smoker's lungs are released into the air.

Children who live with smokers have a higher incidence of colds, bronchitis, ear infections and pulmonary ailments.

Cigarette paper is laden with chemicals that are also toxic when inhaled. Because the paper is designed to ensure that a cigarette will continue to burn slowly even after it has been set aside, cigarettes are responsible for thousands of fires each year, with tragic losses of lives and millions of dollars in damages.

Quitting

Because nicotine is highly addictive, it is extremely hard for any smoker to quit. If you are a smoker, it is imperative that you start a program to quit.

There are many groups that can help you as you give up smoking. Call the American Lung Association, the American Cancer Society, the American Heart Association, your physician or community hospital for more information.

As soon as you quit smoking, your body can start ridding itself of the accumulated toxins. But there are numerous symptoms associated with nicotine withdrawal; but most symptoms will vanish after a few days to a few weeks.
- Dizziness and tingling sensations.
- Frequent coughing, as your lungs try to rid themselves of tar deposits.
- The craving for nicotine will remain for a long time.

How to quit smoking
- Most importantly, believe you can quit, and develop a positive attitude about your future as a healthy non-smoker.
- If you choose to quit "cold turkey," (all at once) *transdermal nicotine patches* can be very helpful. They must be prescribed by a doctor, and must never be worn while smoking.
- Choose one special person who does not smoke to support and help you as you quit. This is the person you call when the urge to light up is overwhelming.
- As you start to cut down on the number of cigarettes you smoke each day, use a brand and type which you dislike.
- Every time you smoke, write it down on an index card. Write the time, place and a word or two to qualify the moment. Keep a new index card for each day. Review your progress by the week and the month. This will also help you determine the times when you are most at risk of wanting to smoke during the day.
- Become aware of how other habits relate to your smoking habit. If you reach for a cigarette every time you answer the phone, try separating the two activities. Do not ever allow yourself to smoke while on the phone. After you have mastered this one, move on to another complementary habit.
- Choose alternative behaviors that feel good to you and can take the place of a cigarette.
- Reward yourself for not smoking.
- Chew on a licorice stick or sugarless gum or an other oral substitute for having a cigarette in your mouth.

- Drink plenty of water to help your body rid itself of accumulated toxins.
- Improve your diet. Eat plenty of fresh fruits and vegetables.
- Exercise. Since your appetite will probably increase, you will want to begin an activity that helps you burn calories and stay within your normal weight range.

Alcohol

Alcohol is a product made of organic chemicals, manufactured through the fermentation of natural sugars. Throughout history, many cultures have had the knowledge to make alcohol from different plants and grains, and have often used alcohol for religious purposes.

But despite its availability and popularity, alcohol is a dangerous, addictive, and toxic drug. It causes cancer, liver disease, heart disease, birth defects, and many fatal accidents.

People are now becoming aware of alcohol's health risks, and cutting down on their drinking. However, it is estimated that there are 90 million social drinkers in the U.S. These are people who enjoy alcohol and drink whenever the occasion arises. In America there are at least 10 million alcoholicspeople who are physically addicted to alcohol.)

Alcohol Intoxication

About 10% of the alcohol we drink leaves the body fairly quickly; the other 90% remains in the bloodstream and is circulated to every organ in the body, including the brain and the liver. Alcohol is metabolized in the liver which can only process a small amount of alcohol at a time. If a person drinks one drink per hour, he or she may not feel drunk. Any more than that cannot be metabolized fast enough, so it will build up in ones blood stream.
- More than one drink per hour will usually cause the drinker to feel less pain, shyness, and sense of propriety, as inhibitions are lowered.
- With continued drinking, the drinker becomes loud and boisterous, and may become overly aggressive and easily angered.
- Another drink or two brings on a lack of coordination. At this stage, the drinker may fall easily and knock things over.

- If drinking continues, it may lead to unconsciousness.
- Under the influence of alcohol the brain first loses its ability to think and judge rationally, then its perception of physical sensations, then its ability to control and coordinate thoughts and movements, and finally its very consciousness. Excessive intoxication may even result in death.
- Alcohol intoxication is a major component in marital discord and violence, public fighting and violent crimes.

The Health Risks

Apart from the dangers of intoxication, alcohol affects every part of us in quite negative ways.
- Alcohol dilates the blood vessels and capillaries. Regular drinking causes fine red lines appear on the skin.
- It also dehydrates the skin, speeding up the aging process.
- Hair becomes dry and brittle, and hair loss will also get worse, because alcohol depletes the body of proteins and B-complex vitamins essential to healthy skin and hair.
- Alcohol is detrimental to teeth and also worsens acne conditions.
- Alcohol prevents the absorption of vitamins and minerals by the body. It can be considered an anti-nutrient, because it draws on the body's vitamin and mineral reserves in order to be metabolized by the liver.
- For dieters, alcohol is bad because it stimulates the appetite at the same time that it lowers control. One martini contains 150 calories.
- Alcohol depresses the body's immune system.
- It shortens the longevity of red blood cells, is detrimental to the health of the bone marrow, and can lead to or worsen anemia.
- Alcoholic drinks contain many ingredients that can cause allergies. These include sulfites, coloring agents, grains, yeast, spices and preservatives.
- Drinking alcohol increases the risk of cancer of the liver, mouth, esophagus, stomach, breast, lung, pancreas, colon and prostate. It could be that alcohol helps carry carcinogens through the body, or that it forms its own carcinogens in conjunction with other elements. Urethane or ethyl carbonate a by-product of the distillation process in certain types of alcohol. It is also a potent carcinogen.
- Alcohol can produce severe irritation of the gastro-intestinal system, causing vomiting, heartburn and ulcers.

- Alcohol, a diuretic, can aggravate constipation.
- Because alcohol impedes the ability of the body to eliminate uric acid, it can provoke attacks of *gout*, a painful inflammation of the joints.
- Alcohol can aggravate hypertension and increase the risk of heart attacks. The risk of a stroke is four times greater in heavy drinkers than non-drinkers.
- Alcohol is the single most frequent cause of liver disease. The liver's main function is to metabolize alcohol and other chemicals. But when the liver becomes unable to handle the level of toxins, it becomes poisoned and cannot perform its other vital functions. It takes only a few short months of drinking several drinks daily to create certain toxic conditions in the liver. First fat is accumulated and creates a condition known as *fatty liver*. Then there may be inflammation of the cells, which become irreversibly damaged and scarred.. The resultant *Cirrhosis* of the liver is fatal, and is now the ninth leading cause of death in the U.S.
- Alcohol inhibits the absorption of calcium, which is essential for strong bones. It may take as little as one or two drinks daily to put one at risk of osteoporosis.
- Even a small amount of alcohol can decrease a person's balance, perception, memory, thinking abilities, motor skills and ability to maintain the proper body temperature. Thousands of car accidents and related deaths each year are caused by driving under the influence of alcohol.

> Do not drink and drive. At social gatherings, designate a driver who will abstain from alcoholic beverages.

Fetal Alcohol Syndrome

Even in early Greece, it was known that drinking wine throughout pregnancy could result in birth defects. In 1973, fetal alcohol syndrome (FAS) was formally identified, as well as other alcohol-related birth defects (ARBD). FAS is the third main cause of retardation stemming from birth defects. Babies with FAS are generally born underweight, with smaller heads and brains than average. They are usually mentally deficient and sometimes have heart defects or other abnormalities.

> Every fetus is extremely vulnerable to alcohol, so pregnant women should completely abstain from alcohol.

Reducing Your Alcohol Intake

You may need professional help to learn to abstain from alcohol. Your doctor, community hospital or health center can refer you to any number of groups that can help you.
- Alcoholics have inherited tendencies for their addiction, and many people now view the condition as a disease.
- Today many programs are covered by medical insurance.
- As you begin an alcohol abuse program, you should also start a program of relaxation and exercise. Relaxation techniques will help you cope with the stresses of work and everyday living.
- Exercising regularly will help you feel better, which in turn will encourage you to continue on a healthy path.

If you do not have a serious alcohol problem, but still wish to reduce your drinking, you could try several things:
- Cut the amount of drinks you have weekly in half. Evaluate the changes in yourself after two or three months.
- If you like mixed drinks, use half a shot of liquor for each drink instead of a whole one.
- Dilute your drinks more by using a larger glass.
- Add more ice to each glass before filling.
- Sip your drink slowly.
- Stop drinking at least two hours before you go to bed.

Non-Alcohol and Low Alcohol Drinks
- Some beers and wines are now available with no more than 1/2% of alcohol.
- They are also lower in calories, and as they are becoming more popular, they are being improved in taste and variety.
- Sparkling cider, a delicious alternative to sparkling wines or champagne, is completely alcohol-free.
- These products are available from most wine merchants, some health food stores and some supermarkets.

Recreational Drugs and Substance Abuse

Any chemical that alters the functioning of the body or mind is a drug.

Legal over-the-counter and prescription drugs are manufactured, tested and dispensed according to strict regulations and laws. These drugs can be harmful if used without the proper care or for the wrong reasons. Almost every drug can have side effects, and some drugs can be addictive or toxic if taken in the wrong dosage.

Other drugs are known as recreational drugs. These are not taken to treat any illness or ailment, but simply to experience the effects of the drug. Alcoholic beverages and tobacco are recreational drugs that are legal and generally accepted by society, at least in moderate amounts. Other recreational drugs, like cocaine and heroin, are illegal in the U.S. and most other countries. Sometimes prescription drugs such as *barbiturates* and *amphetami*nes are used illegally, as recreational drugs.

People take recreational drugs because they make the users feel good or "high," relax them or give them energy, give them a sense of security or allow them to forget the difficulties in their lives. Recreational drug use is usually a form of escape, and can soon become a habit.

- If the habit is formed out of the mental benefits the drug provides, there is a *psychological dependency*. A person who cannot unwind from the day's work and relax without a few drinks is dependent on alcohol, if not an alcoholic. Someone who can't fall asleep without an over-the-counter sleep aid which is probably not strong enough to actually cause sleep at all, is psychologically dependent.
- If the body chemistry has been altered in such a way that the drug has become a necessary element that must be provided regularly, then the habit is physical and is termed an *addiction*. Amphetamines are a good example of addictive drugs: commonly known as "speed," the first few doses of amphetamines will make one stay awake through the night, but the effect diminishes rapidly. When the drug is withdrawn, the person becomes unable to sleep at all.

- While using addictive drugs, people will develop a tolerance, which requires an increased amount of the drug taken to get the same effect.
- All addictive drugs, including alcohol, cause withdrawal symptoms if they are suddenly withheld from the addict. These withdrawal symptoms can be more or less severe depending on the drug. They can include headaches, insomnia, dizziness, nausea, tremors, anxiety and seizures.

Marijuana

The *Cannabis* plant, also known as marijuana, has long been known as a medicinal herb. It was widely used in the past, (as far back as 2,000 years ago) to treat asthma, headaches, fever, glaucoma and many mild ailments. It was also an ingredient in many common household remedies early in this century. Marijuana is illegal almost everywhere in the U.S., but state and local laws vary considerably.

Marijuana is almost always smoked, hand-rolled into cigarettes called "joints," or in a pipe. It can also be made into a tea or added to some foods.

Hashish is the concentrated resin from the cannabis plant which is also smoked, usually in a pipe.

Most marijuana users claim that it relaxes them and makes them more aware as well. But marijuana carries certain health risks:
- Any kind of smoke that is taken into the lungs is damaging, and marijuana is no exception. Smoking it damage s the fine membranes in the lungs, and habitual or heavy use can cause sore throats, bronchitis and other related conditions.
- Even though marijuana is not considered an addictive drug, frequent users often develop a psychological dependence. These people may get so hooked on the relaxing effect of the drug that they have difficulty getting through the day without it.
- One very dangerous aspect of marijuana is that is often sprayed with the defoliant *paraquat*, particularly if it comes from Central or South America. It is impossible to tell if a plant has been sprayed, but this chemical can cause very serious lung injuries.

Cocaine

Cocaine has been used as a stimulant for thousands of years. Native South Americans commonly chew the leaves of the *coca* plant to keep their energy up as they work in their fields. European settlers discovered the coca plant, and extracted from it the whitish powder known as cocaine.

Cocaine was widely used as a tonic, and was part of the original formula of the soft drink Coca-Cola. However, the strong side effects of cocaine were noticed, so the drug was soon restricted to medical use.

- Cocaine has the ability to numb any area that it comes into contact with. Cocaine derivatives and cocaine-like substances are used as anesthetics, such as *Novocain*.
- Cocaine increases the heart rate and raises both blood pressure and body temperature.
- Cocaine has wide appeal as a recreational drug because it is very potent, causing strong feelings of energy, power and control.
- Most users of cocaine prefer to inhale the powder through the nose. It is sometimes mixed with water and injected, particularly among users who mix heroin and cocaine. This mixture can be lethal. It is a frequent cause of death by overdose.
- Another method of cocaine use is smoking or "free-basing." Cocaine is diluted with other chemical products and then heated and dried before it is smoked. This creates the product known as "crack" or "crack cocaine," which quickly leads to relentless addiction and short-lived highs between periods of intense craving for the drug.
- Cocaine in any form is very dangerous, particularly to people with heart ailments or high blood pressure.
- Cocaine can also be fatal if taken in with alcohol.
- Cocaine damages the tissues inside the nose, throat and lungs. Users have a high incidence of severe colds and respiratory infections.
- The pleasant effects of use can be followed by depression, anxiety and irritability, sometimes leading to violence.
- Heavy cocaine use can cause hallucinations and severe personality disorders.

Narcotics

Narcotics are a group of drugs derived from *opium* or similar synthetic drugs. The origin of the word "narcotic" is complex, but it is derived in part from a Greek word meaning "stupor" or "numbness."

Opium is the dried sap of the poppy flower, which is grown extensively in Asia and other parts of the world. Opium is used to make *morphine, codeine* and *heroin*.

Narcotics were used on battlefields and in hospitals for pain relief, in psychiatric treatments, and to cure alcoholism. At the onset of World War I all narcotics came under strong regulations.

- Opium can be smoked or taken orally, to induce a trance filled with vivid dreams.
- Morphine is many times stronger than opium, and is used as a pain reliever for terminally ill patients.
- The synthetic narcotic *Demerol* is also used in pain relief.
- Codeine is often used in cough medicine and pain relievers.

Heroin

Heroin was derived from morphine and used in the early twentieth century as a cure for morphine addiction, until it was realized that heroin is much more potent and addictive than morphine. Heroin is almost never used in the medical field. For recreational use, it is usually mixed with water and injected directly into the bloodstream. It can also be inhaled.

- Heroin decreases the heart rate and narrows the pupils of the eyes.
- It can initially cause dizziness, nausea, breathlessness and other uncomfortable feelings, but eventually the user becomes relaxed, sleepy and euphoric.
- The user will feel totally unaffected by his or her surrounding for several hours.
- After a few hours, restlessness increases as the craving for another dose begins. If the next dose of the drug is not provided in time, the addict's condition deteriorates rapidly. Withdrawal symptoms include back pain, stomach and leg cramps, nausea, sweating, chills and fever, diarrhea, overwhelming weakness and sleeplessness.
- If the user can avoid heroin completely for a few days, most of the worst symptoms will disappear.
- The craving for heroin may remain for months or even years.

- Babies born to heroin-addicted mothers are themselves addicted and must go through the painful withdrawal symptoms during their first days of life.

The physical, emotional and social repercussions of heroin use are many:
- Heroin use damages the nervous system, and may alter DNA.
- An addict's veins may collapse from repeated injections.
- Infections are spread through the sharing of needles among addicts. The spread of AIDS is still virtually unchecked among intravenous drug users. (See *AIDS*.)
- Heroin is always mixed with other chemicals. A common injection of the drug may contain as little as 3% pure heroin, or quite a bit more.
- A stronger dose of heroin than one generally uses may cause respiratory failure and death.
- Many addicts die of sudden reaction to one of the chemicals used as fillers.
- Heroin addiction is an all-encompassing activity that soon takes over every aspect of a user's life. Heroin is a very expensive drug, and addicts almost always resort to theft to support their habits.

Hallucinogens

Hallucinogens are compounds that cause hallucinations or extreme distortions of reality. Many hallucinogens are derived from plants which have been widely used throughout history in certain religious rituals. Some of these drugs are still used in rituals.

Hallucinogens were used by witches in medieval Europe to create the sensation of flying, while *peyote* and *mescaline* are used in some Native American tribes to promote mystical experiences and visions. When using hallucinogens in rituals of this sort, the user is monitored by a shaman or herb doctor, and guided through the experience. Antidotes are available if necessary.

However, the hallucinogens which are now being manufactured are much stronger than the natural plant derivatives, and they are being used without supervision by young people eager for new experiences or entertainment. Of these new drugs, *LSD* (lysergic acid diethyl amide) or "acid" is probably the best-known.

LSD

LSD was first used experimentally for mental disorders. At the same time, it was becoming popular among young people as a recreational drug, sometimes with tragic results. Users sometimes leaped to their death from roof-tops or windows, thinking they could fly, or hurt themselves in various other ways while "tripping." In 1970, LSD was made illegal. Recently its popularity has grown among young people due to its low cost and easy access.

- Chemically, LSD resembles the natural neurotransmitters in the brain, and a very minute amount can cause severe reactions, which vary from individual to individual. These reactions are probably due to the ability of LSD to send false messages across brain receptors.
- LSD is an odorless, colorless liquid that is taken orally, mixed in a drink or dropped onto a tiny piece of blotter paper which is then swallowed (*blotter acid*). It may produce an enjoyable experience of enhanced sensations and interesting visual effects, or it can cause terrifying, nightmarish delusions and hallucinations.
- Some people experience symptoms of serious mental illness while using LSD, and there have been cases of users remaining in these states even after the drug wears off.

PCP (Phencyclidine)

This drug was manufactured in 1956 as a possible sleep inducer for surgical procedures. However, it was shown to cause confusion, high levels of anxiety, hallucinations and possible seizures. It is now restricted to veterinary use as a tranquilizer for large animals. PCP became a popular recreational drug under the name of "angel dust." It comes in liquid form which can be sprayed on marijuana or tobacco and then smoked, or in a powder which can be inhaled or swallowed in a capsule. It also comes in crystals.

- Like LSD, PCP experiences are unpredictable. They can be pleasant or nightmarish.
- PCP can create wide disturbances of perception and sensation. It can cause disturbances in some motor functions as well, particularly speech.
- Sometimes PCP can provoke uncontrollable anger and violence.
- PCP use has resulted in seizures, comas, and death. It is also thought to trigger factors of schizophrenia in some users, sometimes with only one use.

- PCP is not addictive and does not usually lead to any psychological dependence. It is, however, extremely dangerous. It can cause psychosis and death.

Other Hallucinogens

Several hallucinogenic plants, such as *peyote* and *psilocybin mushrooms*, are used as recreational drugs. Another category of products can cause hallucinations and other effects when inhaled. These are the many different gases contained in various household products and other preparations.
- *Nitrous oxide*, or laughing gas, is used in dentistry as an anesthetic, and is sometimes sold illegally in vials.
- Other substances used as recreational inhalant drugs include chloroform, *amyl nitrate* (used as a deodorizer), lighter and cleaning fluids, gasoline, some glues, and some aerosols. Most of us breathe minute quantities of these products without any adverse effect. But excessive inhaling of any of these products or their fumes may lead to severe trauma. Most of these compounds cause a dizzy, intoxicated feeling, sometimes accompanied by a false sense of self-confidence. They may cause hallucinations, anxiety, amnesia, headaches, loss of balance and coordination. They may also cause widespread physical damage to the lungs, liver, kidneys and brain.

Pills

Pills which are used recreationally are usually one of two types: amphetamines, often called "uppers," and sedatives, tranquilizers, and other "downers." These are usually prescription medications.

"Downers"
- Downers calm or depress the nervous system.
- Tranquilizers such as *Thorazine*, *Valium* and *Librium* are frequently prescribed for mental disorders, anxiety and stress. Barbiturates, more commonly known as sedatives, are prescribed for sleeplessness.
- These drugs have many side effects and can be very dangerous if misused.
- Sedatives may cause depression, depressed breathing, forgetfulness, and confusion, which can lead to serious accidents and overdoses.
- *Quaaludes* were the most popular of the recreationally used downers, until they were outlawed in the U.S.

- While all downers cause strong psychological dependence, some cause physical addiction as well.

"Uppers"
- "Uppers" refers to a group of drugs called *amphetamines*.
- They are prescribed under such names as *Benzedrine* and *Dexedrine* to stimulate the nervous system, and to increase energy, alertness and muscle tone.
- They are usually prescribed for narcolepsy (See *Sleep Disorders*.), and can be used to treat hyper-activity in some children. Amphetamines have also been used to assist in weight loss and to treat depression.
- Amphetamines are very dangerous drugs with severe side effects.
- The energizing effects of the drug are followed by immediate depression, since tolerance to the drug builds quickly, more pills must be taken to achieve the same effect.
- After repeated use, certain symptoms may become permanent: tension and elevated blood pressure, heart conditions, constant agitation and irritability. Some users commit suicide or end up in mental institutions.
- Overdoses commonly cause coma and death.
- These drugs are definitely addictive and cause severe withdrawal symptoms.

Steroids

Thousands of people in the U.S take steroids. They are body-builders, athletes, and other people who are concerned with their physique and physical performance. Because steroids are illegal, it is hard to determine who is taking them.

People who take steroids also take a huge gamble with their health. The kidneys, heart, liver and stomach are adversely affected by steroids. Some users are now chronically ill with ulcers, cancer, and organ or bone damage. Some have even had limbs amputated.

There are also very grave psychological dangers to the use of steroids: the feelings of power and invulnerability they induce can be followed by a very deep depression. Many users have attempted suicide.

> **Steroids can destroy the body while making it look and feel good. They are extremely dangerous.**

Light, Color and Sound

Light

Some experts consider light to be second only to food as a factor in our well-being. In studies on the impact of light on health, it has been determined that proper lighting can increase creativity and performance and create a sense of security, whereas bad lighting can cause physical symptoms such as depression, headaches, nausea, irritability, immune deficiency, hyperactivity, hormonal imbalance and vision problems.

Natural sunlight contains the entire spectrum of the electromagnetic wavelength. This means it includes not only the light we perceive with our eyes, but also radio waves, microwaves, gamma rays, x-rays, infrared and ultraviolet rays. On the other hand, any artificial light is restricted to some limited portion of the spectrum.

Artificial lights may produce different psychological effects depending on the their wavelengths. This is because the light that hits the retina of the eye has a direct influence on the functions of two glands inside the brain: the *pineal gland* and the *pituitary gland*.

Fluorescent Lights

Florescent lights are considered to be potentially more harmful than other types of artificial light because of the electromagnetic radiation they emit. Their constant flicker, though not usually consciously perceived, may cause headaches and stress. They have been linked to an increase in certain skin cancers. They are usually too bright and harsh for a home environment.

Incandescent Light

Standard light bulbs give a warmer and more golden light, more like sunlight or the glow of a fire. Regular incandescent bulbs produce more heat and use more electricity than florescent lights, but they cast shadows and are easier to look at.

Quartz-type incandescent light bulbs are relatively new. They are smaller and more intense than standard household bulbs, making them a bit more economical.

It is important to note that all heat-producing lights can release irritating gases and stir up dust particles.

Halogen Lights

Like quartz incandescents, these are also very bright and more economical, but they give off intense heat. While their bright light is closer to daylight, they may be irritating to some people.

"Full-spectrum" Lights

There are now bulbs and fixtures that more closely approximate the glow and color patterns of natural light. They are very expensive, but may be worth the price in terms of health benefits, especially for people who stay indoors.

Sun Light

Natural light is healthiest and most stimulating to the body. It triggers production of vitamin D, and may prevent depression. Its qualities vary in different regions, seasons and times of day. These variations would be hard to duplicate artificially, and our daily cycles can be disrupted by exposure to artificial light of the wrong kind at the wrong time.

Skylights and large windows can bring a lot of natural light into the home. If they are made from some transparent plastics, however, they may let in ultraviolet rays which can cause sunburn and rapid disintegration of synthetic materials, which will then out-gas rapidly. This can lead to a sharp increase of toxic vapors within your home. Window glass blocks about 95% of UV rays.

We can arrange and adjust the use of windows in our home to maximize the changing quality of daylight. For instance:
- Northern light is cool and diffuse. It is indirectly reflected against the sky. A room with a northern exposure is good for reflective occupations such as reading or art work.
- Light from the south is the most direct and can bring a lot of heat into the home. In warm climates it may be necessary to shade windows on the south side to protect from uncomfortable heat and glare.
- Morning light is mostly blue-green and stimulating to mental activity. It boosts energy and is good lighting for a study, office, kitchen, or anywhere else that creative efforts are required.

- Windows to the west will bring in the golden-red glow of evening light, which stimulates the emotions. Western exposures are best suited for family rooms, living rooms, and dining rooms.

Color

Colors are created by the variations in the wavelengths of visible light. The three basic or primary colors are red, yellow and blue. All other colors are called secondary colors, and are created by mixing primary colors in different combinations.
- Blue, green and violet are known as cool colors, while orange, red and yellow are warm colors. When color enters the retina of the eye, the particular wavelength affects the brain and stimulates the production of certain hormones. In this way, colors can influence our moods and overall well-being.
- Reds are associated with the release of adrenaline. Reds will make us feel more energetic, creative and hungry.
- Blues activate hormones which cause relaxation and even sleepiness.
- Colors also affect other senses: the perception of time and temperature can vary depending on the color of a room.
- Dark colors absorb light, and light colors reflect light.

Using Colors

Colors can be used to enhance the purpose of living and work spaces. Different colors can enhance education in schools, relaxation in hospitals, efficiency from employees, and increased appetite in restaurants. Individual considerations must also be taken into account.
- Light colors are essential for people who suffer from winter depression.
- People who are stressed or ill are better off in green rooms.
- Bold primary colors can enhance self-esteem. They are also quite good in children's rooms. Babies are stimulated by the color red.
- Yellows can cause irritation and aggravate anxiety.
- Warm colors (red, orange) can be too stimulating for people who are already over-active.
- Paradoxically, some over-active children find bright primary colors relaxing, while passive children can be stimulated by cool colors.

- Cool colors (blue, green) can be depressing to those who are melancholy.
- It is usually best to use warmer tones in areas of social interaction like living rooms and kitchens.
- Use neutral and light tones in bed rooms or other private spaces, with the color accents coming from furnishings and decorations of the occupant.
- Areas designed for relaxation and quiet times can be done in cool colors.
- Strong, dramatic and bright colors may soon become tiresome and hard to live with. It is often best to start with light and neutral shades.

Sound

Sound waves are another type of vibration that fills the air around us and has an impact on our well-being. Sound is music, speech, or any other auditory stimulus emitted for the purpose of communication or entertainment. Noise is undesirable sound. Noise causes tension and stress, ulcers, high blood pressure, heart disease and mental illness.

Many sounds can be useful or beneficial. The steady hum of a busy office may stimulate and encourage creativity among workers. However, a poorly designed space with clattering machines, ringing telephones and so forth may be very irritating and interfere with work performance. Soft pleasing music can enhance creativity or relaxation.

Quiet Please!

Noise pollution is harmful to everyone. It impairs concentration, efficiency and relaxation. It prevents adequate rest and sleep. It causes anxiety, irritability, frustration and accidents. It can also cause hypertension, headaches, ulcers, insomnia, colitis and heart attacks. Children and elderly people are most affected by noise pollution. There are many ways to make the home or work place more quiet, and to limit street noise entering the home:
- Have noisy pipes, creaky floors and stairs fixed.
- Limit noisy home appliances. Turn them on before buying. Place small appliances on rubber mats.
- Isolate large appliances on a concrete floor or rubber pads.
- Encourage family members to use headphones to listen to music or watch T.V. Inform them of the danger of high volume.

- When using power tools, use adequate ear protection devices and follow all regulations set by employers and the OSHA (Occupational, Safety and Health Administration).
- Hedges, trees, or solid fences create effective noise barriers, especially if they are planted close to the street.
- Ventilation of the home should be done away from the street to avoid both noise pollution and air pollution.
- The use of soft furnishings and carpeting can help absorb interior noises.
- The positive uses of sound: A water fountain can create a wonderful diversion from city noises. Indoors, you can use one of hundreds of natural sound tapes, including seashore sounds, rain, and soft music. They can help diminish anxiety and irritability.

Hearing Loss

Frequent exposure to loud noises will eventually result in some hearing loss. A person may even lose his or her hearing completely, and also develop a recurrent ringing in the ears called *tinnitus*. This last stage is extremely serious and irreversible.

Even common household noises from small appliances, power tools, noisy pipes, loud music and television can cause progressive and irreversible hearing deterioration.

- Sounds are measured in *decibels* (dB) on a logarithmic scale. (If the smallest sound we can normally perceive is measured at 0 dB, then a 10-fold increase in sound level will be registered as 10 dB.)
- Occupational health regulations typically allow only two hours of exposure to noise registering 100 dB, unless one is protected with adequate ear protectors.
- Any noise over 100 dB will cause pain and immediate loss of hearing.

Range of Sounds in Decibels

Range	Decibels	Common Causes
Normal range	0	Smallest sound that can be heard.
	10	Light wind in trees or grass, rustling of leaves.
	20	Rural home environment.
	30	Whispering, quiet library.
	50	Suburban area at a quiet time.
	60	Normal conversation, air conditioner.
Somewhat noisy	70	Normal office routine, suburban home.
	80	Normal street noise, inside a city home, alarm clock.
Noisy: Will cause damage over time	90	Certain blenders, vacuum cleaners, coffee grinders, juicers, truck traffic.
	100	Some power tools, jackhammer at 10 ft., garbage truck.
Very noisy: certain hearing loss	110	Rock concert.
Pain-causing loudness: rapid hearing loss	120	Very loud music through earphones, auto horn, thunder.
	135	Aircraft taxing.
	140	Aircraft lift-off.

CHAPTER 3
MIND

Hippocrates wrote: "Men ought to know that only from the brain arise our pleasures, joys, laughter and tears. Through the brain we think, hear, see and determinate the ugly from the beautiful, the bad from the good and the pleasant from the unpleasant. The brain is the messenger of consciousness."

Your Brain and Your Mind

We now know the brain to be a very complicated organ which generates thought and consciousness, integrates and stores information, and coordinates actions in response to this information.

- The brain consists of groups of cells, which form the *gray matter* and areas of *white matter*, which are connective tissues. Millions of messages flash throughout the brain each second.
- The spinal cord and the *lower brain stem* control reflexes, posture and muscle tone, and activities such as walking, breathing and coughing. They also regulate body temperature.
- The *higher brain stem* receives all sensory data and is the center of sensory-motor reactions. Voluntary activities also originate in the higher brain stem, often traveling through the *cerebral cortex* before passing through the lower brain stem to the spinal cord and the designated muscles.
- The cerebral cortex is divided into two hemispheres that are mostly nonspecific to any particular functions at birth. If a child experiences damage to the cerebral cortex, such as lesions in the major speech area of the temporal lobe, the child will begin to learn to speak again, usually within a year. If such lesions occur after the child has reached the age of twelve, however, the damage will be permanent.
- Major sites of the cerebral cortex carry out the processes of thinking and reasoning.
- Fairly large areas of the cerebral cortex can be surgically removed without any damage to consciousness, but even a minute injury to the higher brain stem can cause total loss of consciousness.

So Where is Your Mind?

If the brain works similarly to a computer, the mind is like the user of the computer.

The brain registers sensations from outside stimuli, but the mind determines what will be noticed, or *perceived*, and recorded in the brain's memory banks. In an instant, the mind can retrieve an item from storage in the brain.

Experiments on the brains of conscious human subjects demonstrate that the mind holds a different energy than the simple mechanisms of the brain. When a small electrical charge applied to certain areas of the brain caused the movement of a subject's limb or hand, the subject invariably described the surgeon as the originator of the movement, saying "You made me do this," instead of "I did this."

No electrical impulse in any location of the brain can cause a person to accept a belief or make a decision. But specific areas can be stimulated to recall sensations, memories and feelings.

The Parts of the Mind

The mind is divided into four parts.
- The *super-conscious mind* is the most powerful of all. It is part of the universal consciousness and knows how to solve every problem.
- The *conscious mind* is your periscope into the world of form. It has the ability to make judgments about what it sees.
- The *sub-conscious mind* is the memory storehouse of everything you have ever experienced, both awake and asleep. It has no ability to judge, but believes everything it is told. For example, if a child is told he will grow to be unsuccessful at his job, the powerful sub-conscious mind believes it is true.
- The *unconscious mind* controls all the automatic functions of the body. These include tasks like walking and even controlling the rhythm of the heart.

Psychology

The word "psyche," from the Greek word for "soul," has come to mean "mind" or "intellect." From this we get "psychology," which is the scientific study of the mind. Psychology is a very broad science, which examines both human and animal behavior in an attempt to discover the rules governing how and why organisms behave the way they do.

Chapter 3 Mind

Psychology began as a subject of philosophy, with Plato and Aristotle being some of its earliest known contributors. It eventually grew into a separate scientific field, incorporating the work of physicians, then physicists, anthropologists and linguists, and now even computer scientists.

The branch of psychology with which we are most familiar is clinical psychology, which applies the general rules of behavior to help individuals to gain self-awareness, and change their behavior as needed. Sigmund Freud was one of the first to apply the theories of psychology in the treatment of mental disorders. His ideas and methods of treatment were known as psychoanalysis.

How Does Psychoanalysis Work?

Trained as a neurologist, Sigmund Freud began his psychoanalytic treatments on women suffering from hysteria. Freud shocked the public by announcing that hysteria, along with many other disorders, was caused by the repression of sexual urges from early childhood.

Freud began by using hypnosis to probe the subconscious of his patients. He soon replaced hypnosis with his technique of *free association*. The patient would lie comfortably on a sofa and simply say whatever came into his or her mind, regardless of logic or decency. The job of the psychoanalyst was to recognize the elements of the subconscious as they were revealed, and then to organize and interpret them, so the patient's repressed desires could be understood. Besides free association, Freud believed that dreams also revealed valuable information about the subconscious.

The Id, Ego and Superego

Freud taught that the personality of each individual is composed of the id, ego, and the superego, and behavior is determined by the interactions of these three subsystems.
- The id contains all the instinctive drives and desires of the person. It operates on the *pleasure principle,* demanding immediate gratification of all desires, with no awareness of morality or reality.
- The ego develops during childhood to protect the individual from the demands of the id. The ego's purpose is to find ways to satisfy the id's desires without

endangering the individual. The ego operates on the *reality principle*.
- The superego, which can be thought of as the conscience, develops as the child begins to understand the moral values of society. The superego works directly to control the id, and makes the ego inhibit desires of the id which the superego considers to be immoral or wrong. The conflicts created by the differing goals of the three subsystems will cause mental disorders if they are not resolved.

Sexual Development

Freud believed that personality is based on five stages of development, each of which is associated with the primary source of libidinal pleasure for that stage:
- In the *oral stage*, from birth to age two, the child derives pleasure through sucking.
- In the *anal stage*, the membranes of the anal area become the principle erogenous zone. This stage lasts from ages two to three.
- The *phallic stage* lasts from age three to age five or six. The child derives pleasure chiefly through self-manipulation of the genitals.
- From about age six to the onset of puberty, around age twelve, the child becomes interested in acquiring new skills and other activities, and loses interest in sexual pleasure. This stage is known as *latency*.
- The *genital stage* begins with adolescence, when the child's sexual interest is directed primarily toward members of the opposite sex.

Each stage causes conflicts within the child, which must be resolved. If the demands of a stage are not gratified, the child may become *fixated* at that level. For example, Freud felt that an adult who eats excessively has probably not resolved the oral stage. During the phallic stage, sexual fantasizing leads to the *Oedipus complex* in boys, and the *Electra complex* in girls. The child feels sexual desire for the parent of the opposite sex, and so develops rivalry and hostility toward the same-sex parent.

Many of Freud's peers and students felt that he placed too much emphasis on biology and sexuality. They believed that social interaction was the primary factor in human development, and that sexuality was just one of many aspects of human relations.

Who is Carl Jung?

Carl Jung was a student and close friend of Sigmund Freud until he publicly disagreed with Freud's theories of psycho sexual development. Jung used the term *psyche* to refer to the mind, which he divided into three levels:
- The *ego,* or *personal conscious,* interacts with reality and enables us to adapt and survive.
- The *personal unconscious,* similar to Freud's ideas, contains repressed or forgotten memories, impulses and desires, all easily accessible to the conscious.
- The *collective unconscious* contains the ancestral memories of the human species, including the experiences of our animal ancestors. The collective unconscious is the part of the mind most responsible for behavior and personality. It is unknown and very powerful.

In cultural comparisons and dream analyses, Jung believed he found evidence of symbols of universal meaning, or *archetypes,* in the collective unconscious. Archetypes predispose people to react in the same way as their ancestors would have. They are associated with the major events and stages of human life, such as birth, death, and puberty, and with reactions to danger. Jung posited four primary archetypes:
- The *persona* is the social self, which hides the true self.
- Jung claimed that all people have elements of the opposite gender in them. These elements are represented by the *anima* (the feminine characteristics in the male) or *animus* archetype (the masculine part of the female).
- The *shadow* archetype comes from the ancient animal heritage. It is sometimes known as the *darker self,* because it contains the immoral, aggressive drives, but it also contains the creativity, spontaneity and emotion that are needed for complete human development.
- The most important archetype is the *self,* which contains and unifies all elements of the unconscious.

Other Contributors to Psychology

While some therapists still practice strict Freudian psychoanalysis, many other therapeutic systems have emerged. Most practitioners incorporate ideas from different fields of psychology in their work. *Humanistic psychology* is now a major influence on therapy, and the ideas of *behaviorism* are also widely used. Abraham Maslow's theory of the *hierarchy of needs* has had an impact on psychological counseling as well.

What is Behaviorism?

In its original form, behaviorism denied the existence of the mind, human consciousness, or self-determination. It tried to show that all behaviors, animal and human alike, could be explained as either automatic or learned responses to environmental stimuli.

The foundation of behaviorism was laid by the Russian scientist Ivan Pavlov, who is best known for his experiments in *conditioned responses* in dogs. Psychologist B. F. Skinner built upon Pavlov's and others' work to create modern behaviorism.

The theories of behaviorism have proved to be quite successful in the treatment of phobias and several other disorders. Behavior therapy deals directly with the problem behavior, and does not look for any underlying causes or subconscious motivations.

Humanism

The humanistic therapists claim that such theories as psychoanalysis and behaviorism are too limited and mechanistic in their treatment of mental disorders. They believe that no real progress can be made unless the whole person is considered, rather than only his or her symptoms. The goal of humanistic therapy is not to simply return a person to normal functioning, but to help all people to realize their full potential for happiness and self-actualization.

The best-known humanistic therapist is Carl Rogers, who developed *client-centered therapy*, in which the therapist and client work as partners in the treatment process, and the client learns the skills for solving his or her own problems.

The Hierarchy of Needs

Psychologist Abraham Maslow theorized that all humans have certain needs which they are driven to fulfill. He explained that the lower-level needs must be reasonably satisfied before energy can be directed towards fulfilling the higher needs. For example, a hungry person will search for food and let the desire for self-actualization wait. As one level of need is filled another takes its place. People have needs at all five levels of the hierarchy.

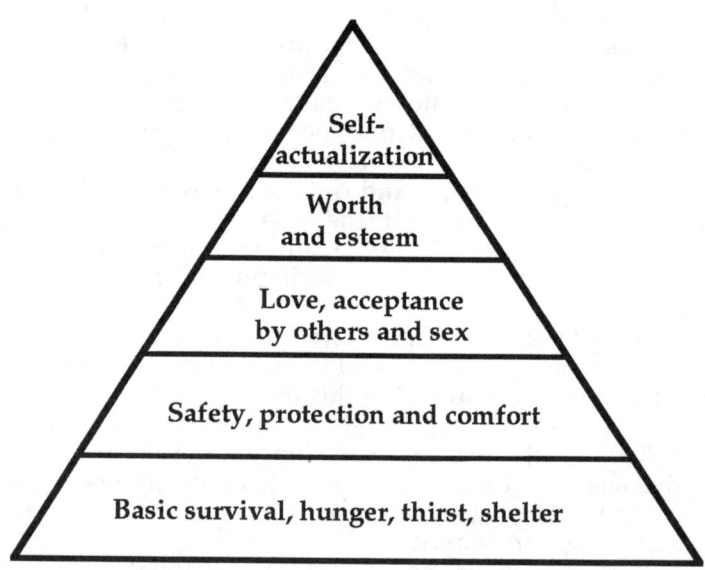

The highest level, self-actualization, is conscious awareness of your relationship with the cosmic creator. The vast majority of people remain in the lower four levels and never reach the highest level of self-actualization. Instead, most people remain concerned with security, money, power, sex and status.

Understanding Yourself with the Enneagram

The Enneagram is a system used by the ancient Sufi Masters for understanding and guiding their people. These Masters discovered personality patterns in their students and identified nine distinct personality types. Each type has its own characteristic ways of looking at life and dealing with the world. Each of us is unique, unlike any other individual that ever existed. Still, we all share certain common traits and behavior patterns with the rest of humanity. These traits were put in a mathematical form called the Enneagram.

The Masters also devised a specialized system of growth instruction based on the individual needs of each personality type. Unlike psychological systems that are based on abnormal behavior, this system looks at individuals as normal. It then provides insights to guide people on their path towards freedom and happiness.

According to the Enneagram theory, each of us belongs to one of nine distinct personality types. By way of heredity, family life and our cultural environment we developed a personality and our own way of dealing with the world. Our real self then became masked by the personality we chose. Now, as adults, our actions are still influenced by these childhood habits of relating to the world.

People of each personality type share a characteristic hidden fear, and they also tend to behave in a similar way to over-resist or avoid arousing this fear.

1. The *Inspector* over-resists boiling-over anger and instead tends to want everything perfect to ensure that this anger will not be aroused. This type of person grows by becoming less critical and serious, and more accepting and playful.
2. The *Helper* over-resists having personal needs and instead takes care of the needs of others. Helpers grow when they recognize their hidden needs and feelings and are dependent less on others for their self-esteem, and more on themselves.
3. The *Achiever* over-resists failure and disgrace and instead gets comfort by identifying with success. Achievers grow when they are more truthful and authentic, and less influenced by others and concerned about status and praise.
4. The *Unique Individualist* over-resists having an average or commonplace life, and instead embellishes his or her life so as to seem unique to others. These people grow when they feel less trapped in their emotional life and less pressured to be special, and begin to accomplish more tasks and projects.
5. The *Sage* over-resists living without meaning and structure, and instead fills life with facts and learning and categorizing. Sages grow when he or she becomes less a loner and observer of life, and more of an assertive participant.

Chapter 3 Mind

6. *Loyalists* over-resist separation or rejection from their families, friends, and co-workers, and instead are loyal and careful to avoid disapproval. They grow when they are less fearful, anxious and defensive, and more trusting and decisive.
7. The *Optimist* over-resists pain and suffering and instead plans ahead carefully and focuses on pleasant things. They grow when they do less planning and daydreaming and become less desperate to be happy at any cost, and become more willing to stop running away from reality and realize that a balanced life contains both pain and pleasure.
8. *Champions* over-resist weakness in themselves, and instead become powerful and stand up for themselves and others. They grow when they are less aggressive, controlling and tough, and become more soft, helpful and self-restrained.
9. The *Peacemaker* over-resists conflict and strife and instead seek harmony and peace at any price. They grow when they are less lazy and procrastinating and less withdrawn, and become more of self-starters and take an increased interest in life.

Psychological Counseling

Our psychological development is dependent on how we balance the conscious part of ourselves with our unconscious part. Often in the challenges of life we need to find a new balance in ourselves. Old thoughts and behavior may be inappropriate for new situations. Psychological counseling helps to unstick blockages that are often beyond our normal awareness. It assists us in going beyond our old limitations to transform our prior inadequate behavior and emotions.

Mental Health Professionals

- Psychologists have a Ph.D. in psychology. However, the term is also used more loosely to refer to many types of mental health professionals.
- Psychiatrists are medical doctors who specialize in psychology, and work with physiological causes and treatments of mental disorders. Only psychiatrists can prescribe drugs.

- Social workers are those with a master's degree in social work (MSW). In many states, they must obtain board certification to practice (BCSW).
- Marriage or family counselors generally have a master's degree in counseling, or some type of training in addition to a bachelor's degree. They should be certified by the American Association of Family Therapists.
- Psychoanalysts are psychiatrists (medical doctors) who specialize in some type of Freudian analysis. There is now a move to expand the classification of psychoanalyst to include Ph.D. psychologists who also study Freudian analysis.
- Anyone can call themselves a psychotherapist or counselor, since these are not legal terms. So check for some form of certification to practice. Certification requirements for some of these professions vary from state to state. Ministers and other religious counselors are exempt from the requirement of specific education.

How to Find a Psychotherapist

Ask someone you trust who has had a positive experience with psychotherapy. You can also ask your physician or minister. Finally you could phone the National Mental Health Association at 800-969-6642 or the American Association for Marriage and Family Therapy at 800-374-2638.

Different Types of Therapy

Psychoanalysis usually takes several years and can be very costly. It is not always necessary or practical to undergo psychoanalysis, and indeed, many mental health professionals question its value as a treatment for psychological disorders.

Many other types and methods of therapy are available, and most clinical practitioners do not follow any specific theory, but incorporate ideas from different fields as needed. There are some very effective forms of therapy that do not examine the client's past or delve into the subconscious. Two of these are *transactional analysis* and *reality therapy*.

Transactional Analysis

This form of therapy, developed by Eric Berne, uses common, every-day language and easily understood ideas.

It is based on the theory that each of us has three different aspects to our ego, which are like three different persons within us:
- The child-like person within us wants all of its desires fulfilled, and is not able to take the realities of life into consideration.
- The parent aspect rules between right and wrong.
- The adult self within us is without feelings, but makes decisions by evaluating all the facts involved. It can be equated to a computer.

Transactional analysis assumes that all adults have all three aspects of the self working at once within them, and can be trained to recognize which aspect is dominant at any specific moment. Clients examine how the parent and the child selves influence their decisions. They are then taught to allow the adult self to weigh the facts and make appropriate decisions.

Reality Therapy

This method of treatment focuses on the client's responsibility for his or her behavior patterns.
- The client is taught to concentrate on his or her own behavior, and to determine on specific changes that must be made, and plans to enforce these changes.
- The patient must commit to making the changes.
- Success brings a strong sense of identity.

Support Groups and Self-Help Networks

A lack of support, particularly during difficult times, can add to the stress that we feel. We need to feel that someone cares about us and is willing to listen to our problems, doubts and fears.

Sometimes we encounter specific problems or situations that our friends and family may not be able to help us with. At this time, a support group or self-help group may be very beneficial. For other problems and disorders, group therapy may be in order.

Self-Help Groups
- A self-help group is designed to provide assistance and support between members, as well as encourage individual personal development.

- The self-help group allows members to share their problems and difficulties with others who are in similar situations.
- Members share their fears, failures and victories. As trust builds within the group, it provides a safe place to release emotions and get support during difficult periods.
- The group also nurtures and encourages one to formulate decisions or establish a direction for the future.
- Support groups also provide a network of practical information and experience from others who have dealt with different aspects of the problem.

There are self-help groups for a great variety of situations: addiction, alcoholism, single parenting, adoption issues, parents of sick children, persons caring for someone with cancer or any other fatal disease, relatives of the mentally ill, recovery from divorce or the death of a loved one, and almost anything else that anyone might ever experience in the course of a lifetime.

Group Therapy

For mentally ill individuals or people who suffer from depression or any other disorder, group therapy is sometimes recommended.

This is also done in a group setting, but it is led by one or several trained therapists, who direct the focus of the group and monitor the interactions between members. Such groups also encourage the building of trust, open communications, empathy and caring among members. They are often of great benefit to the individual.

Mental Illness

In a one-year period, the population of the U.S. will include over 32 million sufferers of active mental disorders, of which 4 million are schizophrenics. Each year, over 10% of school-age children are diagnosed with some type of behavior problem, and about 5% of the elderly develop mental disturbances of physiological origin.

Chapter 3 Mind

It is estimated that one in seven people living in the United States will require professional treatment for a mental disturbance at some time in their lives.

The term "mental illness" covers a very wide range of behaviors. Unlike physical illnesses, which can be recognized as deviations from the normal structure or functioning of the human body, we have no model of normal psychological functioning against which to compare individual behavior.

Another problem in defining abnormal behavior is that norms vary widely between cultures. A behavior which is taken for granted in one society, may be shockingly inappropriate in another.

Most psychologists now agree that mental illnesses should be defined as patterns of thought or behavior that interfere with the well-being, the functioning, or the growth of the individual or of society. These thoughts and behaviors usually cause distress to the individual, and have a negative affect on society, either directly or indirectly. In this way, a behavior such as shop-lifting, which may be accepted by members of a street gang, is considered *maladaptive* because of the harm which it causes to society.

The mental disorders which most often affect people are usually not severe. Many of us live with slightly excessive fears or anxieties, or mildly peculiar habits, which were once termed *neuroses*. While these disorders may cause us to feel quite miserable at times, they do not interrupt work, school, the running of a household, social interaction, and other daily activities. However, the more serious disturbances, such as schizophrenia and multiple personality disorder, represent a complete disassociation from reality. Many of these severe disorders were, until recently, grouped under the term *psychoses*.

What are the Causes of Mental Illness?

There is much debate within the mental health professions regarding the interaction of physiological and social factors in behavior. It is generally accepted that some disorders are almost entirely of physical origin, while others appear to be learned behavior patterns.

Physical Causes
- Some disorders appear to be genetically transmitted, such as Down's syndrome. Other genetic anomalies create predispositions for certain disorders.
- Senile dementia, Alzheimer's disease and other mental disorders associated with aging are often a result of deterioration of the brain tissue.
- Birth defects or difficulties can cause or predispose one to psychological problems. Low birth weight, for example, is associated with hyperactivity, mental retardation and emotional disturbances.
- The ingestion of certain drugs can cause a wide variety of severe psychological symptoms.
- A shortage or excess of certain *neurotransmitters*, the chemical messengers of the brain, has been linked to certain mental illnesses, like depression and other mood disorders.

Environmental Factors
- Maladaptive behavior patterns can be learned in early childhood, from parents or other caregivers.
- Antisocial behaviors, like crime, are often a product of socio-economically deprived environments.
- Disorders such as post-traumatic stress disorder are frequently seen in victims of war, violent crime or natural disasters.
- Physical or sexual abuse in childhood generally contributes to the development of many maladaptive behaviors.
- Alcohol and substance abuse often begin due to peer pressure, although there is now believed to be a physical predisposition to alcoholism, and possibly to other addictions as well.

Stress and Adjustment Disorders

We all face frustration, conflicts and demands on our time and energy. Daily life also confronts us with changes and new ideas. Occasionally, a person may become unduly upset by these common *stressors*, resulting in a stress or adjustment disorder. Generally, the disorder disappears when the stressful situation is alleviated, or when the person learns to cope with it. (See *Stress* and *Stress Management*.)

Post-traumatic Stress
In the event of uncommon and excessive stress, such as surviving a natural disaster, violence, or other life-threatening event, post-traumatic stress disorder (PTSD) may develop. PTSD is frequently seen in combat veterans.
- The person will re-experience the event in dreams and recurring thoughts.
- In an effort to block memories of the event, the person will avoid activities, places, or people associated with it.
- Another common symptom is increased arousal, including sleeplessness, rapid heart beat, and difficulty concentrating.

Anxiety-based Disorders
Anxiety is similar to fear, but without a specific or rational source. Anxiety-based disorders are of three types: *anxiety, somatoform* and *dissociative disorders*. These disorders are believed to be learned behaviors, and are usually not severe. In some cases, however, anxiety-based disorders can be among the most severe of all mental illnesses (as in the multiple personality disorder.)

Anxiety Disorders
There are several types of anxiety disorders, and people often suffer from two or more of them simultaneously:
- *Panic disorder*: Sudden, severe symptoms such as chest pain, labored breathing, choking, dizziness, sweating, and trembling accompany feelings of terror and impending doom, and fears of losing control, going crazy, or dying. The panic attacks occur at least once a week, with no apparent cause.
- *Agoraphobia*: The irrational fear being alone and away from the safety of home, agoraphobia is often accompanied by panic attacks.
- *Simple phobias*: Irrational fears of certain objects or events, such as fears of bugs, heights or drowning.
- *Social phobias*: These are a collection of fears about being in public and being observed. The person is afraid that he or she will do something embarrassing or humiliating.
- *Obsessive-compulsive disorders*: A recurring thought causes anxiety, and the person feels compelled to perform ritualistic behaviors to alleviate the anxiety. For

example, a man who is obsessed with the idea of killing his children may repeatedly count them to make sure they're all still there.
- *Generalized anxiety disorder*: Also known as *free-floating anxiety*, this is a persistent and unrealistic worry about some all-encompassing life situation, such as a fear of financial ruin or a fatal accident.

Dissociative Disorders

In this disorder, a person avoids anxiety by dissociating from his or her personality. It comes in three types:
- *Depersonalization*: This is most common in teenagers and young adults. There is generally a loss of one's sense of self, and the feeling of being someone else. The person may also feel that his or her body has changed drastically, and there are frequent out of body experiences.
- *Amnesia*: The person may forget a traumatic event or period of time, or even his or her entire life, along with the causes of anxiety.
- *Multiple personality disorder*: When the stress, anxiety and guilt caused by conflicting impulses and beliefs become unbearable, an individual may separate the conflicting elements into two or more distinct personalities. The personalities usually have no awareness of each other. Despite its popularity as a movie topic, multiple personality disorder is among the rarest of disorders, with only a little over a hundred cases ever recorded.

Understand Burn-out

The symptoms of burn-out include overwhelming lassitude, anger towards oneself and others (subordinates, associates, clients, patients, relatives) and depression which can be helplessness and hopelessness. This is usually experienced after many years of success. One day a person "wakes up" and for the first time asks very important questions:
- What exactly am I achieving?
- Where do I go from here and exactly where is this road leading?
- Is it really worth all the stress and time away from family and friends?

- Is this really what I set out to do? Is this really me? Who am I, anyhow?

This awakening of sorts often paralyzes us in our tracks.
- We suddenly lose interest in the rewards of our success and career.
- House, cars, boat and club memberships suddenly all seem to have been obtained at too great a sacrifice and have become meaningless.

Because a successful career takes years of study and training, followed by more years of apprenticeship and practice, many other life paths remain unexplored.
Now all the accomplishments and hard-earned rewards seem meaningless. We may come to hate our job, position, responsibilities. We feel burned out.

Recovering from Burn-out

To treat burn-out first of all requires time. Time away from one's job and its responsibilities is of the essence, and must take precedence over everything else. The time off must then be used constructively:
- First we obtain the support of our spouse, children, other relatives and close friends, or preferably all of the above. This is done by expressing our feelings truthfully and realistically without guilt, shame or accusations. (See *Communication*.)
- With their help, realistically analyze exactly what is wrong with the present situation. What has made our life seem suddenly intolerable and what exactly triggered the burn-out?
- Do nothing. Take time out to just live one day at a time, in the present, and let things fall into place. If the understanding and cooperation of our family has been obtained, this should be possible. It's not that hard to do nothing, and often such a moratorium on activity will put all circumstances into perspective.
- Consider the options. Begin to consider a return to structured activity. Once things have fallen into place and we've allowed ourselves some healing and nurturing time, we'll know whether we want to go back to the pre-existing situation or charge ahead into a new future.

Personality Disorders

This category contains some of the most disturbing of mental illnesses. They are also some of the most difficult to treat, largely because the individual blames others for his or her problems.

Those with personality disorders have distorted ways of perceiving and relating to the outside world, due to immature personality development.

In their mildest forms, personality disorders cause troublesome and eccentric behaviors. The individual's history usually includes disruptive personal relationships and problems caused by the person for others. There is frequently a history of trouble with authority figures, including the police.

Antisocial Personality

A person with this disorder is commonly known as a *sociopath* or *psychopath*. There are several characteristics common to the antisocial personality:
- Lack of anxiety and guilt are very common. The conscience is underdeveloped.
- The person is very easily frustrated, and acts impulsively and irresponsibly.
- The person develops great skill at impressing and exploiting others and blames others for his or her own unacceptable behavior.
- There is little or no ability to maintain good personal relationships.
- The person is unable to learn from experience and resents any type of authority.

Traditional psychotherapies have been unsuccessful in treating antisocial and other personality disorders. Various biological treatments, including drugs and electroconvulsive therapy, have also proven all but useless. The only method that offers any hope of success is behavior therapy – giving the patient meaningful rewards for appropriate behaviors, and punishments for antisocial behaviors – in a controlled environment such as a hospital or prison.

Mood Disorders and Suicide

Like stress and anxiety, everyone also experiences changes in mood. But some people experience moods which are so extreme that they interfere with their functioning, and may even endanger their lives. These people suffer from mood, or *affect*, disorders.

Many factors contribute to the occurrence of mood disorders. There appears to be a hereditary predisposition, and some evidence of disturbances in the balance of certain neurotransmitters in the brains of people with more severe mood disorders. Additionally, several hormones are thought to play a role. There is also strong evidence of psycho-social factors in mood disorders, especially situations which lower the individual's self-esteem, increasing one's inability to achieve an important goal, the posing of an especially difficult dilemma, one overwhelming stressor, or a continuous series of stressors. It is now believed that a complex interaction of biological and environmental factors is involved in almost every instance of mood disorder.

There are two types of mood disorders: depression and bipolar disorder.

Major Depression

Someone suffering from major depression will appear to be very sad, yet will rarely be able to name the specific cause of the sadness. This feeling may be so strong that the person will weep for no apparent reason. Other symptoms include:
- Fatigue.
- Insomnia or hypersomnia.
- Decreased appetite and weight loss. (Occasionally, the opposite will occur.)
- Loss of interest in activities the person once enjoyed.
- Decrease in mental and physical activities. (Or, rarely, agitation and increased activity.)
- Extreme feelings of worthlessness and guilt.
- Preoccupation with death and suicide.
- In rare cases, there may be psychotic symptoms, such as hallucinations, delusions or depressive stupor. The delusions and hallucinations are usually *mood-congruent*; they involve ideas of death, illness, inadequacy, guilt, and such.

Many well-known historical figures have suffered from depression, including Moses, Dostoevski, Abraham Lincoln and Sigmund Freud. Estimates for the United States indicate that 8% to 10% of the population – 25 million people – will have at least one episode of severe depression at some time in their lives.

Major depression is often successfully treated with a combination of antidepressant drugs and group or individual psychotherapy.

Bipolar Disorder

This disorder is widely known as *manic-depression*. Bouts of depression alternate with euphoric, expansive moods. The manic phase of bipolar disorder has the following symptoms:
- Frustration, which may result in outbursts of irritability or violence.
- High levels of activity and extreme restlessness.
- Increased mental activity.
- Excessive verbal output (speaking or writing).
- Sleeplessness. The person will sleep rarely, briefly, or not at all.
- Loss of inhibitions.
- Elevated self-esteem, which may produce mood-congruent delusions, such as feelings of grandeur or great power.

The drug *lithium* has proven very effective in treating bipolar disorder. Many manic-depressives are maintained on lithium therapy for very long periods of time, often in conjunction with some type of psychotherapy.

Suicide

Official reports show that every twenty minutes, on the average, someone in the United States commits suicide. This amounts to about 28,000 suicides a year. The actual yearly rate of suicides is believed to be at least twice that number. Most attempts are made by people between the ages of twenty-four to forty-four. While women make more suicide attempts than men, three times as many men as women actually commit suicide.

Suicide is the third most common cause of death for people aged fifteen to twenty-four.

Suicide attempts often occur under much the same conditions as those which trigger depression: chronic or excessive stress, interpersonal crises or conflicts, failure, hopelessness, or loss of sense of self and meaning.

For reasons not yet understood, the vast majority of successful suicide attempts are committed by individuals who are recovering from an episode of depression. For the year in which an episode of depression occurs, the chance of suicide is about 1%, but for a person with recurrent episodes, the chance of suicide increases to 15% over the person's lifetime.

Researchers have divided people who attempt suicide into three categories, based on the degree of intent behind the action:
- The largest group comprises about two thirds of the total suicidal population. It contains those persons who don't actually wish to die, but are trying to communicate their distress or despair to others. They usually use methods that carry little chance of success, such as small drug over-doses, and arrange to be saved by someone. Unfortunately, things don't always go as planned, so deaths do occur in this group.
- About 3% to 5% of the suicidal population is made of people who appear to have a genuine wish to die. The chance of prevention is small, at best, as these people give little or no warning, and most often choose effective and violent methods with no chance of intervention.
- The last group may account for the largest number of actual suicides. This 30% of the suicidal population is the ambivalent group. People in this group often lead stressful, troubled lives, and make repeated suicide attempts with varying chances of success, through moderate drug over-doses, reckless driving and other dangerous behaviors. Unsuccessful attempts are frequently followed by a brief but significant reduction in distress, but the mental state eventually erodes and another attempt is made. The outcome is left to chance, with the feeling that being dead will bring an end to troubles, but being rescued will show that one's death is not yet meant to be.

The Los Angeles Suicide Prevention Center uses the following ten factors to determine the likelihood that an individual will make a serious suicide attempt:

Suicide Potentiality

1	Gender and age: Suicide is more likely if individual is male, also if over age 50, or between the ages of 15 and 24.
2	Symptoms: Sleep disturbances, depression, or alcoholism increase the likelihood.
3	Stress: Increases chance of suicide, especially if stress is caused by divorce or death of spouse, serious illness, increased responsibilities or loss of employment.
4	Acute vs. chronic aspects: Sudden onset of suicidal behavior symptoms increases potential for immediate suicide attempt. Recurring or chronic symptoms, or worsening of chronic mental disorders, indicates an increase in the long-term likelihood of suicide.
5	Suicidal plan: Greater detail of plan, and greater lethality of proposed method of death, correlate with higher potentiality.
6	Resources: Lack of family or friends, or lack of their support, increase potentiality.
7	Prior suicidal behavior: One or more prior attempts, or history of suicide threats and depression increase likelihood of another attempt.
8	Medical status: Potentiality increases with chronic, debilitating illness or with repeated unsatisfactory experiences with physicians.
9	Communication: If communication with family has been broken off and they resist efforts by individual or others to reestablish it, potentiality is greater.
10	Reaction of significant other: Rejection, defensiveness, punishing attitude, or denial of the individual's need for help by his or her spouse or other significant partner increases likelihood of a suicide attempt.

Delusional (Paranoid) Disorder

The ancient Greeks and Romans used the term *paranoia* in reference to almost any mental disorder. Its application is now limited to disorders which involve certain types of delusional thoughts, but without the complete personality disorganization of schizophrenia.

A person suffering from a delusional disorder believes that he of she is being unjustly persecuted, or is better or more special than everyone else. Often both of these themes occur together, and the person may believe that the persecution is due to his or her greatness. For example, a man may believe that his co-workers are plotting to get him fired because they are jealous of his intellectual superiority, or he may be convinced that only he can save the world, but aliens are trying to stop him.

In areas unrelated to the paranoid fantasy, the person functions normally, and is often intelligent and clear-thinking. Even the delusions are well organized and logical. Because of this, it can sometimes be hard for others to see that the person's thinking is delusional.

The parents of the sufferer of a delusional disorder are often found to be dominating, authoritarian, and critical. As a child, the individual may grow to be aloof, suspicious, secretive, and resentful of punishment. Because of these traits, the person is unable to understand the motives and feelings of others. This begins a cycle of social failures, which deepen the isolation and sense of mistrust. By adulthood, the individual becomes rigid, arrogant, domineering, and self-important, and unable to accept responsibility for his or her own problems.

Paranoid disorders are thought to be due to environmental factors. If the person voluntarily enters psychotherapy, at an early stage, there is some hope of treatment. Once the hostility and suspicions become delusions, however, the individual may be beyond help. He or she will not seek treatment, and will only perceive forced treatment as part of a plot. These people may learn to renounce their delusions and claim to be cured in order to avoid extensive hospitalization.

Schizophrenia

The name of this disorder arises from the Greek words *schizo*, or "split," and *phrene*, meaning "mind." This condition is sometimes confused with multiple personality disorder, but schizophrenia refers to the separation of the mind from coherent functioning, which is at the core of this disorder.

The thoughts and actions of the schizophrenic can include the maladaptive patterns of all the other mental disorders, in addition to the disturbances of communication, bizarre delusions and hallucinations, distorted perceptions and emotions, and odd motor behaviors commonly associated with this disorder. There is often no connection to be found between the person's thoughts, moods and actions.

But schizophrenia is more than a large group of odd thoughts and behaviors: it completely consumes the person, so that one becomes inseparable from the disorder. While we can not make any sense of the schizophrenic's emotional responses and behaviors, he or she is not even aware of doing anything unusual.

Causes

Like the effects of schizophrenia, the causes appear to include those of almost every other mental illness known to psychologists. Both physiological and environmental factors are involved:
- Physiological factors include heredity, biochemical and neurological processes and also malfunctioning neurotransmitters.
- Environmental factors include early mental trauma, maladaptive interpersonal and family patterns, faulty learning, difficulties in social or gender roles and excessive stress. Evidence indicates that cultural factors affect the rate of occurrence, type, and symptoms of schizophrenia in different societies.

Types

There are five categories of schizophrenic disorder, in which a certain characteristic dominates, although all other behaviors are possible as well:
- *Undifferentiated schizophrenia*: The symptoms are not those of the other types, or the person has an equal

mixture of symptoms from two or more other types, or alternates rapidly from one type to another.
- *Catatonic schizophrenia*: The person alternates between extreme excitement, during which he or she may be dangerous, and complete withdrawal. The withdrawal phase often includes complete cessation of movement, and the person may remain frozen in the same position for hours or even days.
- *Paranoid schizophrenia*: Along with the usual confusion and fragmentation of thought processes, the individual has illogical delusions and hallucinations regarding persecution, grandiosity, or other themes. The paranoid schizophrenic often is slightly more coherent and socially functional than the other types.
- *Disorganized schizophrenia*: This usually occurs in younger schizophrenics, and is considered to be the worst type, in terms of functioning and treatment. The person is incoherent, silly, laughs or cries at inappropriate times, develops strange mannerisms, and acts in outlandish and obscene ways.

Treatment

It was not until the 1950s that a treatment for schizophrenia was discovered. Until then, patients were simply locked in institutions which resembled prisons as much as hospitals. Less than a third of these individuals were ever released.

The *phenothiazine* drugs were introduced in the mid-1950s. They were very effective in alleviating the thought disorder, withdrawal, and hallucinations central to schizophrenia. The use of phenothiazine and other developments allow most patients to be treated at outpatient clinics. Those rare cases who are hospitalized are usually released within weeks.

Although most schizophrenics are no longer hospitalized for life, only about one third of them ever actually recover. Over half of the individuals who suffer an initial schizophrenic episode continue to have a variety of mental disorders and additional episodes of schizophrenia throughout their lives. However, only 10% still suffer the continued deterioration and permanent disability which was once the norm for schizophrenics.

Common Emotional Issues

We are all plagued, from time to time, by doubts and fears. Everyone must make hard choices and struggle with grief and loss. Just because we do not have some mental disorder which requires professional treatment, does not mean that we are always as happy and well adjusted and sensitive to our own needs and the needs of others as we could be.

Living is a process, and we must stay actively involved in that process, to make sure that we are living the best life we can. We will look at some common problems which confront us, and sometimes hinder us in our emotional development. These problems include fear, envy, loneliness, guilt, and grief. We will also consider the much-talked-about idea of *co-dependency*.

Common Fears

Fear is an automatic response to danger, for humans and animals alike. Fear of things like sharp objects, heights, and tornadoes are all reasonable and necessary for survival; the fear alerts us to possible dangers, such as falling off a cliff, and we take extra precautions accordingly, such as not jumping up and down on the edges of cliffs. Without fear, humans and animals would probably not live very long.

Where do fears come from? There is evidence that some basic, universal fears may be instinctive, such as the fear of sudden, loud noises, or large predatory animals, or a child's fear of being abandoned. However, most fears appear to be learned. A child must be kept from running into the street or playing with matches, until he or she learns of the dangers associated with those activities. But the child does not have to burn the house down, in order to learn.

In the same way that a child learns to fear fire, we can all be taught to fear certain things, and even ideas. We learn from the messages we receive from our families, teachers and peers, and from the disappointments, frustrations and rejections we have suffered from them. But are all of these fears really essential to our survival, or do some of them limit us unnecessarily?

We must learn to differentiate between the real dangers to our well-being, and the unfounded fears we have learned from others.

Fears can sometimes be disruptive and irrational, as in the case of phobias. (See *Anxiety Disorders*.) Most of us, however, suffer from unfounded fears which are not strong enough to interrupt our daily activities, but can still prevent our reaching full potential and enjoyment of life.
- We often hold fears based on false or biased information. We may miss out on knowing many wonderful people because of fears associated with their race, religion, age, or political affiliation.
- Communications between fearful people can become aggressive and defensive. This leads to more misunderstandings, and further serves to reconfirm and strengthen fears. The result of this can be violence between individuals or groups, and even wars between nations.

It's good to be realistic, and to be aware that we can be hurt and disappointed. But if we spend too much time dwelling on the worst possible outcomes of everything we do, we may become unable to take chances:
- If we fear rejection, we may not be able to experience the joys of making new friends and pursuing romantic relationships.
- Fear of failure will keep us from beginning new projects or careers.
- Fear of ridicule or negative feedback from others can prevent us from expressing our opinions and ideas. This can make us miss out on opportunities for advancement at work and in other competitive settings. It will also make us feel frustrated and unappreciated.
- Fear of alienating those closest to us will prevent us from being honest about our own feelings and needs.

We must become aware of how often our lives' circumstances stem from our real choices, and how often from our fears.

Freedom from Fear

There are four basic fears which all of us have felt at one time or another. These fears are the source of most of our worries, doubts and limitations in life. They are the enemy, and they keep us from being all that we can be. Even though these basic fears control us, the average person is unaware of the extent of their control. We can free ourselves from these fears by remembering that they are only states of our mind, and can be controlled with the techniques of positive thinking.

The Four Basic Fears of Humans

1. Poverty and lack (food, money, shelter, etc.)
2. Group disapproval, lost love, failure and criticism.
3. Poor health, pain and suffering.
4. Old age and death.

Anxiety

Like fear, anxiety is a common response to certain situations. But while many things which cause fear can be avoided, anxiety stems from those things which can not be avoided so easily. If a man is fearful of getting mugged in a dangerous part of town, he can avoid that area, or avoid going there at night or alone. But if his fear is more vague, so he often feels anxious about his general safety, it will be more difficult for him to avoid the cause of his fears.

Most of us suffer from minor anxiety at times. We sometimes feel overwhelmed by the worries of modern life: crime, poverty, pollution, wars, overcrowding, the economy, auto insurance, child care, and the depletion of the ozone layer. Even though we cannot solve all these problems, we can take steps to reduce our anxiety about them.

Reducing Anxiety

- Get a big sheet of paper and write down every single thing that you feel anxious about. Be specific. Include rational fears and irrational fears as well. No one will see this sheet but you.
- Go through the list and check off the things you can do something about in the immediate future. (For example, if crime worries you, you can improve the security of your home and take a self-defense class. If the condition of the environment weighs on your mind, volunteer at a recycling center, or contact an environmental group for other ways you can help.)

- Make a plan to deal with one of these problems on each day of the coming week. (For example, on Monday call nursery schools and enroll your child for a few days a week, if a lack of free time is one of your problems. On Tuesday, call the crime prevention office of the police department for information on home security. If finances are a problem you can solve, use Wednesday to plan a realistic budget or polish up your resume´.)
- Shorten your list this way until you are left with only the problems that you cannot solve in a day, such as a relative's chronic illness, serious financial difficulties, the ozone layer and annoying neighbors.
- Though much shorter, your list will now look much more serious and hopeless. Some problems have no realistic solution. You can't prevent a relative from dying of old age or a terminal disease. However, this does not preclude you from doing something to reduce your anxiety, about the situation.
- Find ways to accept the things that you can't change. Prayer, a support group, or the comfort of loved ones may reduce your sorrow over the death of a relative. If you can't quit your stressful job, set aside as much time as possible to relax and have fun, or just to enjoy some quiet time by yourself. Learn to meditate, or practice some other stress reduction technique. (See *Stress Management*.)
- Realize that the one thing you always have control over is your feelings. Others may control certain events, but you are the cause of your own anxiety.

Envy

Envy is the result of believing that comfort, security, love, joy, happiness and everything else that is good comes from outside of oneself. Envy is a sign of low self-esteem and lack of inner security.

Unfortunately, we live in a competitive and materialistic society, which constantly bombards us with the idea that our happiness depends on purchasing the right brands of clothing, automobiles, and personal hygiene products. If we think about this for just a minute, we know it's not true, but sometimes it is hard not to be swayed by the many messages we see all around us. When we allow ourselves to believe that our purchases affect our value as human beings, we open the door to envy.

Just as we may believe that our lives will be better if we buy certain things, we may also believe that certain situations or attributes will make us happy. If only we could lose ten pounds, or have an attractive girlfriend or boyfriend, or be more witty or intelligent or popular, or could have grown up in a different family, or gone to a more prestigious college, then our lives would be fine. We see that other people have these things, and they appear to be happy.

Envy keeps us from dealing with the real cause of unhappiness: ourselves. If a man convinces himself that he would be happy, if only he had a new car, then as long as he doesn't get the car, he has an excuse for his discontent. This way, he can avoid looking at the hurts and fears and insecurities that are the real cause of his unhappiness. But we cannot free ourselves from the fears and doubts we hold, until we examine them, so we will never be fulfilled, no matter whom we date or what we buy.

Each of us is responsible for filling our own lives with interest, striving to achieve our potentials, and making ourselves happy.

Of course, all of us feel a tinge of envy now and then. A little bit of envy can spur us on to work harder, accomplish more, and expect more from ourselves. It can keep us from becoming complacent and bored. Just be careful not to let envy make you feel bad about yourself:
- Whenever you find yourself wishing for something that someone else has, stop and count your blessings. Remind yourself of how fortunate you are. Are you healthy? Do you have a home and food? Do you have time to spend at leisure? Do you have friends and relatives who love and care about you?
- Make a list of things you like about yourself, and things that you enjoy. Include every little thing you can think of.
- If you spend more time examining our own life, you'll be amazed at how much you have, and what a unique person you are!

Death, Loss and Grief

Most people associate grief with the death of a loved one. But grief can also be caused by divorce, separation, or the ending of a romantic relationship; separation from friends or home; retirement; or the disappearance or death of a pet.

Whatever the cause, the pain of loss is real to the person who suffers it, no matter if others think it is unwarranted. While grief may become exaggerated or prolonged until it develops into a disorder, it should never be dismissed by others. The inability to express one's grief can also lead to emotional problems.

Grief is considered to be the normal and healthy response to the death of a loved one. The grieving process lasts up to a year, during which time the person cries frequently, withdraws from activities and social interaction, becomes unresponsive to external events, and exhibits most other symptoms of depression. (See *Mood Disorders*.) The person may also engage in fantasies in which the loved one is still alive. This causes the person much pain at first, but the pain and the fantasizing gradually decreases over time, as the person adjusts to his or her loss.

Those closest to the dead person may feel angry and abandoned by the one they loved. They may also feel intense guilt, especially if they felt hostility and resentment towards the person who died. Guilt may also be experienced by those who feel relieved by the death, even if the deceased had been in terrible pain.

These feeling must be openly discussed if they are to be resolved. If everyone remains silent in the belief that it's better not to bring up painful subjects, the loss and pain can become intensified within the individual and bring on depression.

In many modern cultures, death is often denied or ignored. It is not treated as the inevitable part of life which it is.

- We embalm the dead person's body, apply cosmetics to simulate the appearance of life, and display the body in a cushioned and decorated casket.
- We refer to the "departed ones" as those who have "passed away" or "are no longer with us," and do not

teach our children about death or allow them to witness the experience of death.
- Throughout our lives we continue to deny the inevitability of death, so that we are completely unprepared for it, and react with disbelief when it occurs.

Yet there are two aspects of death we must learn about, so we can achieve growth and maturation within the course of our lives:
- We need to accept the inevitability of our own death, so our lives will have value to us. If you were given a year to live, or a month, what would you choose to do? How would you make the most of your remaining time? How would your priorities change? Accepting the idea of our own death allows us to face these questions realistically, and to make the appropriate choices.
- We must accept the deaths of others: our loved ones, parents, children, relatives, friends, and neighbors. Every time we say good-bye to someone, we assume we will see them again. If we do not accept the inevitability of their deaths, we may not value them as much as we should, or show them how we feel about them.

Elisabeth Kubler Ross wrote about the five stages that people go through when they know they are dying.
- *Denial* takes place when people believe that it can't be happening and that there must have been a mistake or mix-up.
- *Anger* occurs after denial and is directed at doctors, hospitals, relatives and even God.
- *Bargaining* comes next. This is where the person says "If only I get better I will promise to do some wonderful thing with my life."
- *Depression* occurs when they realize they will really die and anger or bargaining will not change that fact.
- *Acceptance* occurs when they become realistic and mature about their approaching physical end. This can be a calm, tranquil self realization that is enlightenment.

"The Traveler" A Poem about Death and Life by James Dillet Freeman

He has put on invisibility.
Dear God, I cannot see–
But this I know, although the road ascends
And passes from my sight,
That there will be no night;
That You will take him gently by the hand
And lead him on
Along the road of life that never ends,
And he will find it is not death but dawn.
I do not doubt that You are there as here,
And You will hold him dear.

Our life did not begin with birth,
It is not of the earth;
And this that we call death, it is no more
Than the opening and closing of a door–
And in Your house how many rooms must be
Beyond this one where we rest momently.

Dear God, I thank You for the faith that frees,
The love that knows it cannot lose its own;
The love that, looking through the shadows, sees
That You and he and I are ever one!

Overcome Loneliness

We all need to be alone at times. Everyone needs private time to relax, meditate, read, sleep, daydream and just to sit and think about things. We must be free of others' demands on our attention, so that we can pay attention to our own needs and desires. But if we are alone more than we wish to be, and find ourselves yearning to spend more time with other people, then we are lonely.

Just as it's important to be alone, it's also important to be able share our thoughts and feelings with someone. We all need to feel loved, cared for and listened to, and to have friends to share our joys and sorrows.

Most people feel lonely at times, especially when they go off to school for the first time, move to a new city, or retire, or have a loved one dies. Then they adjust to the new situation, and go out and make new friends. But some people don't know how to make friends. Their loneliness makes them unhappy, which makes it even harder to reach out to new people. Their unhappiness may even rob them of the joy of having time alone.

Children who are rejected and ignored by their parents often become lonely, insecure, negative, and anxious adults. Their inability to make friends only increases their negative feelings about themselves and the world.

How to Make Friends

- The first step is to acknowledge that the choice is yours. The ability to make friends requires only a set of social skills that can be learned with practice, and some good feelings about yourself. You don't have to be the most charming or happy or beautiful person in the world; you just have to be willing to try and believe that eventually you will succeed.
- Accept others with neutrality, and do not view them as competitors. Most people, after all, would rather make friends than enemies. If they don't respond to your efforts, maybe they also have trouble making friends. They may be even more lonely than you!
- No matter how ready you are to try, you can't meet people by staying at home. You must now go out and find some. Take a non-credit class, join a group that interests you, like a political or environmental group or a softball team or a garden club, or become a volunteer. Try to find something with a regular meeting schedule, so you can't put off going. Besides meeting people who share your interests, these activities will be fun and challenging to you, and will help you feel better about yourself. Not only will you learn to make friends, you'll also become better able to enjoy your time alone.

Are You Co-Dependent?

A co-dependent is a person who needs to be depended upon by others. Lack of self-esteem causes the co-dependent to look to others for a sense of worth. This person will become completely involved in meeting another's needs, while neglecting his or her own.

Co-dependents can't find the love or acceptance they need within themselves, but believe that it must come from being loved and accepted by another person. They find people who have unfulfilled emotional needs, and do whatever they can to make themselves indispensable. But because the co-dependent and the other person are both unfulfilled, their relationship is detrimental to both of them.

The co-dependent lives for and through his or her children, ill parent or sibling, or alcoholic spouse. Because co-dependents rely on being needed, they cannot allow the people they care for to leave them or stop needing them. Without realizing it, the co-dependent undermines others' independence and self-confidence, using caring as a way to control and manipulate.

The following traits are characteristic of co-dependent people:
- They pay a lot of attention to what others feel, think, and want, yet they are unsure of their own feelings, thoughts and desires.
- They put great energy into trying to work things out, and blame themselves for failed relationships.
- They move from one relationship to the next without time in between for themselves.
- Co-dependents remain in hurtful relationships, and do not feel that they deserve better.
- They are unable to ask for love and nurturing.
- People persist in an unsatisfying relationship because they are afraid of losing what they have for the unknown.

Escape and Addictions

We all wish we could just disappear sometimes, and suddenly escape from the problems, dilemmas and annoyances of our daily lives. Sometimes we do have to find a way to escape temporarily, until we are prepared to deal with the tasks facing us.

There are many healthy ways to escape, which renews our strength and clears our minds. Pursuing a hobby, reading a book, exercising, stretching out on the sofa, eating a delicious dessert, taking a long hot bath, or driving off into the country for a day or two can be just the thing to get us going again. But we must be careful not to allow our escapes to turn into addictions.

Escapes become addictions when they are used to deny responsibilities and avoid decisions.

While the healthy person uses escapes for refreshment and renewal, the person who is addicted becomes a hostage to his or her escape behavior.
- The addict denies that anything is wrong.
- Denial keeps the person from taking action to resolve problems, and problems grow and multiply when left unresolved.
- Increasing problems cause an increase in stress, and the person must escape more often or withdraw more completely from the problems.
- Eventually the escape behavior overwhelms the person, and the addiction may become a bigger problem than the original problems that the person was trying to escape.

If an occasional escape does not relieve the pressure you feel, look for a more permanent solution. Escape is not the answer.

Talk to a friend, or seek a support group or professional help. You may be in a career that you are not suited for, or a relationship that is not healthy, or you may be taking on too much responsibility, or perhaps you just need to learn to reduce your level of stress. (See *Stress Management*.) Find out what the problem really is, and find a way to solve it.

Are You Addicted?
- We can be addicted to many things or behaviors: alcohol, drugs, food, shopping at the mall, working, gambling, sex, another person.
- The means of escape themselves can sometimes become addictions.
- Many people think that to have an addiction, to alcohol for instance, you must drink regularly or excessively. In fact, if we require but one drink to unwind after the day's work, bolster our ego before we meet someone important, express ourselves better, or for whatever reason, then we depend on alcohol and it becomes an addiction.
- The same goes for any other form of addiction. If we must depend on something to alter our mood in any

significant way so that we feel better about ourselves, relate better with others, or feel more content, more in control, more able or more relaxed, we are on the slippery path to serious addiction.
- Those enhanced feelings which we get while we are high represent false security. As soon as we come down from the high, sober up, leave the mall or the casino, all that we have left is ourselves again: good old us! And we already know that we are vulnerable, scared, and insecure. (See *Recreational Drugs and Substance Abuse* and *Alcohol*.)

Health and Wellness

Being mentally healthy means that we can adapt to change, maintain our balance and learn from the challenges that life brings.

- It does not mean that we are never sad, angry, embarrassed, hurt, fearful or even devastated at times, in the course of our lives.
- When we are in good mental health we are not immobilized by these reactions.
- On the contrary, we are able to endure or work through our problems, and to emerge whole and renewed.

Good mental health provides us with many benefits:
- The ability to maintain and enrich relationships, as well as establish new ones.
- The ability to let go of things, situations, or people that we have lost, after an adequate period of grieving.
- The ability to maintain our independence, while still being able to express our needs and to help others fulfill their own needs.
- The ability to recognize our own path towards spiritual growth and self-actualization, and being able to follow this path.
- The strength to commit ourselves to our chosen fields of interest, work, goals, and relationships, and the self-discipline to maintain our commitments.
- The courage to face new challenges.
- Flexibility, open-mindedness, receptivity to others' ideas and points of view.
- The ability to explore possibilities and to create.

How to Maintain Mental Health

Before we can attain mental and emotional well-being, there are certain things we need to build upon. We have basic needs which must be met, so we will not become distracted from pursuing our personal growth and fulfillment:

- We have to satisfy the basic physiological needs – air, water, food, sleep, and shelter from the elements – without which we would soon die. We must have a way to ensure continuing satisfaction of these needs.
- There is also the basic need to feel safe and secure. In our society, this often translates into economic security, which is necessary to fulfill most other basic needs. Poverty, homelessness or extreme material uncertainty, as in the case of someone who loses his job and is threatened with eviction, can be very detrimental to a person's sense of well-being.
- Everyone needs a sense of belonging. We can belong with our family, our friends, co-workers, religious or ethnic or political group, as long as we feel that we are a recognized part of some group of people.
- We must love and be loved. Every one of us needs affection from a partner or spouse, children, relatives, or friends.
- We need to feel pride in our selves and our accomplishments. We need to have self-esteem, and also we need the respect of others.
- Once our other needs are met, we can focus our attention on our need for self-actualization. This is the process of understanding ourselves and fulfilling our potential. We must learn to communicate clearly, so that we can understand and explain our needs, dreams and ambitions, and feel sure that others understand us.
- In order to fulfill our maximum potential, we also need to know that only we are responsible for our decisions and our lives.

How to be Happy

Our life is the product of our mind. We create our own circumstances, we choose to be at a certain place at a certain time, we choose our acquaintances and friends.

We all come with certain individual advantages and handicaps which affect our progress toward mental wellness: a specific socio-economic background, a happy or unhappy childhood, wonderful achievements terrible traumatic experiences, a supportive or indifferent environment, and many good and bad habits of thought and behavior.

But we can overcome the troubling memories, childhood deficiencies, doubts and fears and negative thoughts that hold us back and keep us from the happiness we crave. The first step, regardless of where we now stand, is to believe in ourselves. The life we live today and tomorrow and every day thereafter is directly related to how we think today. If we put our minds to it, we can achieve anything we wish to.

The Secret of Happiness

From the Happiness Scale below, choose the list of words that best describes your life.

Happiness Scale

List A	List B	List C	List D	List E
Angry	Tired	O.K.	Secure	Joyful
Lonely	Dissatisfied	Ordinary	Happy	Plentiful
Frustrated	Coping	Content	Relaxed	Fulfilled
Insecure	Needing	Acceptable	Comfortable	Creative

If you choose List A you are very unhappy. List C is average and list E indicates you are a very happy person.

People usually believe they will find happiness by satisfying their wants and desires. But in truth these satisfied desires bring only temporary pleasure. Very quickly new wants and desires arise. People again tell themselves that this time it will be different. This time the satisfied desire will bring real, lasting happiness. But time and time again we achieve only fleeting pleasure. Most of us remain on the never-ending treadmill, searching for security, comfort, sensations, sex, money, acceptance, status or power.

True happiness comes from understanding who we really are and accepting this truth about ourselves and our life. This is an internal understanding, and nothing external needs to be changed.

Life is designed to work and to produce happiness. And now at this moment you have everything you need to be happy. It's not necessary to work and sacrifice for some nebulous future happiness. There is nothing you lack to be happy right now except the realization of what you already have. Discover who you really are and accept the truth about yourself and your life.

The key to happiness is deciding to be happy. It doesn't matter what your life circumstances are. The difference between happiness and misery is your decision. You decide. Happiness happens from your decision. The following three questions will assist you with this:
- Are you where you belong, doing the things that are right for you?
- If so, what keeps you from being happy now?
- If not, what keeps you from being where you want and doing the things you want?

When you can't find peace within yourself, it's useless to seek it elsewhere.

Make Yourself Feel Great

You can change your mood from depression to elation in a flash. You have control over your emotions and you don't need drugs or alcohol to help. There are a number of things people do change their mood. Some people just shake their head and dismiss any negative thoughts. Others sing songs, dance, watch movies, listen to upbeat songs, etc. There are many things you know how to do, but might forget when you need them. Take a few minutes and write a list of your positive mood changing activities on a blank page of this book, so it will be there when you need it.

Communication

Communication is vital to our relationships with ourselves and with others. Without the ability to speak to ourselves clearly and honestly, we cannot know how we really feel, and we certainly can't have any meaningful exchange with others. But communication is often disrupted by fear:

- We often are afraid to say what we mean because we don't feel safe enough to expose our feelings to possible misunderstanding, rejection or even ridicule.
- The truth may hurt the ones we love.
- Sometimes we don't want to share feelings which are painful to us, because we are scared to acknowledge them.

Communication is a very complex skill. Especially when expressing our personal problems, fears, and doubts, it is important to know what we want to say, and not allow emotion to cloud our communication:
- Use the simplest terms available.
- Begin with the statement "I feel," when expressing how you feel.
- Starting a statement with "You make me feel," gives it an accusatory tone and puts the other person on the defensive. You are responsible for your own feelings.
- Remember, others have fears, too. And most of us are not always able to say how we really feel.
- State the problem exactly as you see it from your point of view, but acknowledge that there are as many points of view as there are people involved in any given situation.
- Always remember that others' opinions and feelings are just as valid and real to them as yours are to you. The fact that you did not intend to insult someone, or don't see why they are hurt, does not make their pain any less real.
- The purpose of communication should not be to start an argument or to prove someone wrong, but to exchange thoughts and feelings.
- Be a good listener. Wait until the other person has fully and finally expressed his or her thoughts and feelings. Don't just try to formulate answers to every point, and don't jump in and start talking at every pause.
- Ask questions if you don't understand, and repeat the other's statement in your own words to ensure that you have heard and understood.
- Communication requires the skills of self-expression and of listening. Both are equally important, and both are skills that can be learned, practiced, and improved upon.

Listening

We can practice truly listening to others by paying total attention to what they are saying to us with their words, gestures, postures, attitudes and appearance. Good communication skills include:
- Open-minded and complete listening; truly listening without trying to formulate an answer.
- Listening with empathy; that is, trying to understand the other's point of view and feelings.
- Too often, people talk *at* each other, not *to* each other. Instead, they should hold a real conversation with equal time given to speaking and listening.

The elements of listening are:
- Patience: Biting our tongue if we must, but holding our peace until the other person has truly finished speaking. That means no interruption, no matter what thought has suddenly sprung into our mind.
- Attention: Practicing focusing on the speakers words, facial expressions, gestures, etc. Try to rephrase his or her statements and ask whether our understanding is accurate.
- Being as specific as we can when expressing our own thoughts and feelings.

Learn to Say No

Sometimes taking care of yourself means that you have to refuse someone something. As much as we always want to be there for the ones we love, we don't always have the time, energy or emotional reserves that they ask of us. We have two choices: we can take care of them while neglecting ourselves, or we can say no to them.

Live your own life, for you will die your own death.

Neglecting yourself to help others is not only harmful to you, but also harms the other person. The people who love you should be able to ask things of you and get an honest answer. When you feel pressured into agreeing to do something, you feel guilty and resentful toward the person you are helping, which hurts you both.

Learning to say no frees us to say yes and really mean it.

If you find that you are always putting yourself out for others, you may have an unhealthy need to have them rely on you. (See *Are You Co-dependent?*.) If you feel that someone is making excessive demands on you, on a regular basis, you may need to reassess the value of your relationship with this person. But sometimes it happens that you simply can't do something for someone. You just have to say no.

- Remember that saying no to a loved one is not permanent rejection.
- If you do not take care of your own needs, you may soon find yourself unable to be of much help to anyone.
- Take time to make a decision. Tell the other person that you will think about the request, and then *do* think about it. Examine your needs, and consider what the request would entail. Determine whether there is some other solution to the problem. If you would like to help, but the particular time or task is inconvenient, offer a compromise. You are being asked for a favor: you should be able to say when or how you can do it. This is not a way to punish people for asking for your help, but simply a way to balance meeting their needs with your own. Say something like "I'm going out later; I'll be happy to pick it up then."
- If you must say no, say it firmly and gently so that the person knows that you care and have given the request due consideration.
- Don't begin to doubt your own rights and start offering half-hearted excuses. You do not need any excuse to take care of yourself.
- If someone is asking something of you, that person should be aware that "no" is a possible answer. Trust your loved ones to be able to accept that answer, and to tell you (instead of asking) if they really *need* you to do something.
- Be careful not to overextend yourself in a time of crisis. Take time to think before offering or agreeing to anything.
- Follow your intuition and your judgment. Never say yes to something you feel may be wrong, dangerous,

unethical, or distasteful to you. Think through all the possible outcomes.
- Allow others to be responsible for themselves.

Have Better Relationships

Our relationship with ourselves will determine our relationships with others. If we want to build satisfying relationships with others, we must begin with self-awareness, self-examination and willingness to take responsibility for our own lives.

- Notice each time a negative thought enters your mind. Which thoughts recur most often? Do they concern something you don't like about yourself? Or do your negative thoughts center on someone else? Someone you can't forgive? Someone you care for and worry about? Someone who makes you feel insecure, depressed, angry or resentful?
- Each time you notice one of these thoughts, scrutinize it to see how it makes you feel.
- Remind yourself that you are solely responsible for your own life. You choose your own thoughts.

We can learn to love ourselves and take care of ourselves in the same way that we love others and take care of them.

We can love others and care for them without neglecting ourselves. We need not jeopardize our own integrity, our self-esteem, or the fulfillment of our own needs.
- We can choose to trust and love others, and to share with others.
- We must learn that we have the right to say no, to refuse requests and demands on our time and attention, without having to give an excuse or explanation.
- We can be comfortable with ourselves, physically, mentally and spiritually.
- We must accept total responsibility for ourselves, alone and in our relationships with others.
- We can choose happiness and enjoyment in life and in relationships.

- But we must begin by ridding ourselves of our own negative thought-forms.

Happiness comes to those who wish it and make room for it in their lives.

Forgiveness

Forgiving those who hurt us is not just something we do for them; it is something we do for ourselves.

The ability to forgive is essential to mental wellness. When we forgive, we let go of all the negative, angry, vengeful and paralyzing thoughts and feelings that have been consuming us.
- Even if you never forget a harm done to you, forgiving the person who did it allows you to move forward again.
- Only when you forgive can the pain begin to dissipate.
- You may choose to speak to the person who has hurt you, explaining that you were hurt, and how you feel now. This is not an opportunity to make the person feel bad, and if you use it as such, you have not yet reached forgiveness. You are still controlled by your pain.
- If you can't or don't want to confront the person, you can visualize yourself saying the things you need to say. Imagine yourself explaining your feelings to the person, and imagine his or her response.
- True forgiveness does not need to be repeated. But to help yourself reach the point of forgiveness, you can use meditation, visualizations and affirmations.
- Tell yourself that all is well now; that you recognize the past and choose to move beyond it. Acknowledge the power of forgiveness.
- Forgiveness applies to ourselves, as well as to others. You must learn to forgive yourself for the hurts you have caused yourself, and the hurts you have caused others. We cannot take back the things we have done; we must learn from our mistakes and move beyond them, so that we don't make the same mistakes again.

Change

Our mind is responsible for the current condition of our body. This condition is not an accident or coincidence. Before change can occur, you must first identify why you have chosen your current condition. You probably chose it with your sub-conscious mind long ago.
- Determine how your illness, lack or limitation serves you. If you have disease, why did you chose it?
- Change is difficult because the familiar seems safer than the new. There is a natural fear of the unknown results of change.
- Once you decide to change, you must determine the actions necessary to implement the change.
- You must be committed to go beyond your fears and accomplish the change.
- Commitment is possible when your thoughts, words and actions are in alignment.
- Are you willing to take the actions necessary for your commitment?

"The world is moving so fast these days that the man who says it can't be done is generally interrupted by someone doing it."
— Elbert Hubbard

Behavior Modification

Replacing old, negative behavior with more positive behavior is a matter of reconditioning your mind. Personal behavior modification can be reinforced by the following:
- See yourself in the new behavior whenever you think of the future. Feel absolutely positive that you can replace the old behavior with the new behavior.
- Associate pain with the old behavior you want to change. When you think of that old behavior also imagine and feel painful memories from your past.
- Associate pleasure with the new behavior that will replace the old behavior. Imagine and feel pleasure when you think of the new behavior.

Improve Your Memory

Repeated exposure over time will help you retain material more easily than a single intensive session. According to the latest findings, it is wise to avoid concentrated periods of time for careful study. Simply look over the material, let some time pass, and look over it again. Next, double the time. Then, double the time again, and so on. Other keys are:
- Sustaining an even pace improves memory. Exhausting oneself tends to fog the memory the following day.
- Study before sleep increases retention the next day.
- Early risers are generally most attentive in the early morning. Late risers tend to be most alert in the evening. Take advantage of peak times for mental ability.
- For many, memory is keenest on Friday and Saturday. This is thought to be due to the fact that people tend to be relaxed and have more time on weekends.
- Many of the relaxation techniques of yoga help achieve the right level of alertness for optimum memory performance, and also boost brain power.
- Memory tasks are easier to perform when one is alone.
- Write down items you want to remember. For many of us who are visual instead of auditory learners, writing things improves the clarity of our memory.
- Never ask others to do your remembering for you. Don't agree to remember things for others.

To Remember Names of People
- When introduced, say the name out loud.
- Think of an image or word that reminds you of the person's name. For example, you might think of Big Al for a tall person whose name is Alan.
- In conversation, periodically use the person's name.
- When ending the conversation, use the name again.

Create Prosperity in Your Life

The concept of prosperity includes not only abundant money, but also the prosperity of health and happiness. Even if you currently have very little money

you can now create in your mind the illusion of enormous abundance. If you see your life as abundant, it becomes so. The keys to manifesting prosperity are:
- Create the vision of what you want. Be sure your vision is detailed and is exactly what you want.
- Create the plan to bring reality to your vision. It's wonderful to have a great vision, but also vital to have a plan to turn that vision into reality.
- See your vision as already accomplished. Invest your vision with your complete faith, as if there were no doubt of the positive outcome.
- Follow up with the actions that accomplish your plan and bring your vision to fruition. Persistence is the key to manifesting your vision.
- Be thankful that your vision is accomplished. Give thanks that your vision is becoming reality.

The man who believes he can be prosperous is probably right, and so is the man who believes he can't.

Supply is limitless, and there is no real shortage of food, shelter, love, etc. However, we often hinder ourselves by believing in the illusion of limits to our good. There are three steps to a more abundant life.
- Help others grow and prosper so that you may prosper. This act of helping others takes our mind off of our illusion of lack or limitation. Encourage others so that you will be encouraged.
- Give thanks in advance, before you receive your good. Give thanks, as if you were already prosperous. Thank God or the universe as if you had already received your goods. "Be thankful and the things of the earth will be added to us 100 times more." See yourself already receiving your good.
- Affirm that "prosperity is the truth of my world." Life responds to what we think and say. Your words are law, so say "yes" to your good. Then any lack or limitation will be transformed into a rich, abundant supply.

Truths Connected with Prosperity
- It is your right to choose abundance. Be willing to accept yourself and receive your abundance.
- Never embrace thoughts of poverty, scarcity, lack or limitation.
- Never undervalue yourself by charging too little for your services. Always charge properly for your work.
- Giving and receiving are both part of the same energy flow.
- Abundance is not a function of how much money you have, but of how you relate to the money you do have.

Positive Thinking

> *"Some men see things as they are, and say, 'Why?' I dream of things that never were, and say, 'Why not?'"*
> – George Bernard Shaw

In nature we accept the order and inevitability of certain reactions to certain causes, but in the realm of our minds, we do not want to believe that the process of cause and effect exists. Yet it is so. For instance, we accept that if we overeat we will get a stomachache or heartburn. If we do so regularly, we will become overweight. Yet most of us do not understand how negative thought patterns deteriorate our self-esteem and make us more susceptible to despair, failure, unhappiness, and a host of mental disorders. Emotional pain is a call to change our thinking habits and to re-establish positive thoughts, harmony and wholeness.

Some will object: "But what if things don't turn out as I had planned? What if I fail anyhow?" Such doubtful and fearful thinking is a guarantee of failure. When we first begin on the road to positive thinking, we may still have doubts deep within us, so it is very possible that we will encounter some failures at first. We still lack focus, determination, and belief in ourselves.

We have all made errors of judgment in the past. But these mistakes are in the past, where they are bound to stay. They can only interfere with the present life if we choose to let them. Positive thinking does not entail negating our mistakes by blaming our circumstances on other people who influenced us. Positive thinking requires that we face up to our mistakes and analyze them, so we can comprehend the lessons which they hold. Then we simply apply these lessons to the present and to our plans for the future.

Positive thinking involves much more than just vague affirmations and meditations. It entails taking all of this general and specialized knowledge and creating a plan by which to live our life.

Once you truly decide to, you can produce almost any results.

As soon as you really commit yourself to achieving a result, it will happen. It may not be perfect the first time, and you may have to learn from less-than-perfect results. But if you truly commit, you will learn from those results and change something so you will come closer to what you want the next time.

The Power of Positive Thinking

Whenever we have doubts about ourselves or our own worth, we can reflect about the past and see that:
- We have been up against tough times before and we found a solution.
- We had whatever it took to remedy or bear with the situation.
- We moved on from there, to where we are now.
- We still have choices. There are always other options.
- Someone who cared then is surely an ally today, to be trusted to support and understand us.

Thought Patterns

Negative Thought	Consequence
Fear, Doubt	Weakness, Failure
Resentment, Envy	Mental exhaustion
Anger	Sorrow, Self-loathing
Laziness	Lack of progress, Depression
Selfishness	Isolation, Loneliness

Positive Thought	Consequence
Courage	Success, Self-worth, Esteem
Self-control, Temperance	Independence, Grace
Patience, Compassion	Self-esteem, Growth
Seriousness, Creativity	Progress, Success, Esteem
Generosity, Selflessness	Harmony, Love, Happiness

We can use positive thought-forms as reinforcements in meditations or relaxation exercises. But life cannot be scripted, programmed and expected to run its course without a hitch.

- Changes – unplanned, unsuspected events – will take place, whether we like it or not. Life turns, twists, jumps ahead and leaps out of bounds, from moment to moment. We cannot have planned for every possibility and we cannot put off sudden occurrences. Yet, we fear the unexpected; we fear change, sudden obstacles and the possibility of failure and loss.
- Using positive thought-forms throughout the day or as part of a meditation practice can help us affirm our strength.
- Positive visual imagery can work alongside verbal affirmations.
- Real positive thinking comes from always being able to draw from our own past, take responsibility in the present and create our own future.
- We can learn to develop self-confidence through the positive tests of life.
- The only negative elements in life are those which have taught us nothing at all. How many of those can we really remember? Obviously none, because all of life's events contain some lesson, however small.

Positive thinking and the resulting self-esteem can help us develop a plan for attaining those things which we want and know are within the realm of possibilities for us.
The key is to know that we are worth our own effort.

Athletes, great performers and discoverers all know that each morning must be greeted with positive thoughts and attitudes, and some progress must be made each day if the end goal is to be reached or the all-important discovery made.

Today, when we are faced with new advances in technology, split-second world-wide communications, as well as greater threats of natural and man-made disasters, violence and sorrow, a similar attitude of day-to-day positive thinking can benefit each and every individual and ensure a better world for future generations.

We are always free to choose, and choosing a positive path makes sense.

Your Bill of Rights

- I do not have to feel guilty just because someone else does not like what I do, say, think, or feel.
- I have the right to say "I don't understand," without feeling stupid or guilty.
- I have the right to say "No," without feeling guilty.
- I have the right to refuse requests which others make of me.
- I have the right to make mistakes and to be responsible for them.
- I have the right to refuse additional responsibility without feeling guilty.

Affirmations

Affirmations are positive statements which we repeat to ourselves. They help to change our negative attitudes and self-defeating thought patterns, by changing and replacing the bad things we used to tell ourselves.

Remember that all affirmations must be:
- Set in the present.
- Worded in the positive form. Never use a negative form such as "I won't allow self-neglect," but replace with the positive: "I always take care of myself."
- Phrased to yourself and for yourself, by using the pronoun "I."
- Worded as specifically and personally as possible. For example, "I play a great game of volleyball. My serve is always on target," instead of "I am good at sports."
- Memorize your affirmations and if possible, say your affirmations out loud. Even better, look at yourself in the mirror as you say them. This may be hard at first, but it will soon become easy and enjoyable.

- Repeat each affirmation at least five or six times, several times a day. You can do this anywhere: in the shower, on the bus, whenever you pass by a mirror, while waiting for the copier or your lunch, before you go to sleep, or while you exercise.

If you don't have a plan for yourself, you'll be part of someone else's.

The following sample affirmations are called "The Twelve Pathways to Higher Consciousness," reprinted from *The Handbook to Higher Consciousness*, by Ken Keyes, Jr. (Fifth Edition, Copyright 1975, by the Living Love Center). Since its printing it has changed the lives of countless numbers of people.

When the word "addiction" is used, it means any desire that makes you upset or unhappy if it is not satisfied. Even if an addiction brings you pleasure, it is usually short-lived. For you will then begin to perceive threats to that pleasure and worry about potential changes in your life that will deprive you of the pleasure. You also compare today's pleasure with yesterday's pleasure – and often find today's pleasure is not quite as satisfying.

The Twelve Pathways to Higher Consciousness

Freeing Myself

1 I am freeing myself from security, sensation, and power addictions that make me try to forcefully control situations in my life, and thus destroy my serenity and keep me from loving myself and others.
2 I am discovering how my consciousness-dominating addictions create my illusory version of the changing world of people and situations around me.
3 I welcome the opportunity (even if painful) that my minute-to-minute experience offers me to become aware of the addictions I must reprogram to be liberated from my robot-like emotional patterns.

Being Here Now

4 I always remember that I have everything I need to enjoy my here and now – unless I am letting my consciousness be dominated by demands and expectations based on the dead past or the imagined future.

5 I take full responsibility here and now for everything I experience, for it is my own programming that creates my actions and also influences the reactions of people around me.

6 I accept myself completely here and now and consciously experience everything I feel, think, say, and do (including my emotion–backed addictions) as a necessary part of my growth into higher consciousness.

Interacting with Others

7 I open myself genuinely to all people by being willing to fully communicate my deepest feelings, since hiding in any degree keeps me stuck in my illusion of separateness from other people.

8 I feel with loving compassion the problems of others without getting caught up emotionally in their predicaments that are offering them messages they need for their growth.

9 I act freely when I am tuned in, centered and loving, but if possible I avoid acting when I am emotionally upset and depriving myself of the wisdom that flows from love and expanded consciousness.

Discovering My Conscious–Awareness

10 I am continually calming the restless scanning of my rational mind in order to perceive the finer energies that enable me to merge with everything around me.

11 I am constantly aware of which of the Maslow need centers I am using, and I feel my energy, perceptiveness, love and inner peace growing as I release the lower centers. [See *The Hierarchy of Needs*.]

12 I am perceiving everyone, including myself, as an awakening being who is here to claim his or her birthright to the higher consciousness planes of unconditional love and oneness.

> **Other Sample Affirmations**
> - My life is my own to live. I choose my own path. I take responsibility for my choices and my actions.
> - I respect others' opinions, but I give myself permission to create my own life as I see fit.
> - I have genuine talents and abilities.
> - I welcome change and challenge.
> - I choose the best for myself and my loved ones, and encourage others by my examples.
> - I respect others' choices, goals and visions and encourage them to give their best towards the creation of their lives.
> - I forgive myself for past errors. I value the things I learn from the past.
> - I acknowledge my accomplishments, my beauty, and my uniqueness.
> - I take full responsibility for my own feelings in my relationship with (my parents, my children, my spouse, my co-workers) at the same time that I allow them their own feelings and thoughts.

Positive affirmations are the path to positive thinking. They help reinforce our good thinking habits and prevent us from falling into self-doubt.

"Our individual potential is limitless. We can achieve any goal which we can envision for ourselves."
– Professor Hal Cohen

Daily Practice

This is a kind of self-examination which can easily be adapted to any situation or area of your life that you're working to improve or gain confidence in. It will help you to identify any areas you need to pay specific attention to, and keep your affirmations current.

Set aside some time each day to evaluate the events of the day. Answer the following questions, or make up your own. The questions should have a positive emphasis on your choices, responsibilities and abilities:

- Who did I speak to who is a real friend or supporter, worthy of my trust?

- What was the worst moment of the day? What did I fear most? What happened?
- What did I choose to do about it?
- What did I learn about myself?
- Is there anything to be corrected about the situation?
- What qualities do I have which I wish to increase?
- What did I do well which bears continuing?

Write your answers on an index card and re-read them carefully to make sure that you have not overlooked anything.
- Add any thoughts that come to your mind which have a positive impact on the situation.
- Then turn the card over and write down the goals you wish to achieve for the new day.
- Below that, add one or two positive affirmations that can help you on your way towards those goals..
- Re-read aloud your positive goals and affirmations a couple of times, putting feeling into them and visualizing yourself achieving them easily as you move through the day.
- Keep this card in your pocket throughout the day and take a peek at it whenever you need to realign your thinking or whenever you get a chance to be by yourself.
- At the end of the day, put the card away and relax until it is time for your new self-evaluation; then start a new index card.

This kind of daily practice can help you make very rapid progress in the direction you have chosen, and help redefine your direction. You are learning about yourself through the information provided by your own day-to-day life. Daily feed-back provides encouragement, and shapes your plans for improvement to your immediate needs.

Hypnosis

Hypnosis is an induced sleep-like condition in which an individual is extremely responsive to suggestions made by the hypnotist. Under hypnosis, a person is able to bypass the conscious mind, with all its chatter, and go directly to the subconscious mind.

Used for therapeutic purposes, hypnosis can help achieve deeper states of relaxation, overcome stress, control weight and break smoking habits. Many forms of self–

improvement can be achieved through hypnosis, from improving concentration to improving a golf swing.

Hypnosis is the process of relaxing your mind and fixating your attention on something. We are in a spontaneous hypnotic state thousands of times during our life, so we don't feel any abnormal sensations during most hypnotic experiences.

Hypnosis is basically safe, and people cannot be forced to do anything against their conscious will during hypnosis. However, hypnosis is not a magic wand that always produces conclusive results. Often a number of sessions are needed to achieve anything substantial. And in some people who have poor concentration, hypnosis does not work at all.

Much can also be accomplished using *self-hypnosis*. This eliminates the live hypnotist and instead uses an audio tape or just self-talk.

The Law of Attraction

We each attract everything that comes into our experience of life. Often it seems that someone else or some external force is controlling our experience. However it is our own thoughts, feelings and actions that attract various situations into our life.

When we give thought to something, feel its excitement, and perform action to attract it, we then create that in our life. When we give thought to something we do not want and feel the fear or anger of it, we then attract this negative experience into our life.

If we feel good about love whenever it appears, we will attract it. If we are thinking more about the lack of love in our life, we are creating negative thoughts. If we feel bad about never having enough love, then we will repel opportunities to develop love.

To change our thoughts about love or anything else, use the Flip-Flop Technique described in the next section. Rather than struggle against the lack of love, allow your natural abundance of love to flow. Remember that the Law of Attraction affects how we experience outer reality. When we look into our life and see lack or limitation, we can be sure that it was attracted with negative thoughts. Change negative thoughts to positive thoughts and we can attract whatever we want.

The Flip-Flop Technique

The images in our mind affect the way we think and act. The image comes first, before the behavior. The Flip-Flop Technique is a powerful method to substitution the images you choose to change.

For all its power, this technique is surprisingly easy. You simply create, in your mind, an image of the thing you do not want, and also an image of what you do want. Then you just flip-flop the two images. This is easy to understand by way of an example.

Let's say you believe you spend too much of your time and energy at the local pool hall and you would rather go home and spend that time with your family. To use this technique, you put the pool hall in the large blue frame on the left side of the paper. Visualize the pool hall in full color, in 3–D, and with smell and sound.

In the small black and white frame on the right visualize yourself at home with your family. This picture is small, obscure, two-dimensional, and without color or smell.

```
┌─────────────────────────┐
│                         │
│   Large blue frame      │
│                         │         ┌──────────────────┐
│                         │         │ Small black and  │
│                         │         │ white frame      │
│                         │         └──────────────────┘
└─────────────────────────┘
```

Count to three and then flip-flop the frames and pictures. Now the small black and white frame is on the left and the pool hall is in it. Now the large blue frame encloses a bright, colorful family scene.

[Large blue frame]

[Small black and white frame]

Now is the time to enhance the large family picture on the right. Make it 3–D, crystal clear, with bright, vibrant colors. Increase its emotional intensity by adding smells, tastes and sound. Now diminish the pool hall in the small picture now on the left. Make it become fuzzy and out of focus. Make it black and white and two-dimensional.

This conscious flip-flop of images will go straight into the subconscious and actually change the way we think and react. It will be necessary to repeat this exercise a few times.

All manner of unfavorable activities can be controlled by the Flip-Flop Technique. Overeating, stress, laziness, smoking, drinking, and drug addiction are just a few. The list is limited only by your imagination.

You Can Succeed

Taking risks willingly and making changes in life gives us strength, integrity and balance. Through this process we learn to become responsible and to trust ourselves more and more.

- We find out that we do not fail as often as we once might have thought, or as much as others would have made us believe.
- We discover that even when we fail, we always learn something valuable from the experience. There are no failures in being responsible for one's own life.
- We find that we can never please all the people all the time. Yet if we constantly demonstrate our personal power, integrity and responsibility, we'll soon become a source of real strength and support to others.

- We develop flexibility by learning to adjust and adapt to success and failure, to new events and new coordinates.
- Flexibility strengthens us and gives us more balance.

> **Words to Erase From Your Vocabulary:**
> Can't, Try, Limitation, If only, Ought to, Should, Never.

Increase Your Personal Power

When we are able to recognize our own needs, fulfill them in comfortable and adequate ways, and request help from others when we need it, then we have mastered personal power.

Now if we can keep this pattern going, fluctuating and flowing with all that comes in to the course of our life, we will remain in balance, whole and constantly adjusting ourselves without losing integrity. The benefits of such personal power are many:
- We are happy with ourselves. We know and accept all our good points as well as our faults.
- We are able to give more and more freely because we are not depleted by others. We keep enough energy for ourselves.
- We are more creative in finding solutions to life's problems.
- We grow mentally, emotionally and spiritually. Others are more attracted to us and grow with us.

Your Psychological Growth

The purpose of maintaining mental and emotional wellness is to grow.

Without awareness of our problems and assets, we remain limited and held back.
- Growth is not possible when old patterns of behavior are still locked in place. Yet as we have seen before, our ability to come to grips with our problems depends on the degree of emotional strength already present.
- Everyone is different, and some individuals may presently much more love and nurturing to gather up

emotions. The personality – thoughts and emotions – determines how we fare in our environment, in society, in love, and in work.
- Our mind is the most powerful tool that we'll ever have.
- Our mind fashions our personality as well as the circumstances around us.
- We create our own circumstances which can then nourish further thoughts.
- The direction of our thought process is of our own choice. We can always choose to cultivate our minds and tap the power of creativity which resides in our mind. By choosing to think positive thoughts we create positive results for ourselves.
- On the other hand, through the habit of negative thinking, we receive negative feedback which soon causes a deterioration in ourselves and our environment.

Our circumstances mirror our true self. We find ourselves in the circumstances which we have chosen for ourselves, which we believe we deserve and which reflect our beliefs.
- But we can become aware of how we think, what thoughts we bring to fruition within our own minds and how a change of thought pattern, attitude and priorities, can turn around a bad set of circumstances and create successes which we had not even believed possible.
- Being stuck in our own negative thoughts is like sentencing ourselves to a prison term, when in fact there are open doors and windows through which we can explore the world.
- Each positive change, affirmation and constructive attitude gives us new avenues of discovery, and new opportunities.
- We choose to be or not to be successful.

After all, if we have no control over our own thoughts and are pushed to and fro by doubts, insecurities, opinions and other criticisms, how can we plan and control any course of action, be it to complete a project, manage an enterprise or anything else?

the necessary strength and resilience to move forward confidently into life.
- We must learn to love ourselves and to speak to ourselves with our honest internal voice of the higher Self, the voice that knows us best.

Life is not a straight and uneventful continuum, but a series of ups and downs, crests and valleys, cycles that end and begin anew. We cannot expect to always be on top, and never experience failure, set-back, rejection, emotional upheaval, loss and so on. But we can remain aware that all failures hold important lessons. We can learn to recover from all the trials of life with even more strength, compassion and determination.

Freedom

Taking responsibility for our actions and our life can lead us to a feeling of great freedom.
- There is no freedom in being overwhelmed by problems and difficulties which we feel unable to resolve.
- Trying to please everyone can keep us going in circles, unable to focus in any one direction.
- As we learn to objectively look at our past actions and plan for the immediate future, we will find ourselves steadily moving forward.
- There are no guarantees that we will never make the wrong decision or choose the wrong path. But wrongs can be made right again, and even the worst situations allow choices and possibilities.
- Handling problems ourselves gives us a great feeling of freedom. We learn to depend upon ourselves and our own sure judgment. Because even if we are mistaken once, we will encounter another opportunity to face similar challenges. The second chance we will have learned to resolve the situation more positively.

Learn to listen to the inner voice of your higher Self.

Our mind reveals itself through our thoughts, the way we think as well as the specific content of individual thoughts. When we add our thoughts together, we form the outline of the personality. Thoughts also engender

Mental Wellness

No matter how well-prepared we are to handle ourselves in the world, life is full of improbable, unforeseeable events as well as cyclic changes which come to all of us. In essence, mental wellness is a dynamic path of challenges, strength, fearlessness, risk-taking, letting go and growth. Mental wellness includes:
- Adapting to always changing circumstances, which is life itself.
- Maintaining one's self-esteem or to re-establish full self-esteem after a temporary period of self-doubt brought on by any trial.
- Drawing from our own past to always take responsibility in the present and create our own future.
- Choosing our own goals which generate enough enthusiasm to start right away and give your best efforts.

A clever person turns great troubles into little ones and little ones into none at all.

Take Control of Your Emotional Balance

The remedy to making changes in our feelings about our own selves entails two main components: how and when.
- How can we remedy feeling the way we do? By choosing a course of action determined by us. How do we determine the course of action? By visualizing ourselves feeling the way we want to feel and be.
- When is the next opportunity to change? It may be when we receive our next paycheck or a bonus, have a day off, or something else. Once again, we follow our own rules, our own agenda. We take control of the changes to please ourselves. Establishing a definite time commitment also makes sense; the sooner we create change, the sooner we will be on the road to recovery.

Rules for Wellness and Growth
- Take responsibility for your own feelings. You will listen to your heart, mind and soul in all important matters.
- Reserve the right to say no to someone and not bear unnecessary guilt.
- Reserve the right to your own opinions and to change your mind if you believe it is right for you to do so.
- Make time for yourself to spend as you please.
- Do not take on any more responsibilities than you can carry.
- Take time off to relax, treat yourself and share with friends and loved ones.
- Always remember that you are the master of your own mind, life and destiny.

Be the Master of Your Own Life.

Service to others is beautiful and gratifying only when it is offered freely. If service to others is demanded of us to the extent of short-changing our own needs, we will not be able to give adequately. Our gifts will be poorer and of lesser quality. Maybe we will be filled with guilt, resentment or anger. To refuse help to others when they ask (or manipulate or beg) does not need to involve harsh rejection or a flat no. We can emphasize the things which we are willing to do for them and explain that we need time and energy for ourselves as well.

Say no and resist others' needs whenever the following happens:
- Any sudden crisis puts an unnatural urgency to our actions. We must be able to devote solitude time to think things out to decide what is best for us and others. It is very easy to overextend ourselves in time of crisis.
- Our own perception of a situation gives us a different opinion of the facts at hand. We need to follow our intuition and not participate in any action that goes against our own better judgment.
- We feel manipulated, guilty, embarrassed or shameful about our own reaction. We should reexamine the situation, determine the proper adjustments to be made in our actions and maintain our own integrity.
- Being responsible for our past and present errors equates taking risks. If we're not making our own

decisions, how can we be held responsible? We need reclaim our personal power.

Others are responsible for their feelings about us. If they find us ugly, does that make us ugly? Of course not. Beauty – and ugliness – are both in the eyes of the beholder. If they find us without generosity, does it make it so? As you know we are the only one that can set the means and limits of our own generosity?

It is important to remember that we have the right to say no; we are not responsible for how others choose to feel. We choose only our own feelings and situations; thus we become responsible for ourselves emotionally and mentally.

We can remain sympathetic, compassionate, generous and loving. In fact, remember that the stronger and steadier we are the more positive we have to share.

Separating ourselves from others in our mind (no matter how much we love or care for them) allows us to remember that we alone are the maker of our happiness. Others may disappoint, fail or desert us, but our own inner peace and happiness depend on us only.

- Anger, guilt, shame as well as joy, contentment and self-assurance all come from within.
- Even in a time of conflict or crisis we can retain our inner strength and peace of mind.
- This does not mean we will be able to banish all negative feelings out of our life. We will experience worry for those we care about, momentary guilt if we err and hurt ourselves or others, and sorrow for the losses we will encounter.
- But being well and whole, and remaining so, means that we will be able to do something about it.
- We will be able to focus on the hurt, guilt or grief and make a decision about it and re-establish our inner balance.

Achieve Serenity through Quiet Meditation

Meditation is one of the most powerful techniques known to man. Amazingly it is something that takes only a little time but will pay great dividends in your physical and mental health and well being. To begin the meditation, take a deep breath (filling your lungs completely) and let it out slowly, Repeat three times. This will automatically begin to relax you.

Continue to breathe slowly and deeply but now shift your attention to just "watching your breath." Shallow, rapid breathing and holding one's breath indicate tension instead of serenity.

"Watch your breathing" means to just be aware of your abdomen rising and falling as you breath in and out. When other thoughts come into your mind ignore them and go back to just watching your breath. This powerful meditation technique will calm you down and bring you serenity in just ten minutes. If your attention wanders in any way, gently return your focus to your breath.

CHAPTER 4
MIND–SPIRIT

"Our real journey in life is interior; it is a matter of growth, deepening, and of an ever greater surrender to the creative action of love and grace in our hearts."
— Thomas Merton

Overview of Chapter

Even when we are in good physical and mental health, satisfied with our work and enjoying the support of family and friends, we may search for something more: a supreme happiness, peacefulness, or sense of security which we feel is attainable, but only glimpse every now and then.

There is an unending reservoir of peace, happiness, joy and security within each of us. Some of us seem to have an easier time tapping into this reservoir than others. Yet for all of us, it is there. This is the real self, which many people call the soul or Spirit. Each of us must find this higher inner self and create a solid bond with it, in order to fulfill our search for happiness and peace.

When we define ourselves, we often describe in great detail our physical and mental attributes, our skills and gifts, our activities, personal relationships, likes and dislikes. Yet we may remain quite unaware of the elements of our real inner selves.

Our bodies get older, but our real selves are ageless. As we grow and learn, we become wiser and more knowledgeable. But the real self is beyond knowledge. It is the source of all wisdom. The inner self remains whole and unchanged, even as we mature, age, suffer, grow, experience the joys and sorrows of life and change in other ways.

As difficult as it is to describe or locate the mind, it is even harder to define the true self. Many of us may feel with certainty that it exists, and have a definite idea of what it is, without being able to explain it in any logical way. We sense that like the mind, it is without any apparent physical existence. Perhaps it is some product or extension of the mind.

Throughout human history, the nature of the true self or Spirit has been a topic of great importance. Its study has been central to religion, which is based on the connection between the individual spirit and an infinite, all-powerful Spirit, commonly referred to as God. Religion is the structure through which most people seek to discover their true selves, and acknowledge their connection to God.

Why a Spiritual Quest?

At times we may wonder about our own consciousness, and its origin, purpose, and uniqueness. As we contemplate the nature of our minds, we may wonder how the mind is able to question itself. These same questions have puzzled philosophers, scientists and theologians throughout human history.

We may also wonder who we really are. Each of us seems to have a definite sense of identity: we know the difference between ourselves and others; we all have a deep understanding of our meaning when we use the terms "I" and "me." Yet is our self-perception ever identical to others' perceptions of us? How is our understanding of ourselves influenced by our culture or other external forces? The mystery of who we are, of which self-concept is the most accurate, is an extremely important but complex question.

Our minds perceive, analyze, categorize, reason and decide. If provided with enough information, we can solve almost any problem. But our minds do not have the necessary information to answer such questions as:

- "Where do I come from?"
- "Who am I?"
- "Where do I go when I die?"
- "Is there a purpose to life?"

Our inability to answer these questions creates anxiety in us. In an attempt to alleviate our anxiety, many of us look to religion. Religion allows us to express our spirituality, and look beyond restraints of logic and reason for answers to our questions.

Many people believe in their experiences of intuition and precognition. Some people also claim to obtain revelations from God. These communications from God to the human mind usually occur during meditation or prayer. For people who experience revelations, it is evident that there is a greater energy beyond what we perceive in the physical world. If the mind can connect to this energy and transcend the body, then it is possible that something of the mind is able to survive in some form after the death of the body.

Establishing spiritual harmony gives us the ability to live a happier and more productive life.

In today's fast-paced technological society, we often feel alienated from the world around us, from nature, other people, and our own spirituality. Modern-day life and stresses dull our sensitivity and distract us with more pressing practical concerns. Yet as our feelings of alienation grows, we become more and more ill at ease with a mechanical, monotonous and superficial culture. Increasing anxiety can deteriorate the image we have of ourselves; in other words, it can damage our identity.

A spiritual quest is necessary to answer our questions of identity and purpose. We must strive to discover our true selves, and celebrate our connection with humanity and the Divine.

Why a God? The Mind Questions the Existence of God

God is the focus or personification of that spiritual energy which is greater than our individual selves. It is the omniscient consciousness we attach to the unknown. The superior intelligence is conceived by humans, yet we recognize that it is not comprehensible to humans. God, known throughout the world as Allah, Yahweh, Brahma, or any one of a hundred other names, remains an abstract entity which we cannot fully understand, because it is greater than the realm of our minds. Yet God, the creative Spirit behind everything, manifests in everything, and these manifestations can be perceived by humans.

Not everyone believes in God. *Atheists* deny the existence of any type of god or gods, and have no religious beliefs or practices. *Agnostics* do not reject the possibility that a God exists, nor do they accept it; they feel that there is not enough information to draw any conclusions about God.

On the other hand, believers, have faith in the existence of a higher spiritual entity or force of some sort. By believing in God, a person's universe becomes more comprehensible.

- The existence of God gives people a sense of purpose and continuity. The idea that we are created from divine energy, and will return to the Spirit realm, helps us see all life as sacred.

- In times of difficulty and tragedy, belief in God and a divinely ordered universe provides solace: one knows that everything happens according to God's plan, even if the reason is unclear.
- A benign God who is omniscient and omnipotent will listen and care, help, heal, and offer answers to the mysteries of life.
- God provides an ideal of spirituality towards which we can strive. This inspires us to expand our knowledge of ourselves and to fulfill our potential. As our world becomes increasingly complex, the path towards inner peace and contentment becomes all the more important to our well-being.

The Proofs of God

Many philosophers and theologians throughout the ages have tried to demonstrate or refute the existence of God. St. Thomas Aquinas, in the thirteenth century, proposed the following arguments as the ways through which the mind can unequivocally reason the existence of God:

1. Argument for the "unmoved mover": The world is made of motion. Everything we know is moved by the action of something else. This something else must therefore have been put into motion itself at some previous time. If we continue to trace back to the first mover, we see that the first mover must be something which was capable of putting itself into motion. This could only be God.
2. Argument for the "first cause": Everything we know is caused or brought into being by another: the pot is fashioned by a potter, who came to be from the union of his parents, who were the product of their parents and so forth. Everything can be traced back through a chain of causes to the first cause: God.
3. Argument for time and eternity: Everything on earth (even mountains and rivers) eventually disappears. Even stars are born and collapse. We can reason that our own planet will one day cease to exist. If all things are caused by another, there must be at least one eternal cause which is independent of time, birth or death: God.
4. Argument for a goal: Everything we know of in the world is in motion towards a goal. In the same way that a

man directs an arrow toward a target, there must be a divine intelligence to direct all things towards their goals: God.

Of course, throughout the ages, there have been many arguments against the existence of God as well. Some have reasoned that the existence of God does not match what can be observed in nature. Similarly, there are many arguments against the need for a God to explain the creation of the universe.

Why a Religion?

Looking back upon the great living religions – those which were founded hundreds, even thousands of years ago, and still have millions of followers – we see the many ways in which they are beneficial to society:

- Gods, spirits and religious myths have been the source of many artistic masterpieces, such as the cave paintings of Lascaux in France, Michaelangelo's frescoes, Mozart's Requiem and the Reclining Buddha of Sri Lanka.
- A code of behavior based on the will of God provides structure and direction in life. All known religions have rules of morality to guide our relationships with others in society.
- Religion brings people together and creates a form of social commitment between them, even as each pursues his or her individual religious path.
- The rituals of religion mark the passage of time and validate the changes and events in life. The sharing of joy and sorrow gives people a sense of self-worth, and increases community cohesiveness and pride.
- Rituals and prayer give believers a sense of control over their environment. Today, as was true in primitive societies, one can beseech God for assistance. If God does not respond (by not sending rain, healing the sick, providing solutions to financial difficulties etc.), it is thought to be due to one's own lack of faith or incompetence in performing a ritual. Our feeling of control, however unwarranted, does reduce anxiety.

Religion binds people to God by celebrating the Spirit in each person, and its connection to the greater Spirit, of which we all are part. Recognizing our connection to God gives us a sense of belonging, purpose, and common destiny.

Origins and Development of Religions

We do not know precisely when or how religion began, but it appears to have existed in all human societies of the world.
- Among Neanderthals and Cro-Magnons, elements of burial practices and the possible existence of a bear cult suggest religious beliefs.
- Ancient rock paintings indicate the presence and leadership of shamans.
- Female clay figures are linked to rites of fertility and beliefs associated with a mother-goddess or goddess of bounty.
- Early religious beliefs were closely linked to the forces of nature.

With the development of agriculture and settlements, the tools that permitted humans to work the earth or dominate nature (axes, plows, spears, etc.) took on religious significance. Burial sites also became increasingly complex. Stone monuments became more prominent. Stones were not only worshipped as part of nature, but also manipulated to create sacred sites. Archeologists have discovered many monuments built to allow astronomical sightings as well. The best known example of these is at Stonehenge, in England. Astronomy plays an important role in the history of many religions.

Religions gradually evolved into complex, highly structured systems of symbols, myths, and rituals which established an order that humans could comprehend, influence, and depend upon. The word "religion" itself, from the Latin, speaks of observances that promote a tie or bond, and mutual obligatory reciprocity.

Common Elements of Religions

Religions are like different rays of the same light, separated as the light travels through a prism, each appears a different color and quality.

The religions of the world, from the prehistoric past to the present, are structurally similar in many ways. Their practices require prayer, worship and other rituals.

Rituals

Religious rituals are used to communicate with God in worship or supplication, or to acknowledge events which are part of the divine plan.
- A ritual common to all known religions is sacrifice or offerings. Worshipers endure some hardship or give something they value to pay homage to their God. The Aztecs sacrificed prisoners of war, believing that the Gods needed blood to maintain their strength. Catholics abstain from eating meat at certain times of year. Many cultures give offerings of food and other necessities to their priests, who accept the offerings on behalf of God.
- Most religions hold regular public services, in which rituals are performed for the purpose of worship. Attendance is often required by religious law or tradition.
- Many religious rituals celebrate the change of seasons and other natural occurrences. In primitive agricultural societies, rituals were performed to bring rain and to ensure a bountiful harvest. Hunters ritually entreated the gods for plentiful game.
- Other rituals celebrate the important events of human life, and serve as *rites of passage*. They help to diminish one's anxiety as he or she prepares to take up a new role in life, and officially announce the new role to the community. Most religions ritually commemorate the birth and naming of children, puberty or some other passage into adulthood, marriage and death. Many cultures have rituals of *ordination* for persons who assume a religious office or other important community role.
- Rituals also celebrate important dates in the history of the religion, such as the birth or death of its founder and

other important persons; visions, miracles and other profound events; and times of great suffering or triumph.

Parables

Religions rely on parables to explain their origins, beliefs and customs. Creation parables explain the origin of the world, its laws of operation, and the role of humans in it. Many rituals and customs are parables or symbolic reenactments of events. The custom of placing the star on the top of the Christmas tree, for example, signifies a star which was said to appear on the night of the birth of Jesus Christ.

Mysticism

An element of mysticism is common to all religions. All known religions have procedures for obtaining control over events or manipulating natural and supernatural forces.
- Ritual imitation of mythical figures can fill a person with their powers.
- Objects that belonged to, or were closely associated with a sacred spot or person can still hold power.
- Certain objects, often called *fetishes,* are thought to hold powers because of their appearance or origin. Relics from saints and martyrs are among these. Native American children were given small bear figurines carved from red stones – red bear fetishes – to prevent them from getting lost. The Christian priest performs a ritual which imbues the communion wafer with the sacred powers of Christ's body.

Prayer & Worship

Some form of prayer is used in all religions to address sacred spirits or gods. Prayers can contain some or all of the following elements: adoration, confession, promises, thanksgiving, and supplication. They can follow a ritual formula or be like an informal conversation with God, can be spoken or sung aloud (in groups or alone) or recited only in one's mind.

All religions entail worship. While some religions worship objects as sacred in themselves, others worship the Spirit or sacred energy inherent in an object. Still other religions worship a more abstract sacred force, of which certain objects are only symbols or tools to focus the mind. The God or sacred energy of these religions is more powerful and transcendent than the others.

The Holy Ones

God is too great to be fully understood. How can we as individuals communicate with a God who is beyond our comprehension? How can we know what God expects of us? How can we discover the will of God?

These questions have given rise to the classes of religious officials and specialists who act as intermediaries between the people and their gods. We know them as priests, shamans, nuns, monks, ministers, and other types of clergy people. In the history of many cultures, the religious specialist also acted as a healer, leader, diviner, philosopher, or teacher. The holy man or woman of primitive societies was often responsible for the physical and spiritual well-being of the tribe and its individual members. Even now, religious specialists are often seen as community leaders, and many are involved in education and health care.

Religious specialists guide the prayers and rituals used to communicate with God. They study and interpret the scriptures of their religion, and with enhanced knowledge guide their people in spiritual growth. The leaders assure us that the experience of God is within our reach. They also maintain sanctuaries and shrines, and care for religious objects.

Common Elements of the Great Living Religions

Sacred Places

Sacred places are believed to help us concentrate on our spiritual endeavors. Some special event may have happened there, or a sacred object may be kept there. (These include the grotto of Lourdes, the Bo tree of the Buddha, birthplaces of saints and prophets, relics of saints).

Places of Worship

Places of worship (churches, temples and mosques) are chosen or built in order to establish a sacred place, conducive to meditation, prayer or illumination.

Sacred Texts and Scriptures

These are considered to be divinely inspired. They may have been orally transmitted for thousands of years before being written down, and therefore remain anonymous. (The Vedas, the Old Testament.) Or they may have been told to a prophet through revelation, or be a compilation of discourses, prayers, hymns, and myths. (The Koran, the Guru Grant Sahib of the Sikhs.) These texts often explain the relationship of the creator and its creation, as well as the rules of spiritual and social behavior.

Clerics and Holy People

These individuals devote their lives to their religion. They can be spiritual leaders, readers and interpreters of sacred texts, counselors, or intermediaries between laypersons and God. They may also live as hermits and devote themselves entirely to prayer.

Rituals and Ceremonies

Rituals appease, supplicate, or bind people to their God. They establish a predictable order of events that mark life with successive milestones of commitment to God and the community.

The Great Living Religions

Learning about spiritual beliefs and practices other than our own teaches us respect, compassion, and love for humanity.

Today there are hundreds of religions in practice throughout the world. Of the major religions, four were founded in India: Hinduism, Buddhism, Jainism and Sikhism. Taoism and Confucianism originated in China. Shinto was the religion of Japan. Iran gave birth to

Zoroastrianism. The Near and Middle East saw the founding of Judaism, Christianity and Islam.

Of all these religions, Hinduism, Shinto and Judaism have existed for so long that we have no historical documentation of their origins, although Abraham is believed to be the founder of Judaism, and the sages of India (known as *Rishis*, are said to have created Hinduism from the direct inspiration of God. Even less is known about the origins of Shinto.

Confucianism and Zoroastrianism take their names directly from their founders: Confucius, the sixth century BC philosopher who preached ethical conduct and devotion to family and society; and Zoroaster, a Persian religious teacher from the sixth or seventh century, BC. Jainism, Buddhism, and Christianity refer to the titles given to their founders: a Jain is a conqueror who overcomes in a spiritual way, as did its founder, Vardhamana. Buddha, the Enlightened One, was born Siddartha Gautama, and Jesus became known as Christ, the Anointed One.

Taoism, Sikhism and Islam refer to a certain path prescribed by the religion itself. Tao is Chinese for "the Way," implying the harmonious way the universe exists, and the way humans should live, in harmony with all things. A Sikh is, literally, a disciple; one who follows the religious path of Sikhism. Islam is an Arabic word which means "submission"; in terms of the religion, it means "Submission to the Will of Allah."

Religious Affiliations of the People of the World	
33%	Christians
	Catholic 19%
	Orthodox 3%
	Protestant 11%
17%	Moslems
13%	Hindus
6.5%	Buddhists
1%	Taoists
0.5%	Jews
9%	other religions
20%	non-religious

Hinduism

Hinduism is always changing and adapting to its cultural environment. It is not so much one religion, as a whole family of faiths shared by the many people of India.
- Hindus can choose from many systems and practices. They can select to belong to a temple and become members of a congregation, or to establish a direct mystical connection with the Brahma, the name of God.
- A Hindu can choose a quiet lifestyle of asceticism and contemplation, or a more active life as a householder and member of society.
- Because Hinduism is extremely complicated, a personal *Guru*, or spiritual master, is of great importance in practicing the proper devotions and following the path to God through this religious system.

The Sacred Hindu Texts

The oldest Hindu sacred writings are the *Vedas* or "Sacred Knowledge."
- The Vedas are made up of four parts, which together form the *Samhita,* and are believed to have been written between 3100 BC and 2000 BC.
- These texts are the oldest religious scriptures known today.
- Three of the Vedas are books of hymns, and the fourth book contains magic spells.
- The Vedas were later supplemented by the *Brahmas,* which explained the proper uses of the hymns and prayers.
- The Forest Books, *Aramyakas,* were created for those who chose to live in isolated areas for the purpose of devotion to meditation and prayer.
- Philosophical treatises known as the *Upanishads* are the most recent addition to the Vedas. They elaborate on the use of hymns, and explain the relationship between Brahma and the individual soul or *atman*. The Upanishads date from around 900 AD.
- The Vedas and the commentaries are considered to be the original, divinely inspired texts of Hinduism. The Vedas describe the belief in Brahma, the absolute God, who can be reached through the invocation of his manifestations as the numerous Hindu Gods, and by the

use of special ceremonies, prayers, and sounds. (See *Mantras*.)
- In the *Bhagavad-Gita*, (a poem that is part of a longer epic) the method for achieving oneness with God is revealed in a dialogue between Lord Krishna and Prince Arjuna. It entails proper knowledge (Jnana), pure devotion (Bhakti) breath control (Prana Yana), and right action (Karma).
- The Upanishads, which take the form of a dialogue, were probably written at least in part by members of the military caste, *Kshatriyas*, who were second only to the Brahmans. The Upanishads portrayed women as equal to men in their ability to succeed in spiritual endeavors. They also advocated asceticism, at a time when many Brahmans retreated into the forests.

Asceticism and Moksha

Asceticism is greatly valued in Hinduism, where self-inflicted deprivation and renunciation is considered equal to the sacrifices made at the altar. It is up to the individual to choose modes of renunciation that are compatible with his or her situation in life; however, certain renunciations are commonly expected:
- Intoxicants, illicit sex, and all types of violence are abhorred.
- Vegetarianism is strongly encouraged, both as an austerity and to avoid harm to animals.

Asceticism and meditation together can free one to move from the material body into the realm of the spirit. There one can join with Brahma, the all-inclusive and eternal being, with whom humans long for reunification.
- Union with God provides deliverance from life and its pain.
- All manifested things are not completely real; they constitute *maya*, (illusion) as opposed to Brahma, the only real, undeniable, and eternal being.
- The human soul is part of the eternal soul of Brahma: it is *Sat-Cit-Ananda*, Being, Consciousness and Bliss, and as such it longs for mystical union with God.
- Material things are of only passing value: they cannot be shared without decreasing; they cannot be kept after death; even during one's lifetime, riches, health or

happiness are easily lost. Material wants are never satisfied: the more one acquires, the more one desires.
- Spiritual attainments, however, are of eternal value. Once acquired, they remain with one and assure a better situation in the next life, as explained in the Law of Karma. If one shares spiritual values, he or she gains in generosity, compassion, and mercy.
- Only total absorption in spiritual practice can guarantee *Moksha*, liberation from the material plane. Such liberation will automatically bring consciousness of one's real being, and consequently, Bliss (Ananda).
- Moksha is the highest and most sought-after goal of any Hindu. By attaining Moksha, one experiences Nirvana, the sweetness of which cannot be described by words. The cycle of rebirth ends, and one escapes the Law of Karma.

The Law of Karma

The universe goes through cycles of creation, followed by total destruction, when the souls of all beings leave their bodies and remain suspended until a new cycle begins.
- During any cycle, the soul migrates from body to body after each death.
- One can be reborn in any other body – vegetable, animal or human – and into any caste.
- According to the Law of Karma, all of a being's thoughts, words and actions in one life have direct and absolute influence upon its future incarnations.

The Caste System

The four original castes of Indian society gradually separated into hundreds of sub–castes. The lowest group of people was pushed out of the castes altogether: they became known as *untouchables*. The Law of Karma gave a sort of moral justification to the caste system: No one should feel pity for people of the lower castes or the untouchables, because their situations were the direct result of their thoughts and actions in past lives. They were only getting what they deserved.

The Hindu God

Brahma is the eternal, undefinable, supreme God, who also manifests himself as Vishnu, Krishna, Shiva, and a number of other Gods and Goddesses. The Hindus believe in only one God, yet they worship the many manifestations of God. This is similar to the Christian doctrine of the Holy Trinity, in which the Father, Son, and Holy Spirit are different and simultaneous manifestations of the one God.

Quotes on Bhakti and the Availability of God, from the *Bhagavad-Gita*

The Blessed Lord said:

Attach your mind to Me; put your trust in Me; listen how you may come to know Me in my entirety with all doubt dispelled.

These sacred writings are derived from the wisdom of experiences I shall proclaim to you, leaving nothing unsaid.

Knowing these things, never again will any other thing remain that needs to be known.

Only one in a thousand will strive for self-perfection; and even among those few who strive, but one, maybe, will come to know Me as I really am.

Eight fold divided is my Nature – thus: Earth, water, fire, air, space, mind, soul and the ego.

This is the lower, but I also have a higher Nature. You must know this also.

And this Nature is seen as the life by which this universe is kept in being.

From these two Natures all beings take their origin. Be very sure of this.

In the whole universe the origin of the dissolution too am I.

Higher than Me there's nothing whatsoever.

On me the universe is strung like clustered pearls upon a thread.

In water I am the flavor, in sun and moon the light, in all the sacred words I'm the sound. In man I am.

Pure fragrance in the earth I am. A flame's beginning in the fire. In life I am in all contingent beings, in ascetics their fierce austerity.

Know that I am the eternal seed of all contingent beings: reason in the rational, glory in the glorious I am...

Buddhism

Buddhism came about as an effort to understand the nature of life and the suffering of the human existence. Westerners often believe that Buddhists do not believe in God, but this is not true. Buddhism does not have a set concept of God because it holds that one particular concept would be too limiting. Buddhists believe that such a limited view could not do justice to the absolute God. This absolute God is beyond the concepts of our human mind. They believe that a limited concept of God can only show relative truths, and not the real truth of God that is absolute and beyond logic.

The Buddha's Life

Buddhism was founded by Siddartha Gautama, who became known as the Buddha, the Enlightened One. Siddartha was born in 563 BC in the city of Kapilavastu, Northern India. He was the son of a king. His father was told by a diviner that the young Siddartha would either become the greatest king of all India, or he would give up the worldly life altogether. His father took great pains to ensure that his young son would not encounter any distressing sight that could lead him to renounce his great and glorious destiny.

Yet on an outing to the nearby village, young Siddartha saw a very old and frail man. Another time he saw a sick and infirm man. On a third outing he saw a corpse, and so the young prince came to know of the universal human fate of old age, disease and death. On a fourth outing however, Siddartha encountered a holy man, devoid of all luxury or even comfort, who seemed, none the less, totally content.

Siddartha continued to live a princely life, and was married at the age of sixteen to a distant cousin. Yet he was more and more attracted to the thought of leaving his household to pursue a spiritual quest. In his late twenties, Siddartha left home to begin a life of intense renunciation, which he would follow for six years.

Siddartha studied with various spiritual teachers and began a period of asceticism so severe that he became very emaciated and nearly died. Yet he did not feel any closer to enlightenment. Finally realizing that the path of starvation and denial would bring death sooner that enlightenment, he gave up his asceticism. This caused his companions to abandon and denounce him.

Left alone, Siddartha started a quiet meditation at a place now called *Bodhi-Gaya,* under a fig tree which became known as the *Bodhi tree,* or tree of knowledge. Through his meditation, Gautama suddenly received the revelation that became the Buddhist doctrine.

The essence of the Buddhist doctrine is that all suffering in life is due to the never-ending desires which cannot be fulfilled.

After his enlightenment, the Buddha faced a crucial decision: to enter Nirvana, or to remain on earth and help others to attain enlightenment. He chose to remain. The Buddha went to Benares, where he found his companions again. He won them over and they became his first disciples.

The order of monks grew rapidly, and was governed by definite rules:
- The initiates pledged to take refuge in the Buddha, the *Dharma* (Truth), and the *Sangha* (Order).
- The monks wore yellow robes and shaved their heads.
- They carried begging bowls, with which to beg for their food, and spent most of the day in meditation.

The Buddha continued to preach to a growing number of disciples, monks and nuns, including his son and many of his relatives. At the age of eighty, he died in the town of Kusinara. Buddha left his doctrine to those who came after him, and enjoined them to work out their own salvation.

The Buddhist Doctrine

Release from the pain of life, with its unending and unfulfilled desires, requires that one break the bonds of wrong attitudes and beliefs. One must then accept the *Four Noble Truths,* and live by the tenets of the *Eight-fold Path.* According to the Buddha, this would assure enlightenment.

Bonds that Need to be Broken to Ensure Salvation
- The three intoxications: greed, hatred and ignorance.
- The five hindrances: desire for sense-pleasing, ill will, sloth, restlessness and doubt.
- The ten fetters: belief in the existence of the self, doubt, trust in ceremonies and rituals, lust, anger and ill will, desire for rebirth in another form, desire for rebirth without form, pride, self-righteousness and ignorance.

The Four Noble Truths
1. Life is filled with suffering from birth to death.
2. This suffering is caused by a ignorance of the nature of reality and attachment and craving for worldly things.
3. Suffering will stop when one learns to overcoming ignorance and attachment.
4. The way to end suffering is by following the Eight-fold Path.

The Eight-fold Path
We can learn end suffering by following the Eight-fold Path:
1. Right belief (in the Four Noble Truths).
2. Right aspiration (purpose; overcoming sensuality and desires, and the belief in the sanctity of all life).
3. Right speech (speaking kindly and truthfully to all).
4. Right conduct (acting skillfully and righteously).
5. Right means of livelihood (earning one's living without harm to others).
6. Right effort (remaining alert and being discriminating).
7. Right mindfulness (controlling one's thoughts and emotions).
8. Right meditation (daily meditation that will lead to enlightenment).

Nirvana
Nirvana is the final goal of the Buddhist path. It is release from all illusion with its inherent suffering. Nirvana is an enlightened state in which greed, hatred, and ignorance are no longer in control.

Divisions of Buddhism
As Buddhism spread through India, it divided into two distinct traditions: *Mahayana* Buddhism, the greater

raft, and *Theravada* Buddhism, the lesser raft, which follows the teachings of the elders. These divisions were based on the way in which one was believed to reach Nirvana: alone, on a raft only big enough for one; or on the greater raft, with many other people.

Buddhism was also influenced by the countries to which it spread. It branched into *Zen* Buddhism in Japan, and into *Lamaism* in Tibet.

The Lesser Raft

In traditional or Theravada Buddhism, the all-important monk preaches self-reliance in the path towards enlightenment. It is believed that the Buddha has entered into Nirvana, and can no longer help anyone.

- Meditations on love, pity, joy, impurity and serenity are practiced daily.
- Buddha images are part of the Theravada tradition.
- Buddha is revered as a divine, perfect, and all-knowing being who came to Earth to preach the way. He has appeared on Earth many times before, and will return in the future.
- Sanctuaries exist for the purpose of pilgrimages, and special holidays are celebrated, principally on the Buddha's birthday, the day of his enlightenment, and the day of his death.
- In countries where Hinayana Buddhism predominates, most men are expected to spend three months of each year in monastic life.
- Yet for all the prayer, devotion, meditation and celebration, Theravadan Buddhists do not expect divine intervention. The name Hinayana itself, the lesser raft, represents the individual crossing the river to enlightenment alone, guided by no one, and guiding no one else.

The Greater Raft

Mahayana Buddhism believes that the greater raft, piloted by the Buddha, transports large numbers of devotees simultaneously. Mahayana Buddhism became popular in Northern India.

- In this tradition, Buddha is a divine being who has come to earth out of compassion for humans.

- Buddhas have come before, and those who will appear in the future are *Boddhisattvas*, (an individual who has attained perfect enlightenment.)
- or enlightenment is the standard that Buddhist should strive for.

Mahayana followers profess that Buddha himself, in his private teachings, described three kinds of Buddhas who can help one attain salvation:
- The *Manushi* Buddhas appear on earth, like Gautama himself.
- The Boddhisattvas exist in great numbers, and answer the appeals of mortals, like angels of compassion.
- The *Dhyani* Buddhas reside in heaven to inspire contemplation and peace.

Mahayana Buddhism spread into China, where it assimilated parts of Taoism and Confucianism, the religious systems already there. Later the Buddhist ideals of humanitarianism spread to Korea and Japan. China and Japan host a great pantheon of Boddhisattvas, including Goddesses of Mercy who parallel the Virgin Mary of the Catholic church.

In Tibet, Buddhism took on a third form. Here it is called Lamaism, after its high priest, the *Dalai Lama* or *Mantrayana* Buddhism, due to the importance of the mantras in the devotional service.

In Tibet, the Buddha of Mercy has a consort: Tara. From this arose *Tantra Yana* or the Buddhism of Tantra:
- Tantra holds a quasi-magical character, with elements of secrecy and the vital role of the spiritual master or guru.
- Sacred rites involving the body and mind must be performed in order to reach illumination. Such rites can include chanting mantras, consuming certain foods and beverages, and even performing sex acts.
- The belief that all things are produced by the union of male and female forces leads to the use of sex as an affirmation of the Oneness. Similarly, each God has his consort, and it is in union with his consort that he achieves the utmost power.
- Tara is generally the symbol of compassion, purity and piety, qualities which the Buddhist woman is expected to exemplify. Yet she can also take on other aspects, such

as the red Tara, who symbolizes wealth, or the yellow Tara, the embodiment of anger.

Zen Buddhism
Another form of Buddhism prevalent in Japan is Zen Buddhism, which uses meditation to attain sudden insight into the nature of the self.
- As in Hinayana Buddhism, salvation is an individual and solitary endeavor.
- Zen emphasizes practice and personal enlightenment rather than scripture study.
- Zen teachings are passed orally from Master to students.
- To achieve sudden awakening, one must get away from thinking in terms of duality, and go beyond the intellect and its questions.
- Sometimes a *koan*, or seemingly illogical problem, is given to students to encourage the necessary and sudden shift in thinking.
- Contemplation of nature and humanity is paramount to the practice of Zen; this has given rise to the celebrated Japanese art forms of poetry, flower arranging, decorative arts and the tea ceremony.

The Great Way
by Sengstan, Third Zen Buddhist Patriarch
The Great Way is not difficult
for those who have no preferences.
When love and hate are both absent
everything becomes clear and undisguised.
Make the smallest distinction, however,
and heaven and earth are set infinitely apart.
If you wish to see the truth
then hold no opinions for or against anything.
To set up what you like against what you dislike
is the disease of the mind.
When the deep meaning of things is not understood
the mind's essential peace is disturbed to no avail.

The Way is perfect like vast space
where nothing is lacking and nothing is in excess.
Indeed, it is due to our choosing to accept or reject
that we do not see the true nature of things.
Live neither in the entanglements of outer things,
nor in inner feelings of emptiness.

*Be serene in the oneness of things
and such erroneous views will disappear by themselves.
When you try to stop activity to achieve passivity
your very effort fills you with activity.
As long as you remain in one extreme or the other
you will never know Oneness.*

*Those who do not live in the single Way
fail in both activity and passivity,
assertion and denial.
To deny the reality of things
is to miss their reality.
To assert the emptiness of things
is to miss their reality.
The more you talk and think about it,
the further astray you wander from the truth.
Stop talking and thinking,
and there is nothing you will not be able to know.
To return to the root is to find the meaning,
but to pursue appearances is to miss the source.
At the moment of inner enlightenment
there is a going beyond appearance and emptiness.*

*The changes that appear to occur in the empty world
we call real only because of our ignorance.
Do not search for the truth;
only cease to cherish opinions.*

*Do not remain in the dualistic state;
avoid such pursuits carefully.
If there is even a trace
of this and that, of right and wrong,
the Mind essence will be lost in confusion.
Although all duality come from the One,
do not be attached even to this One.
When the mind exists undisturbed in the Way,
nothing in the world can offend,
and when a thing can no longer offend,
it ceases to exist in the old way...*

*With a single stroke we are freed from bondage;
nothing clings to us and we hold to nothing.
All is empty, clear, self-illuminating,
with no exertion of the mind's power.
Here thought, feeling, knowledge, and imagination*

are of no value.
In this world of Suchness
there is neither self nor other-than-self.

To come directly into harmony with this reality
just simply say when doubts arise, "Not two."
In this "not two" nothing is separate,
nothing is excluded.
No matter when or where,
enlightenment means entering this truth.
And this truth is beyond extension or
diminution in time or space;
in it a single thought is ten thousand years.
Emptiness here, Emptiness there,
but the infinite universe stands
always before your eyes.
Infinitely large and infinitely small;
no difference, for definitions have vanished
and no boundaries are seen.
So too with Being and non-Being.
Don't waste time in doubts and arguments
that have nothing to do with this.

One thing, all things:
move among and intermingle,
without distinction.
To live in this realization
is to be without anxiety about non-perfection.
To live in this faith is the road to non-duality
Because the non-dual is one with the trusting mind.

Words! The Way is beyond language,
for in it there is
>*no yesterday*
>*no tomorrow*
>*no today.*

Taoism

Taoism began in China around 500 BC. It has since influenced every aspect of Chinese culture.

The object of Taoism is to move closer to the divine way of life. The Taoist often avoids the worldly pursuits of money and power and devotes himself or herself to more fully understanding the Tao.

Taoism teaches that everything is basically one, despite the appearance of differences. It also states that problems arise only when people lose sight of this oneness. This concept is shown in the principle of yin/yang.

Yin forces are described as yielding, moving inward, darkly colored and concentrating. They are symbolized as feminine forces. Yang forces are described as confrontive, moving outward, expansive, lightly colored and are considered masculine. And the Universe is recognized as being formed of yin and yang forces in balance. This is represented by a circle divided into two half by an S-shaped line. One half of the circle is black and the other half is white. The white and black dots represent that yin contains an element of yang, and yang contains an element of yin.

Yin/yang Symbol

Tao Te Ching

The Tao Te Ching was said to be written about 2500 years ago in China by a man named Lao Tzu. *Tao* means path, way or truth. *Te* is power, and *Ching* means book. Tao Te Ching thus is translated *The Book on the Way and the Power*. The Tao Te Ching is short, (only 5280 Chinese characters) yet it is one of the greatest and most influential books ever written.

From chapter 1
The Tao that can be told of is not the Absolute Tao.
The names that can be given are not Absolute Names.
Naming anything relegates it to being a material thing
And not the creation of the Mother of all Things.

Therefore:
Reduce needs in order to see the Secret of Life.
Yet also live with passion in order to see its manifest forms.
Both actions are the same
but they are given different names.
They may both be called the Cosmic Mystery.

From chapter 2
When people know beauty as beauty then there also arises ugliness.
When people know good as good then there also arises evil.
So:
Being and non-being inter depend in growth
Difficult and easy inter depend in completion
Long and short inter depend in contrast
High and low inter depend in position
Tones and voice inter depend in harmony
Front and behind inter depend in company.
Therefore the man of wisdom:
Manages affairs with non interference
Preaches the doctrine without words.
All things flourish without interruption
He gives them life, but does not take possession of them.
He accomplishes but claims no credit.
Because he claims no credit
then credit cannot be taken away.

From chapter 9
Stretch a bow to the very full and you will wish you had stopped in time.
Temper a sword-edge to its very sharpest, and the edge will not last long.
When gold and jade fill your hall, you will not be able to keep them safe.
To be proud with honor is to sow the seeds of one's downfall.
Retire when your work is done.
Such is the way of the Tao.

From chapter 11
Thirty spokes unite at the hub.
From their loss of individuality
arises the utility of the wheel.
Mold clay into a jar,

and from its not-being (hollowness)
arises the utility of the jar.
Cut out doors and windows in a house,
from their emptiness arises the utility of the house.
Therefore by the existence of things we profit,
and from the non-existence of things we are served.

From chapter 67
All the world says that teaching the Tao is folly.
Because it is great it resembles folly.
If it did not resemble folly
it would long ago have become petty.
I have three treasures, guard them and keep them safe.
The first is love.
The second is moderation.
The third is humility.
Through love one drops fear.
Through moderation one is ample.
Through not presuming to be first in the world,
one develops full growth.

From chapter 76
When man is born he is tender and weak,
At death he is hard and stiff.
When plants are alive, they are soft and flexible.
When they are dead they are brittle and dry.
Hardness and stiffness are the companions of death.
Softness and gentleness are the companions of life.
Therefore when an army is too stiff it will lose in Battle.
When a tree is hard, it will be cut down.
The big and strong position is low.
The gentle and weak position is high.

From chapter 78
There is nothing more yielding than water.
Yet the soft water overcomes the hardest rock.
Weakness overcomes strength,
and gentleness overcomes rigidity.

Judaism

Deuteronomy 6
"Hear O Israel! The Lord our God, the Lord is One!
"And you shall love the Lord your God with all your heart and with all your soul and with all your might.
"And these words, which I am commanding you today shall be on your heart.
"And you shall teach them diligently to your sons and shall talk of them when you sit in your house and when you walk by the way and when you lie down and when you rise up."

Jews base their monotheistic religion on the belief in an omnipotent and unknowable God named Yahweh. Yahweh created everything: space and time, light, humans and animals, the planets, the sun, and the stars. This is explained in *Genesis*, the first book of the Bible.
- Yahweh is a benevolent God, most often portrayed as a merciful and caring father figure. He is a God of love, which is directed towards his chosen people, the Jews.
- Because God cannot be seen, attained or directly experienced, the proof of his love for his people must be found in his gifts to them of the land of Israel, and his laws to guide their lives.
- No matter how bad one's situation or sorrow may be, faith in Yahweh is a source of hope: a meaning can be derived from any situation, and a solution can be found.
- In Judaism, the material world is not dismissed, but rather incorporated into the constant search for meaning. All aspects of the world are important, because even the body and nature are part of salvation, and can be inhabited by God.
- Because life is considered to be good, and human society worth participating in, Judaism gave rise to a positive attitude towards progress and the ability of humans to change and improve their lives. Judaism has influenced both Christianity and Islam in this way.
- Humans are thought to be capable of self-direction; they have the ability to become almost Godlike, but they do not always have the strength or will to do so. They are created in the image of God, and can struggle to become sublime, yet they are frail and perishable, and easily led astray.

- Humans are seen as God's beloved children; God yearns for their love, and in turn they can be confident of always being accepted, loved and cared for by God.

Much of Western culture is influenced by Jewish thought.
- Our ideas about God and our moral values are shaped by Jewish ideology.
- Legal systems in the Western world are often based on Jewish philosophies.
- Both Islam and Christianity stem from Judaism.
- Our sciences, art, philosophy and other intellectual pursuits owe much to Jewish minds such as Albert Einstein and Sigmund Freud.

Abraham and the Origins of Judaism

Yahweh appeared to Abraham and made a special covenant with him. He made a promise of everlasting love and support for Abraham's people, and their descendants, as long as they continued to abide by His law.

Yahweh also promised Abraham a son. At the age of eighty-six, Abraham's son Ismael was born to his wife's slave girl, Hagar. When Abraham was one hundred, his son Isaac was born to his wife, Sarah, who was ninety years old at that time. Yahweh later demanded the life of Isaac as a sacrifice from Abraham as a test of faith. Because Abraham was willing to sacrifice even his son, Yahweh spared Isaac from death.

God demands the utmost obedience from his people, and their complete trust is ultimately rewarded.

Abraham was the first Jew chosen by God. Since God's covenant with Abraham, the Jewish people believe that they are God's chosen people, and that they receive the eternal love of their God.

The Torah

The Torah contains all the religious writings of Judaism. Many of these writings were given to the Jewish

people from God through revelations in words, and revelations in the history of the people themselves, through the acts of God. For example, God revealed to Abraham his covenant with the Jews. God led the Jews out of Egypt. He also revealed the *Ten Commandments* to Moses. The Torah contains all the following things, and much more.
- One part of the Torah is the *Talmud*. In the third century AD, the writings on Jewish civil and religious law were gathered to form the Talmud. It is composed of the *Mishnah*, which contains the laws themselves, and the *Gemara*, a collection of commentaries on the laws.
- These commentaries were written by different religious scholars, in Babylon and in Palestine.
- The Torah also contains the *Holy Scriptures*, known to Christians as the *Old Testament*.

The Ten Commandments

Over 600 commandments are found in the *Book of Leviticus* in the Bible. Of these, ten commandments are said to have been revealed to the prophet Moses by God himself. The Ten Commandments form the basis of the moral code of Judaism. They are listed as follows:

The Ten Commandments, from Exodus Chapter 20

Then God spoke saying all these words:

I am the Lord your God who brought you out of the land of Egypt, out of the house of bondage. You shall have no other gods before Me.

You shall not make yourself an idol or any likeness of anything that is in heaven above or on the earth beneath or in the water under the earth.

You shall not bow down or serve them; for I am a jealous God, visiting the iniquity of the fathers on the children, on the third and fourth generations of those who hate Me, but showing steadfast love and kindness to thousands, to those who love Me and keep My commandants.

You shall not take the name of the Lord your God in vain for the Lord will not leave him unpunished who takes His name in vain.

Remember the Sabbath day, to keep it holy. Six days you shall labor, and do all your work. But the seventh day is a Sabbath of the Lord your God. In it you will not do any work, you or your son or your daughter, your servant or your cattle or your sojourner who stays with you. In six days your Lord made heaven and earth, the sea, and all that is in them, and rested the seventh day. Therefore your Lord blessed the Sabbath day and made it holy.

Honor your father and your mother, that your days may be prolonged in the land which your Lord God gives you.

You shall not murder.
You shall not commit adultery.
You shall not steal.

You shall not bear false witness against your neighbor nor covet your neighbor's wife or his servant, or his ox or his donkey or anything that belongs to your neighbor.

The Hallowed Life

Psalm 23
The Lord is my shepherd; I shall not want.
He makes me lie down in green pastures,
He leads me beside still waters.
He restores my soul;
he guides me on paths of righteousness, for His name's sake.
Though I walk through the valley of the shadow of death,
I shall fear no evil, for You are with me.
Your rod and Your staff do comfort me.
You prepare a communion table before me in the presence of my enemies.
You anoint my head with oil, my cup overflows.
Surely goodness and mercy shall follow me all the days of my life;
And I will live in the house of the Lord forever.

Jewish teachings include many rules and rituals. These must be followed to ensure that one's daily life is sacred, or "true to the Torah." The practice of the rituals and observances has been tremendously relaxed in the Western world, but orthodox Jews still follow them in the strict, traditional manner.
- Prayers are said three times a day.
- A blessing must be said over every meal.
- All newborn males are circumcised, as a sign of God's covenant with the Jews.

- Marriage is sacred, because the union of man and woman brings forth children for the glory of God. Procreation in marriage is seen as the duty of all Jews.
- A good family life is believed to ensure happiness and longevity.
- Dietary laws are complex. For instance, one may eat cows but not camels, because cows are cloven-footed, whereas camels have a solid hoof. Aquatic animals can only be consumed if they have fins and scales. Scavengers such as bottom-feeding fish and shellfish are not permitted. Animal flesh and dairy products cannot be served together, or from the same dishes. Animals must be killed quickly, followed by a ritual blood-letting.
- Food that is obtained or prepared according to Jewish dietary laws is said to be *kosher*.
- Being charitable and helpful to others is required of all Jews. Forgiving debts, tithing, giving alms, and so forth, are thought to be very pleasing to God.

Ecclesiastics Chapter 3

For everything there is a season and a time for every event under heaven:
A time to be born and a time to die;
A time to plant, and a time to harvest;
A time to kill, and a time to heal;
A time to tear down, and a time to build up;
A time to weep, and a time to laugh;
A time to mourn, and a time to dance;
A time to throw away stones, and a time to gather stones;
A time to embrace, and a time to shun embracing;
A time to seek, and a time to lose;
A time to keep, and a time to throw away;
A time to tear apart, and a time to sew together;
A time to be silent, and a time to speak;
A time to love, and a time to hate;
A time for war, and a time for peace.
What profit has the worker from his toils?

Islam

The word *Islam* means peace or surrender. To be Islamic is to be at peace with the will of Allah (God) or to surrender or submit to the will of Allah. The credo of Islam tells much about the religion: *"La ilaha illa Allah, Mohammedan rasul Allah,"* which means, "There is no God but God, Mohammed is His prophet."

Followers of Islam believe that there is no reality except God; and nothing but God exists. This belief dominates all aspects of life in Muslim countries, where laws and traditions are defined by the essential act of submission to Allah. Social interaction, family relationships, and private life are all subject to Muslim law.

The Life of Mohammed

Mohammed was born around the middle of the sixth century AD in Mecca, which is now the religious capital of Saudi Arabia. Mohammed grew up amidst political and spiritual chaos. There was little social cohesion, and no predominant legal system, moral code, or religion to regulate behavior.

Mohammed spent long hours in solitude, meditating and praying to Allah. He believed Allah was the only true God. Mohammed was concerned with the gross immorality of the teeming city, and hoped, through his prayers, to find a way to bring order to Mecca.

An angel appeared to Mohammed one night, and proclaimed to him that Allah was the only God. This night is known as the Night of Power, when peace fell over the entire earth.

Mohammed is said to be he last of a long line of Muslim prophets that include Moses and Jesus. Because he is the last, he is known as the Seal of the Prophets.

Mohammed received his first revelation when he was forty years old. The revelations continued over the next twenty-three years, sometimes through voices, sometimes as a single voice of the angel Gabriel. Often the revelations had a physical effect on Mohammed: he trembled, shook and cried out. These revelations were repeated by Mohammed and written down by his disciples on whatever was at hand. (There was no paper in Arabia at that time.)

Mohammed also told of having been flown to the highest realm of Heaven, where God himself entreated him to ask men to pray fifty times each day. Upon his descent, Mohammed met Moses, another prophet of Islam, who sadly acknowledged that the common man was incapable of such dedication to God. Mohammed was sent back several times to negotiate with God, until it was agreed that men would pray five times each day.

The Koran

The revelations of Mohammed were recorded by his disciples as verses. Verses were grouped into chapters or *surahs*, which together form the *Qu'ran* (or the *Koran*, as it is more commonly known), the holy book of Islam.

Because it came directly from God to Mohammed, and was transcribed immediately by the disciples of Mohammed, most Muslims believe in the absolute authenticity and infallibility of the Koran.

- The Koran is comprised of 114 surahs.
- It is meant to continue the teachings of the Old and New Testaments of the Bible.
- The Koran is best recited in its original Arabic, in which it has an especially rhythmic and poetic form.
- Unlike the Bible, historical events and heroes are usually only alluded to in the Koran, often out of context.
- In the Koran, God explains that he is forever forgiving, and always accessible: at any time a person can ask God for pardon, courage, and hope. There are no barriers between God and his people.
- God is absolute good, therefore his creation is also good. In this way, material possessions and wealth are considered to be good.
- Each Muslim has a unique path to follow, through which he can glorify God.
- Muslims believe that they are free; that their souls are free. Each individual is responsible for living right, or for going astray into forgetfulness and sin.
- No one can hide from God. On Judgment Day, everyone's actions will be recalled and examined, and people will be sent to Heaven (a cool place of waterfalls and fountains) or to Hell.
- The Koran speaks more about action than about ideas: its doctrine focuses upon the creation of the world by Allah, the freedom of the individual soul, the judgment to come, and most of all the omnipresent, omniscient, omnipotent nature of Allah.
- The Koran allows a man to have up to four wives, but today most unions in the Muslim world are monogamous.

- Women were enjoined to cover themselves and remain modest in appearance and behavior.

Islam does not preach pacifism. It advocates defending against "enemies." But it does not encourage conversion by force: only by right example and rational persuasion can non believers be brought to join the ranks of Islam.

Quotes from *The Koran*
Sura 9:1-10
By the white forenoon and the brooding night!
The Lord has neither forsaken you nor hates you and the last shall be better for you than the first.
The Lord will give to you and you will be satisfied.
Did He not find you an orphan and shelter you?
Did He not find you erring and guide you?
Did He not find you needy and suffice you?
As for the orphan, do not oppress him. And as for the beggar, scold him not. And as for your Lord's blessing, declare it.

Divisions in Islam

The most predominant groups are the *Shi'ites*, the *Sunnis*, and the *Sufis*. The Shi'ites are growing at a faster pace than other groups of Muslims, though Islam in general is growing rapidly. Today there are as many as 900 million Muslims.

Sunnis and Shi'ites

Sunnis, the traditionalists of Islam, comprise 85% of the Muslim population, while Shi'ites make up most of the remaining 15%. The Shi'ites differ with the Sunnis primarily on the basis of the order of succession of religious leadership. The Shi'ites believe that Mohammed's son-in-law Ali should have succeeded Mohammed directly, as the first supreme ruler of Islam. Instead, Ali's succession was delayed by three others. This is a division of historical character. The Shi'ites are much more fundamentalist in their beliefs, than are the Sunnis.

Sufis and Whirling Dervishes

The Sufis (from *suf* or wool, because they wear coarse woolen garments) arose in protest to the worldliness

of later Islam. These mystics spend a great amount of time in the contemplation of Allah, hoping to know him during their lifetimes.
- The Sufis have developed their own rituals of worship involving music, dances, prayers and group repetition of the names of Allah. (Such repetitions are called *dhirk*, or remembrance.)
- Sufi poetry is known and admired throughout the world; it describes the longing for God.
- Through love and the opening of the heart to all creation, one encounters the Divine.
- Much symbolism is used to ascend towards God by degrees, until a complete extinction of the self is accomplished and separation from God disappears.
- Some Sufis claim direct knowledge of God, which goes against Muslim orthodoxy.
- Most Sufis receive their teaching from sheiks of a certain line of transmission of the tradition. The *whirling dervishes* of Kona in Turkey represent such a line.
- The dervishes dedicate themselves to a life of poverty and chastity. As a religious act, they may chant or whirl.

A Sufi Prayer

Towards the One
The perfection of love, harmony and beauty.
The only being.
United with all the illuminated souls,
who form the embodiment of the Master.
The Spirit of Guidance.

When you pray, enter the room as if for the last time.
When you love, give all that you are, saving none for yourself.

When you desire, desire me so completely that you are totally dependent that I come.
Every time you come to me, let part of you die in my heart.

Seek me, knowing there is no other way out.

Fall down and collapse in my presence so that I have no choice than to pick you up and carry you.

When you prepare to join me, say good-by to everything you know.

Every time you approach me be certain that you will never leave the same.

And when we have union, hope that no part of you survives to again separate, needing to pray, love, or desire again.

Have no thoughts, no trust, no vision of tomorrow, for it does not exist.

Spread yourself entirely before me, hiding nothing from my view.

Let your heart scream of peace, singing in the silence, until everything ends and I begin.

Christianity

The Old Testament prophecy of the appearance on Earth of the Messiah, who is the son of God, forms the basis of Christianity. Christians believe that it was fulfilled by the birth of Jesus of Nazareth two thousand years ago. Jesus, born in a stable in Nazareth, was called by his followers Christ, the Anointed One. At the time Jesus Christ was crucified, he had only a few hundred followers. Today there are about 1.6 billion Christians throughout the world.

The Life of Jesus

Around the age of thirty, Jesus started preaching. He also healed people with his touch, and raised the dead. Jesus was a Jew and, at first, his attraction was mostly to Jews by fulfilling what God had promised to Abraham, Isaac, and Jacob. A few years later, his teachings incurred the wrath of the Romans who had him executed as a criminal.

- Jesus taught that the day of judgment was approaching. He called for drastic changes in the way people lived so they might be judged worthy of going to Heaven.
- Through the use of parables, Jesus encouraged people to be compassionate and forgiving, and to care for the poor and sick. He believed that everyone was capable of choosing to live a peaceful and loving life.
- Jesus exemplified his teachings in his own life by loving and caring for everyone he met, refusing to use violence

even to protect himself and by forgiving those who hurt him, even those who had him put to death.
- Jesus loved all people, regardless of class or condition.
- Christians believe that Jesus was resurrected after his death. Several days after his burial, his tomb was found empty. Some of his followers claim that he appeared before them in the flesh, with a solid body and apparent wounds from his crucifixion. Others said that he appeared to them as a spirit. After that he is believed to have ascended into heaven.
- While Islam and Judaism view Jesus as only one of God's chosen prophets, Christianity was founded on the belief that Jesus is actually the son of God, who came in fulfillment of the prophecies of the Old Testament.

The Gospels

The Bible is the sacred book of Christianity. It contains the *Old Testament,* written before Jesus, and the *New Testament,* which is based on the belief that Jesus was the prophesied Messiah and the son of God. The Old Testament is identical to the Scriptures of the Jewish Torah, and explains how God created the world.

The miracles and teachings of Jesus are known through the *Gospels,* which are said to be the accounts of four of his disciples: John, James, Mark, and Luke. The Gospels are a part of the New Testament, which also contains the *Acts of the Apostles,* the *Epistles,* and numerous writings and discourses added throughout the ages by philosophers and mystics, telling of their personal knowledge of God, or attempting to prove his existence.

Jesus' famous Sermon on the Mount (recounted in Matthew, Chapters 5 through 7) incorporates much of the essence of Christianity. (Another account of the Sermon on the Mount can be found in Luke, Chapters 11 and 12.)

The Sermon on the Mount

And when he saw the crowds he went up on a mound and sat down. His disciples assembled near him and he began to teach them saying,

Blessed are the poor in spirit for theirs is the kingdom of God.

Blessed are those who suffer for they will be comforted.

Blessed are the meek for they will inherit the earth.

Blessed are those who hunger and thirst for righteousness for they will be satisfied.

Blessed are the merciful for they will receive mercy.

Blessed are the pure in heart, for they will see God.

Blessed are the peacemakers, for they will be called the sons of God.

Blessed are those who have been persecuted for the sake of righteousness for the kingdom of God is theirs...

You have heard that it was said "An eye for an eye and a tooth for a tooth." But I say to you do not resist an evil man. If he slaps you on your right cheek, turn the other cheek to him also.

If he wants to sue you and take your shirt, let him have your coat also. If he forces you to go one mile, go two miles with him.

Give to him who asks of you and do not deny he who wants to borrow from you.

You have heard that it was said "You shall love your neighbor and hate your enemy." But I say to you love your enemies and pray for those who persecute you so that you may be the son of your father in heaven; for it is He who causes the sun to rise on the evil and the good and sends rain to the righteous and the unrighteous.

For if you do good only to those who do good to you: Don't even tax collectors do the same?

And if you greet your brothers only what do you do more than others? Don't even the Gentiles do the same? Therefore be merciful, just as your Father is merciful.

Beware of doing your righteous acts in public to be noticed by others. When you give charity don't sound a trumpet as the hypocrites do in the churches and in the streets so that men will praise them.

But when you give charity do not let your left hand know what your right hand is doing. Keep your charity a secret; and your Father who sees in secret will compensate you.

And when you pray don't be like the hypocrites who love to stand and pray in the churches and street corners so that men will see them. But when you pray go into your inner room and shut the door and pray to your Father in secret and your Father will repay you.

And in your prayers don't use meaningless repetition as the non-believers do, for they suppose that they will be heard because of their many words. Don't be

like them; for your Father knows what you need before you ask Him. But pray in this way:
> *Our Father who art in heaven*
> *Hallowed be Thy name.*
> *Thy kingdom come*
> *Thy will be done,*
> *On earth as it is in heaven.*
> *Give us this day our daily bread*
> *And forgive our debts as we also have forgiven our debtors.*
> *And do not let us enter into temptation, but deliver us from evil. For Thine is the kingdom and the power and the glory forever. Amen.*

Do not lay up treasures on earth, where moth and rust destroy and where thieves break in and steal. But lay up treasures in heaven where neither moth nor rust destroy, and where thieves do no break in or steal. For where your treasure is, there will your heart be also...

For this reason I say to you, do not be anxious for your life, for what you will eat, or what you will drink, or for what you will wear. Is life not more than food and the body more than clothing?

Look at the birds of the sky: They neither sow nor reap, they have no storeroom nor gather into barns and yet God feeds them. Are you not worth much more than they?

And which of you by being anxious can add a day to his life? And why do you worry about clothing? Consider the lilies of the field, how they grow: They neither toil nor spin. Yet I say to you that even Solomon in all his glory did not clothe himself like one of these.

Therefore if God so arrays the grass in the field, which is alive today and tomorrow is thrown into the furnace, won't he do much more for you, O men of little faith?

So don't be anxious about these things for your Father knows that you need all these things. But seek first the kingdom of God and all these things shall then be given to you. Do not be afraid for your Father has chosen to give you the kingdom. Therefore do not be worried about tomorrow; for tomorrow will care for itself.

Do not judge and you will not be judged. For in the same way that you judge people, you yourself will be judged.

And why do you look at the speck of sawdust in your brother's eye, but do not notice the log that is in your own eye? Or how can you say to your brother, "let me take the speck of sawdust out of your eye," and behold, the log is in your own eye? You hypocrite, first take the log out of your own eye, and then you will see clearly enough to take the speck out of your brother's eye.

Do not give what is holy to dogs, and do not throw your pearls before swine, lest they trample them under their feet, and turn and tear you to pieces.

Ask and you will receive; seek and you will find; knock and the door will be opened to you.

For everyone who ask receives, and he who seeks finds, and for he who knocks, the door will be opened. For what man is there among you, that when his son shall ask for a loaf would give him a stone? Or if he asked for a fish would give him a snake?

If you being man know how to give good gifts to your children, how much more does your Father in heaven give what is good to those who ask.

Therefore always treat others as you would have them treat you. This is the essence of the Law of the prophets...

The Christian Church

After Jesus' death, his followers continued to spread his teachings as he himself had done. This formed the basis of the Christian Church, with a mission of converting all people to Christianity. It was not enough to live by the teachings of Jesus; one must also accept Jesus as a part of the *Holy Trinity*, (three manifestations of God) and believe that he died to redeem humanity. Only in this way could one be judged worthy to ascend to Heaven after death.

Atonement

Christian doctrine teaches that all people are born in sin, sharing the sins of Adam and Eve (the first humans of Biblical myth.) Because of this *original sin*, all people are separated from God, and cannot redeem themselves. The Virgin Mary (the mother of Jesus) is said to be the only person ever to be born free of original sin.

It is believed that Jesus sacrificed himself to make amends for original sin. *Atonement* is the reconciliation between God and his people, made possible by Jesus' death. Jesus taught people what they must do to redeem themselves, and gave his life so they would have an opportunity for redemption.

The Holy Trinity

The doctrine of the Holy Trinity states that there is only one God, but God is also three entities the Father, Son, and Holy Spirit who are united in one substance or being. This leads many non-Christian theologians to question the Christian claim to monotheism.

Jesus' disciples were Jews and worshipped their one God, Yahweh. Christianity diverged from Judaism in its belief that Jesus was Yahweh's son, and Yahweh's manifestation on Earth. Thus Christians can pray to God as Yahweh in the form of Jesus.

The Holy Trinity compares the Christian conception of God with the concept of a source, a coming forth, and a return

Divisions of Christianity

Early Christianity eventually developed into three major branches: the Roman Catholic Church, the Eastern Orthodox Church, and the Protestant Church.

The Roman Catholic Church

The Roman Catholic Church is under the authority of the Pope, its highest religious official.
- The Pope is said to be the successor to Saint Peter, the founder of the Christian Church.
- Roman Catholics consider the Pope to be infallible regarding matters of faith and morality. The Pope may have erroneous views on other subjects, such as politics or history, but his religious opinions and his pronouncements are believed to be the will of God.
- The Catholic Church practices seven rituals instituted by Jesus as ways one's faith is affirmed and one's life path dedicated and strengthened. These seven sacraments are baptism, confirmation, matrimony, holy orders for clergy, penance, the Eucharist, and Anointing of the Sick, or last rites.
- Many sacraments are performed only once in a person's life, while penance and the Eucharist occur regularly throughout one's life. Penance requires that a person confess all his or her sins to a priest and then pray or

perform some other task in reparation, to earn God's forgiveness. In the sacrament of the Eucharist, or Holy Communion, the priest re-enacts Jesus Christ's last supper with his apostles. Bread and wine are consecrated to become representative of the body and blood of Christ, and then distributed to the congregation members for spiritual nourishment.

The Eastern Orthodox Church

- The Eastern Orthodox Church officially broke away from the Roman Catholic Church in 1054. It predominates in Eastern European countries such as Albania, Bulgaria, Greece, Romania, and Russia.
- The Eastern Orthodox Church administers the same seven sacraments as the Roman Catholic Church.
- There is no supreme and infallible religious official, like the Catholic Pope. Spiritual guidance and decisions on religious issues are provided by a consensus of bishops. This Church believes that the Holy Spirit guides and protects the spirituality of Christians, so a human leader is not necessary.
- Bishops meet regularly in councils to resolve questions of doctrine. They address the interpretation of existing doctrines, rather than instituting new doctrines.
- There is less separateness among members of this Church, and each member's salvation is tied to all others within the Church. The feeling of community may be stronger, as the members of the Church are considered to be its voice and its essence.
- Eastern Orthodox priests do not always follow the strict code of celibacy practiced in the Roman Catholic Church.

The Eastern Orthodox Church encourages individuals to seek union with God in this life, making this realization more prone to mysticism and mystical teachings.

The Protestant Church

Protestantism began as a movement to reform the Christian church in the 16th century, resulting in the Protestant Reformation. The term Protestant is applied to any Christian who is not a member of the Roman Catholic or Eastern Orthodox Churches, and is based on the religious faith of the individual.

Protestants believe that faith is first and foremost, and all else will naturally follow if one loves God and has deep, abiding faith in Him.

- The principle thrust of Protestantism rejects idolatry and all else that takes away from God. God alone should be the focus of religious worship.
- God must therefore become manifest to each individual. The Bible, God's word (called the Living Word) should speak directly to each of us, and its teachings should be applied to our daily lives.
- The hundreds of different churches in Protestantism often reflect diverse ethnic or social groups.
- The pursuit of spiritual knowledge and revelation of God's truth is an individual path for the Protestant. It can at times be a very lonely path, without the sense of community wholeness and unity that other Christian Churches offer.

Spiritual Choices and Practices

Awareness of our own spiritual needs is necessary to our happiness and fulfillment.

Religion helps most people throughout the world explore and satisfy their spiritual needs. It offers techniques of prayer and rituals through for expressing our spirituality, and provides guidance and encouragement to help us individuals on their chosen path of enlightenment.

Choosing a Religion

Most of us follow the religious traditions in which we were raised. But some of us have had little or no religious training, or found our parents religion do not answer our current spiritual needs.
- The Western world's obsession with technology, logical thinking, and materialism has left some of us with a feeling of alienation from our spiritual selves.

- Exploring and adopting an Eastern tradition, with its different values and beliefs, can sometimes help us understand and express our spirituality.
- Choosing a religion outside of one's own culture can be a form of revolt against parents or society, or it can be a crucial step in strengthening one's identity and fulfilling emotional needs.

Modern travel and communications have allowed us a greater exposure to the myriad religions practiced throughout the world. Any religion we investigate will probably contain elements we concur with and also elements we cannot accept or feel unsure of. The practice of a single religion may vary greatly among different congregations and geographic, ethnic, or social groups. The many available choices can seem overwhelming.
- Many people, especially in the Western world, are culturally conditioned to view God as an abstract, omnipotent being, as portrayed in Judaism or Christianity.
- To someone raised in Eastern culture the many representations of divinity found in Hinduism or Tibetan Buddhism may seem more acceptable.
- An increasingly prevalent theory suggests that all religions are simply facets of the universal belief in Divinity. In this view, each religion developed to fit the geographical, historical and traditional values of the region of its birth.

The Benefits of Religious Faith

As we study the major religions of the world, we find many similarities:
- All religions teach that we are of divine origin.
- The true essence of the self, resides in the soul rather than the body, and it is capable of existence beyond or without the body.
- Our souls can merge with the Divine Infinity.
- Techniques of prayer and meditation help us focus on our true selves, and encourage our spiritual growth and fulfillment.
- Religions offer answers to our questions about the cause and the purpose of life and death. We are reminded that there is some power greater than ourselves, of which we are a part.

- Religions give us models of humanistic behavior, that encourage and inspire us to contribute to our communities and help those in need. Most religions promote such qualities as humility, charity, kindness and truthfulness. They also condemn behaviors which are detrimental to the community and to individuals, such as murder, lying, theft, and greed.
- Shared rituals and worship services give practitioners a sense of belonging.

Religions are like the different rays of a single light, separated into all its component colors as it passes through a prism. As worshipers of one specific faith, we may bask in our own ray of color, and mistakenly believe that we know the full light.

Take time to identify your spiritual needs and explore your choices. If you have drifted away from the religious tradition of your family, you may want to try it again, as your needs have probably changed over time. You may find some ideas or practices that help you in your spiritual quest, without adopting the entire religion Only you can decide how best to fulfill your own spiritual needs.

A path of healthful and moderate living ensures progressive advancement towards enlightenment. There is no need for renunciation, deprivation or extremes of any kind.

Practices to Strengthen the Spirit

There are thousands of exercises and methods for finding or acknowledging the Spirit self. They are usually designed to strengthen the bond between the individual spirit and the Divine Spirit or Life Force or God. Most of these practices, were first developed as religious rituals or prayers. They may be performed as part of a religious devotion, or used alone, or in combination with other spiritual practices.

Yoga

The Indian sage Patanjali refined the techniques of yoga and compiled them in a treatise in the second century AD. Yoga is a Hindu discipline which promotes unity of body and mind. Certain physical postures and breathing patterns are used in conjunction with intense concentration and meditation. Eventually a state of *Samadhi*, or total absorption, is reached.

As we have seen in Chapter 2, Body-Mind, there are many different forms of yoga. Some focus on physical postures, while others concentrate on elevating the mind into the realm of the spirit.
- *Jnana* yoga uses techniques of study and contemplation to develop spiritual wisdom.
- *Raja* yoga, "the Royal Road," involves the practice of austerities, selfless actions, and meditation.
- *Bhakti* yoga is centered upon love and devotion to God. This love is manifested in selfless action, prayer, contemplation, and chanting of the name of God.

Meditations

The purpose of the meditation is to empty the mind of random thoughts, so it can become open to awareness of the Spirit, beyond thought.

The mind is very powerful. It determines how we perceive events. It is constantly busy with wonderful ideas and fascinating perceptions. However, it also creates worries and distractions which block out the communications of the spirit. We worry that we will become poor or ill, lose our loved ones or be lonely.

This power of the mind is the reason why spiritual exercises are necessary, and always include some method to still the mind's activity.
- A quiet mind allows us to return our thoughts to the Spirit, the creative principle behind all things we are attached to.
- Instead of being dependent on external forces such as material wealth, beauty, good luck and affection of others, we can come to know Spirit within ourselves, and rely on it for our happiness.

Mantras and Sacred Words

Some meditations use mantras (words and sounds) chanted aloud to achieve a higher consciousness. Even as little children, we are fascinated with the sound and power of words. We are especially interested in magic words; that make things happen.

As a child cries, its mother appears with nourishment, love, and comfort. We read stories in which doors open magically, and transformations occur through the sound of magic words.

> *We learn in the Bible and other scriptures that the Word was with God and that the Word was the beginning of everything.*

Mantras are simply certain words or sounds that carry a special vibration. The vibration released when one chants a specific mantra creates certain responses.

We often think of mantras only as exotic sounds from foreign tongues. But even in our own language we can easily demonstrate the power of words.
- Angry words repeated over and over will soon erode one's self-confidence and incentive.
- Positive and loving words will nurture the person, and help to uncover talents and determination.

Chanting the names of God or praising Spirit will engender subtle transformations, from calming the fears of the mind to opening the heart which unveils the light within us.

- Mantras are often taken from sacred languages such as Sanskrit or Aramaic (the common root language of Hebrew and Arabic), because it is believed that the abundance of open vowels (*a* and *o*) in those languages creates a vibration helpful to stilling the mind and opening the heart.
- However, we can create our own mantras with any positive image, word or sound that feels appropriate, or any name of God that we find meaningful.
- A mantra can be repeated at a whisper or more loudly. The sound vibrations not only have an effect on our mouth, tongue and lips, but also reverberate in the ear. If done in a group, these vibrations can be very powerful.

Chanting or repeating a mantra is not meant to create magical changes, but simply to soothe and open the mind so our own spiritual self can be more easily contacted.

Letting Spirit Heal

The force of Spirit within us can help us to heal ourselves in body and mind.

The Power of Spirit

If we accept that we each have a spiritual self, then we must realize that this Spirit force is not limited to our heart or brain or any other physical body part, but extends into each and every one of our cells.
- Our spiritual self is everywhere within us, and it is also part of the infinite and immeasurable Spirit.
- Therefore we can use our own spirit to draw upon the universal store of health and wellness, to strengthen and even heal ourselves.
- The universe vibrates with life. Similarly we are vibrant with life: each cell within us is vibrant with life. If any one cell or group of cells sickens, we can renew them with life-force by using our spiritual power.

Aligning Our Spiritual Energy

It is true that we do become tired, ill, and depleted of energy. This happens because we sometimes act in opposition to the natural flow of energy. We create friction and tension in our own lives. This is clearly the case when we become sick due to anxious thoughts, worries, or extreme stress. Our minds often lead us astray from our spiritual truth, causing our spirits to become ill at ease and dis-harmonious, and our bodies to become diseased.

However, simple techniques can help us realign our energy and strengthen ourselves:
- Deep breathing and relaxation exercises are invaluable.
- We must become aware of the natural rhythms around us, and relax our breath and very being into those rhythms. We find natural rhythms everywhere: the waves of the oceans, the songs of frogs or crickets at dusk, a water fountain, rain, our own heartbeat and any other vibration of the natural world.
- We must also practice awareness of the life-force inherent in all things.
- Awareness of our own life-force comes from visualizing and concentrating on our centers of energy (or *chakras*, in the study of yoga): the navel, the solar plexus, the

heart, the throat, the Spirit center between the eyebrows, and the crown center at the top of the head. While concentrating on the centers of energy, repeat their corresponding affirmations (working up from the navel center): I create, I live, I love, I speak, I am, I bless.
- In every spiritual tradition in the world, these centers of energy have been used (though often subconsciously) as focal points for prayer and meditation.
- Very potent spiritual healing is realized by focusing one's intent upon the chosen energy center, and visualizing a strong white light and powerful healing energy there.
- Complete charts of the body's energy centers and their corresponding colors for visualizations are available in many books on yoga or meditation, and can be taught by most yoga teachers.
- One healing technique is done by visualizing that one is inhaling and exhaling a white light. The white light is the divine force that can be directed through the energy centers, the spinal column or even over the entire body like a fountain of health and wellness. (It is interesting to note that many religions use a blinding white light as one representation of God.)
- Such powerful visualizations, practiced regularly, can bring great calmness, vitality, balance, harmony and mental and spiritual strength.

Healing
Three practical steps to change disease to health:
- Help others so that you may be healed. This act of helping others takes your mind off your personal illusions of illness.
- Give thanks, as though healing has already happened. This will increase your faith. You must believe that you will heal. But how do you get this faith? You simply give energy to the results by visualizing them as having already occurred. If you give thanks and see something as already happening, this allows faith to go with your affirmations. Your faith will allow you to make the leap into your new reality.
- Call forth the Spirit. Affirm that "I am healed now." Whatever you say after "I am" is sent directly into the sub-conscious and is very powerful.

Spiritual Decision

Living means having to make major decisions, about everything from buying a house to choosing a religion. Even not deciding is actually a decision to remain unchanged in your current situation. Evaluating options based on incomplete information and changing emotions can lead to bad decisions. Accessing your higher wisdom will help you find the best solution.

Techniques for Spiritual Decision Making

Get in a relaxed, comfortable sitting position and still your mind. Silently state the problem that you face, and ask what you need to do to take the next step forward. Listen to that small voice within. Without thinking about it, write down whatever you are given as the next step forward. If you have the courage to follow the instructions from your higher self, your life will unfold perfectly.

But how do you know if what you write comes from Spirit or somewhere else? There are four characteristics that indicate that the answer came from Spirit rather than ego. If your answer does not have the following four characteristics, try again until you get an answer that fits.

Answers from Spirit

1. Does the answer have the ring of truth? Does it feel like the right thing to do?

2. Is it a brief answer? A short, simple answer is more likely to come from Spirit, while a long complicated answer is more likely to come from ego.

3. Does the answer show the qualities of higher wisdom? Qualities such as love, forgiveness, kindness, and understanding are likely to come from the Spirit.

4. Does the answer give you a sense of upliftment? Your ego may create an answer that is a put-down to yourself or someone else. Destructive and negative answers do not come from the Spirit.

CHAPTER 5

SPIRIT

> "A human being is a part of the whole called by us universe. A part limited in time and space. He experiences himself, his thoughts and feelings as something separate from the rest – a kind of optical delusion of his consciousness. This delusion is a kind of prison for us. Our task must be to free ourselves from this prison."
> –Albert Einstein

Overview of Chapter

The highest experience of fulfillment in life is to realize our direct connection with the divine. Mystical teachings of all major religions prescribe various ways to achieve this direct connection. Neither logical nor emotional, this connection requires a leap beyond everyday normal knowing. It requires the realization that we are more than just our bodies and our minds. We are actually children of God, an outflowing of the Divine Spirit. As we learn more about spiritual truth, we are bound less by the physical and mental laws of man and more by the laws of Spirit. Physical and mental laws no longer hold their former degree of power over us.

Looking within to find the key to Self is like penetrating a maze to find its center. Questions may only lead to more questions. Yet with a pure heart and clear vision, one can find the center of the maze, the Reality of the Self, a sense of wholeness and belonging, the key to answering all questions, the still quiet place within, where one can truly see and hear and know. How are we to acquire this pure heart and clear vision?

In this chapter you are given the priceless opportunity to understand the spiritual nature of life. This chapter's lessons can guide you to your true identity.

Spiritual Meditations

This chapter on spirituality is extremely potent. The mind is powerful; it controls the body and creates health and happiness. Spirit is even more powerful than either the mind or body; it is the ultimate source of all power.

It is difficult to logically explain spiritual wisdom because spiritual consciousness requires an understanding beyond logic. Spirituality exists on a higher plane of awareness than the mechanical thinking of the mind. Therefore a different type of training is necessary. Spiritual principles taught in this chapter may at first seem illogical or even incorrect. However, they will be catalysts for us to grow beyond conditioning and logic into awareness of spiritual truth.

Almost all of the world's spiritual masters and teachers have said that meditation is the way to peace, joy and spiritual illumination. So the purpose of these meditative spiritual exercises is training to go beyond the limitations of our mind and into an alignment with the spiritual view of Reality. We normally live our life in an illusion, with a sense of separation from Spirit. We each usually become mesmerized by the events of everyday life and forget our spiritual nature. The meditations assist in awakening us from life's hypnotic trance, which is so powerful that we need some type of spiritual meditation on a daily basis. Although there are rare cases of spontaneous alignment, most of us must learn some formal method to free us from our trance.

In this series of fifty-two spiritual meditations, we simply focus our whole attention on a spiritual concept. At the same time, we remain receptive to the flow of information coming to us from infinite Spirit. We accomplish this by reading about the theme of the week. Sitting in regularly-scheduled meditations and contemplating the specific weekly concept, all the while listening for that still small spiritual voice within us. If distracting thoughts come to your mind – as they surely will – acknowledge them briefly but remain unattached, and return to the theme of the week.

The meditations provided in this chapter are designed to facilitate a profound spiritual growth within one year. The meditations are non-denominational and use the general name "Spirit." However, you may substitute other names such as God, The Great I Am, The Eternal All-Powerful, Christ, etc.

In this section there are a total of fifty-two spiritual meditations. Study each for an entire week. Choose a day of the week, possibly Saturday or Sunday, to begin a new spiritual meditation. Try to consciously practice the spiritual meditation twice every day, but don't "beat yourself up" if you miss some days. Generally about ten minutes is sufficient. The meditations are to be done in order. Don't skip any. Whatever posture you assume is okay. Most people prefer sitting in a comfortable position. Noises are very distracting, so choose a quiet place and ensure that you will not be disturbed. The preferred time for the first daily spiritual meditation is as soon as possible after awakening in the morning. Do the repetition of the spiritual meditation any time you choose. Also throughout the day, whenever you have an opportunity, think about the week's meditation.

Begin by reading everything in the weekly spiritual meditation, and then concentrate on the statement in the box for five minutes with your eyes closed. Say this statement a number of times to yourself, and consider how it applies to your life and the people and things around you.

Understanding the truth of Spirit requires embracing a larger perspective than just logic. You don't have to understand the statements, just reflect on them during the week. Certain key concepts are repeated in various ways during the course of the year.

One Year Spiritual Training

Exercise for Week 1 (Reality)

Each person views the world through his own perspective. As though each individual wears filtered glasses with different color filters, and therefore reports seeing different colored objects.

The problem is that we almost never remove our personal filters, and consequently we have a distorted viewpoint of Reality. An example of this is to look at a tree and note our observation. We might see it as a large umbrella that provides shade from the sun. Other individuals might see a log to turn into lumber. Others might see a source of beautiful flowers, tasty nuts, leaves to rake, etc. Birds may consider the tree their home, and termites may consider it their food. The true Reality is all of the above and much more!

> "The world I see is only a very small part of total Reality."

Once we see one thing differently, we then have the ability to begin seeing yet other things differently. We will understand that there are different ways to perceive the world. While our five senses give us information, we interpret this information in various ways. We give the meaning to what is there. In the past we have chosen to focus on those things that our conditioned mind dictates. Now we begin to recognize that the reality we see is only a very small part of total Reality.

Exercise for Week 2   (*Reality*)

We generally think dreams occur only at night when we are sleeping. In fact dreams also take place during the day. We actually see things as if viewed through a filter, distorting our perception of Reality and limiting our ability to perceive the world. Reality is much more than what we believe we see or touch in the external world. This week's spiritual meditation will help us realize that we see "through a glass darkly."

Certain thoughts remind us we are dreaming instead of being focused in Reality. They are there to remind us that there are other ways to understand our experience.

Replace dream thoughts of fear, separation, lack and limitation with Reality thoughts of love, unity and abundance.

> **"What I see is distorted by my dream thoughts."**

Our internal filter distorts our perception of experience. This filter is created by our unconscious mind. Most people are unaware of how to control the unconscious mind. By repeating this spiritual meditation during the week, we can begin to see particular events in our life from a different perspective.

Exercise for Week 3   (Reality)

The human condition can seem like one problem after another. Our freedom from needless pain and suffering in life depends on our becoming awakened from illusion. Perception is a choice; we can consciously choose to focus on pain and suffering, or we can choose to focus on joy and happiness. We can choose to transform negative and dysfunctional beliefs into more positive ones that work for us.

> "Liberation from illusion brings joy and happiness."

Some people think that suffering is the way to grow, but it does not bring us closer to Spirit. Understanding the truth of our being brings liberation and lasting peace and joy and happiness. This liberation can come only from our conscious choice to be free.

The challenges and conflicts of the illusionary outer world cannot bring lasting happiness. We may have noticed that the goals set by our old conditioned mind do not bring lasting happiness. Successful completion of our individual goals may bring fleeting happiness, but we quickly seek a new and more difficult goal to accomplish. Only liberation from illusion brings enduring happiness.

Conflicts and suffering offer us opportunities to choose to transcend the illusions. Many people awaken after a period of intense suffering. At these times of pain our choices become more obvious. Conscious choice for liberation often follows when we feel that we can't or won't take any more suffering.

Exercise for Week 4 (Reality)

Sometimes it seems we are controlled by life's events. It seems like all we can do is react. The onslaught of happenings can eventually overwhelm us. It takes courage to realize that we can learn to see life's challenges in a different way. Our mechanical mind tells us one thing, but a small voice deep within us says that we can indeed see things differently. It says that we are the masters of our destiny and do have a choice.

> **"I can change my perception and choose joy and happiness."**

We have a variety of thought systems with which to experience life. We can choose separation, fear, lack and limitation. Or we can choose love, harmony, abundance and peace.

This week when you think of something negative, try to observe it from another viewpoint.

Exercise for Week 5 (Reality)

Holding on to outdated viewpoints of life limits our ability to realize our higher self. By removing our old limiting ideas, we can expand our consciousness to include a more comprehensive understanding of life. What more is the purpose of life than growing from infancy into adulthood and progressively seeing things more fully?

> **"I am committed to growing, and will release my outdated concepts about life."**

Once we can see an expanded reality in one area of our life, it becomes easier to see an expanded reality in other parts of our life. This is because we begin to understand that our preconceived ideas about things are only a small portion of the total picture. We soon understand that we can withhold initial judgments about initial perceptions and thereby observe a larger Reality. This encourages us to continue to awaken from our sleep and to know the truth even more fully.

Exercise for Week 6   (*Reality*)

It is impossible to understand infinite Spirit with our finite, logical minds. Sometimes certain events occur repeatedly and we can not understand the reasons. Some people are married and divorced a number of times to the same type of spouse. Others held a series of similar jobs, which ended quickly. These types of events continue to occur until we finally learn the lessons that we are meant to learn from the experience.

Occasionally seemly dreadful things happen and we ask why these things happen to us. We would much prefer only pleasant events to occur. Why do "bad" things happen? And why do they continue to happen? If everything in life was picture perfect we would never learn anything. The various circumstances we confront during routine living are opportunities to learn to see Reality.

> "All events hold lessons of truth."

We have taken form in human bodies to learn truths necessary to the evolution of our spiritual beings. The specific events we experience are not as important as the truths that we learn from them. Try to consider all events as opportunities to learn and to grow. Whenever faced with challenges of any kind, be thankful for the opportunity to learn and grow. Don't reject the powerful lessons that we can learn from all life's events, whether positively or negatively perceived.

Exercise for Week 7 *(I am)*

Most of the world's spiritual teachers agree that all things were made by the one infinite Spirit. They believe that human life was created in the image and likeness of Spirit. Our humanness is the life given to us by Spirit. We were created by Spirit and therefore live in relation with Spirit.

> **"I come from Spirit."**

Spirit did not create us just to abandon us. We maintain relationship with Spirits. When we don't see this truth, we are living in a dream. Our true being is in the image and likeness of Spirit. We are an outpouring of Spirit.

Exercise for Week 8 *(I am)*

Our old thoughts of being not good enough, or of somehow lacking, only occur due to our conditioning. In fact Spirit made us perfect, in Its image, and gave us the choice to confirm or deny this perfection. Unfortunately, most of humanity denies its perfection. Nevertheless, the truth of our being is always within us. It is only necessary to take off the false blinders of our old conditioning, in order to recognize our kinship to Spirit.

> **"I am perfect now, just as Spirit created me."**

Once we really learn this week's spiritual meditation we will be free of the world's illusions of our imperfections. There will be nothing in us that needs fixing. Awareness of our source will free us from sickness and disease. Knowing our perfect being will free us from the world's illusions of lack and limitations. We were created as part of the perfect Spirit, and are perfect as such.

Exercise for Week 9   *(I am)*

Success comes from being steadfast and not quitting. In today's busy world, so many demands are made upon our time and energies that we often feel almost overwhelmed. We feel that we have no control over our lives. But we can decide to set aside a few minutes twice a day, during which we can begin to take charge of our lives. If we practice our spiritual meditation on a regular daily schedule, we will be successful. All those who truly want to know and remember their true identity will be motivated to continue and ultimately succeed.

> **"I remain steadfast in my desire to remember my true identity."**

For most of us this is an important element of spiritual growth. To have a strong desire and be steadfast in that desire will enable us to complete any task. It will assist us in our leap of awareness from the material to the spiritual plane. It will help us remember our true nature as part of Spirit. This is the most freeing experience in the world. It brings us peace and happiness.

Exercise for Week 10 (I am)

We generally ignore the cycles of change that occur in our lives. An example of changing cycles can be seen in the egg that hatches into a caterpillar. This caterpillar spends its life eating large quantities of plant matter necessary for its growth. The larva's life purpose is to feed upon vegetation and grow. This is like the unconscious portion of man's life during which he consumes elements of the material world.

Eventually the caterpillar spins a cocoon spending this phase of its life in this pupal case in quiet metamorphous. This is like the quiet time a man spends when he is devoted to contemplating the world of illusion and the world of Spirit.

Finally a butterfly emerges from the cocoon. The beautiful butterfly no longer eats plant matter, but now visits fragrant flowers and drinks their sweet nectar. This compares to man's enlightenment after he realizes his connection with Spirit when his existence miraculously changes.

> "I am more than my body. I am part of Spirit."

Our body also developed through cycles. It began as a sperm and egg that combined to form a one cell animal in our mother's womb. Was that really us? Once it was a crying baby. Was that really us? Do we have the same thoughts today? Scientists tell us that each molecule in our body is replaced every few years. Where are we?

As we grow older we continue to change. Who are we? The only answer is, that as part of Spirit, we are more than those things.

Exercise for Week 11   (*I am*)

We don't have to travel to mountain tops or holy places to communicate with Spirit. Spirit is always within us, closer than our hands and feet. When we don't feel Spirit within, we are just not alert to its presence. But Spirit is still there. It is like radio waves that surround us, but that we can't hear unless we use a radio to tune in to one particular wave and tune out the rest of the signals. We need to "tune us" to Spirit, and tune out other distractions.

> "Spirit is forever with me, closer than my own hands and feet."

At the center of our being Spirit has incarnated itself. Spirit is part of our very core. We all share the same Spirit. Spirit has given us individual outward expressions in material form. But in our very core we are the infinite Spirit. Our true self is part of the Spirit.

Exercise for Week 12   (*I am*)

Honor yourself acknowledging your true identity as part and parcel of the unlimited Spirit. Wherever you are, Spirit is. Accept your true nature and joy, and freedom becomes your birthright.

> "My true identity is part of the unlimited Spirit."

We will never die because our true self is part of Spirit. The body and mind exist in time and will eventually age, decay and die. Spirit exists beyond the concept of time. It exists in the infinite here and now. It always existed and always will exist. Our real identity as a part of that infinite Spirit is ageless.

Exercise for Week 13 *(I am)*

When we experience fear, it means that we see ourselves separately, as body or mind and not as part of Spirit. When we remember our true nature as more than our body and our mind, we are not afraid. We are part of Spirit and nothing can harm our true identity.

> "I remember my true identity and do not fear the world's illusions."

Spirit is infinite and all-powerful. It can not be harmed by anything that man or nature does. When we remember that we are more than simply our mind and body, our fear will lose its power.

Exercise for Week 14 *(One Spirit)*

Spirit is the only power and the only law. This may seem confusing since each of the various belief systems, are filled with different laws and traditions. The realized person is not bound by the millions of man-made laws. These are set up for those who don't yet recognize their true nature as being part of Spirit. We invented them ourselves in an attempt to protect ourselves from the multiple worldly powers. As long as we believe in worldly powers they will control us. Once we realize that we are not bound by these man-made laws, we will experience a tremendous sense of freedom.

> "There is only one Spirit, one power, one law."

It is not possible for the one infinite, perfect Spirit to be divided against itself. The only laws are the laws of Spirit. All other laws come from the human mind. Freedom is recognizing that we do not need to obey all the beliefs and rules drilled into us from the first moment of our birth. Though they were necessary in our earlier, formative years, these old rules now enslave us. We may no longer reach for our mother's hand before we cross the street, but there are still thousands of apparently "logical rules" that interfere with our awareness of the one true power.

Exercise for Week 15 (*One Spirit*)

This week we will learn that Spirit is everywhere that it is realized. Wherever we accept the presence of Spirit, it is!

> "There is only one Spirit and it is everywhere."

Look slowly around the room, and focus attention on various items, and repeat this spiritual meditation. Spirit is even in the chair, the desk, the door, etc. Affirm that Spirit is in every item that comes into our awareness. Spirit is literally within every thing that we can perceive.

Apply this week's spiritual meditation periodically throughout the day. Repeat it whenever we have a few free moments.

Exercise for Week 16 (*One Spirit*)

Sitting in a room with drawn curtains in complete darkness. we might feel alone and separate. We may feel the pain and suffering of human existence. But throw open those curtains, and the room is flooded with light. The warm loving light that has been within us since the beginning is revealed. It shines forth as our experience of the infinite Spirit. The white light of Spirit will sweep away the terrors of darkness. Darkness cannot survive when illuminated by this light. So when light comes, darkness loses its appearance of Reality. Darkness does not exist except as the absence of light. The light of Spirit brings its awareness of who and what we are. We are part of Spirit and Spirit is part of us.

> "Spirit is part of me and I am part of Spirit."

If we view ourselves as separate from Spirit, we also feel separate from other humans. When we realize we are part of Spirit, we view other humans as part of us. This enables us to perceive them differently – on a higher level, and acknowledge our oneness. We realize that getting angry at others is the same as getting angry at ourselves. Loving others is the same as loving ourselves.

Exercise for Week 17   (*Love*)

When you feel the love of Spirit you will see the entire world through new loving eyes. Your fresh vision is very different from the fearful and angry world of your past. This world you see now is free from danger, hatreds, pain, suffering, separation, failure, conflict and strife of the world you once knew.

> "I feel the love of Spirit."

The love of Spirit varies greatly from the conditional love of the material world. The love of Spirit has no degrees or limits, and is unchanging and forever. It is accepting and non-judging. This love actually comprises who you are.

Exercise for Week 18   (*Trust*)

Feelings of loneliness, suffering and depression come from one's sense of separation from Spirit. Unity with Spirit instantly restores peace and happiness. The light of Spirit illuminates the darkness. Just as there can be no darkness where there is light, there is no suffering when we realize Spirit.

> "Spirit protects and watches over me."

Spirit is perfect, and acceptance of this perfect Spirit will cure all our suffering and depression. Spirit protects us in all circumstances. We have nothing to fear because Spirit is our strength, and its strength is infinite. If we fear something, it shows that we are attempting to rely upon our own strength and not upon the strength of Spirit. Spirit sustains our very life; without Spirit, we could accomplish nothing. Spirit is all-powerful; there is nothing Spirit cannot do. We need only ask Spirit for direction. Turn over all worries and problems to the all-powerful Spirit that watches over and protects us.

Exercise for Week 19 *(Error)*

Let us never forget who we truly are. We are one with Spirit, and not under the power of the illusory material world. Our kingdom is not of this world of illusion, but of the world of truth. Once we recognize this, we no longer suffer from loss and limitation.

> "I take full responsibility for what I think and feel."

If we suffer from pain, either mental or physical, it is because we choose to suffer. Pain exists only in the illusionary world where our negative thoughts and resistance bring forth suffering. Suffering is not possible when we elect to live in the truth, instead of the material world. Remember, we choose for ourselves whether to be sad or glad.

Exercise for Week 20 *(Error)*

Suffering, lack and limitation grow from desiring for things to be different from the way they are. Sometimes we are able to see that we want things which we believe will eventually bring us happiness. But when we finally achieve these things, we get only a fleeting kind of happiness. Soon we desire new and better things. We still don't get the lasting happiness which we so long for. Our old mind soon desires bigger and better things.

> "I choose to be free from suffering."

Only Spirit can bring lasting happiness. Spirit is responsible for the universe, and made it perfectly and without error. Any error exists only in our minds when we think things should be different from what they are. Pain and suffering are an illusion of the mind.

Exercise for Week 21 *(Error)*

We cannot cure lack, limitation and suffering. It does not truly exist. All we can do is recognize that the appearance of suffering is not real. The choice between joy and suffering is ours. It's our dream. We can decide!

> "I choose the joy of Spirit instead of the suffering of illusions."

There is no lack or limitation to fight against. You don't overcome suffering by overpowering anything, but by remembering that there is no real power in the illusion of suffering. Suffering has only the power of the belief that you give to its appearance. Choose joy instead and the suffering disappears, much like darkness disappears.

Exercise for Week 22 *(Error)*

Let us not be fooled by the rewards of the material world. Millions of dollars in the bank do not bring us any closer to Spirit than someone who may not even have a bank account. The true and lasting demonstrations of abundance, peace and happiness are internal, not external. The true riches come from Spirit and have nothing to do with more money, a bigger car or a higher position.

> "Spirit gives me life and releases me from all illusion."

Most people believe that there are two powers in the Universe. One is the power of the material world, and the other is the power of Spirit. But in fact only the power of Spirit exists. The material power is only illusion created by our dream thoughts.

The belief in two powers comes from the misperception of a power separate and apart from the One Spirit. The belief in two powers presents itself as lack, limitation, sin, separation, sickness and death. These states were not created by Spirit, but dreamed by the mind of man. Our realization of the emptiness of what we see in the material world is the only way to dissolve this illusion. Awaken and see through it!

Exercise for Week 23 (*Error*)

As humans, we believe we were created involuntarily and can be destroyed at any time, without our consent. We are like frightened children who hear a ghost story and look everywhere for the imaginary ghost. Like children, we see life as filled with danger, and seek help wherever we can find it. But the human help we find is temporary at best, and soon new ghosts frighten us.

> "Fear no longer controls me."

Fear means you see yourself as a limited being controlled by unpredictable worldly illusions. But you are much more than a limited mind and body. The infinite Spirit did not create you to forever suffer in fear and limitation. Spirit created you with the free choice to see yourself as much more than the physical self. As your Reality expands to more fully understand your true eminence, your fears drop away. The gruesome ghost stories no longer control your reactions.

Exercise for Week 24 (Error)

When we are angry and think about attacking others, we do it from a state of fear. We believe in some threat, become afraid, and attack the object of our fear. Attack stems from our fear that we will be hurt by some force. We believe that we need to defend ourselves against that force.

When we remember our true identity we know that there is but one power and others' thoughts of attack cannot hurt us. Let us behold the One Spirit in everyone that we encounter. When we go to work, the grocery store, the restaurant, let us remember that Spirit is in everyone. Whomever we meet, let us recognize Spirit within them.

> "I replace thoughts of fear and attack with thoughts of love."

Attacking others is really attacking ourselves because we are all one in Spirit. Loving others is really loving ourselves. Let us disregard the appearance of fear and attack, and greet people with love. Let us disregard the appearance of human identity and greet Spirit within all beings. People will react in a positive way and reflect back to us the loving energy that we have released.

Exercise for Week 25 *(Error)*

Throughout history people have dedicated their lives to the erroneous cause of fighting evil. But Spirit is the only power and there is nothing that needs to be resisted.

What we resist will persist. What we focus on grows in importance. When we defend ourselves we create conflict. Defense arises from fear that we are unsafe. But our true Self is one with Spirit, and cannot be harmed. Our true Self always existed and will always exist. Our true Self is the one and only power, and no other powers can be aligned against this one power. Any other powers are just illusionary, and are only perceived as real and powerful by those who don't yet understand the truth of their being.

> "In my defenselessness is my freedom."

Our defenselessness is our safety. Carrying guns and building missiles will cause our defeat. We will spend all our time seeking to be defended from the threats of the illusionary material world, rather then learning about the true world of Spirit. This will sow the seeds of our destruction. Strong defenses really show our weakness, because they show that we don't understand who we really are.

When we fight the appearance of evil, we create an enemy in our mind that is greater than ourselves. When we fight this appearance of evil we actually give it the strength that it did not previously have. Since we defined this evil, it has all the strength we possess ourselves. We need not attempt to change the appearance of evil into good. Instead of fighting, let us look beyond appearances to the spiritual plane, where there is only good.

Exercise for Week 26 (*Error*)

The cloudy illusions of everyday life evaporate when illuminated with truth. These illusions become insignificant and vanish in the face of spiritual truth. It is not easy to view the lack, limitation, disease and horrors of the world and remember that they have no power. We do not understand the reason things happen as the do, but infinite Spirit has its reasons. However, the first time that we are healed because of our belief in Spirit, we will gain renewed faith in the power of the truth.

Our everyday confused and unsure thinking creates the errors in the way we lead our life. The spiritual truth fixes these errors and allows us to go forward free of future errors.

> "Spiritual truth will heal errors in my thinking."

Separation from the truth of the infinite Spirit creates illusion and error. But separation is not real. Hearing and living truth will free us from confused thinking.

Exercise for Week 27   (Error)

It is the pleasure of Spirit to bring us health and abundance. However we must decide to accept this gift from Spirit and not believe in sickness and limitation. We must remember our true being. We must remember that we are not separate and apart from Spirit, but one with Spirit. Spirit created everything and all that it made was good. Spirit did not make concepts such as sickness, lack and limitation. Healing occurs when we remember that sickness has no power. The hypnotic trance of everyday life attempts to convince us of the power of sickness, but this is not truth. When we remember this truth, sickness disappears.

> "I am healed now."

A rich man does not affirm that he is not poor. Affirmations made through denial will not work, so make only positive affirmations. Don't affirm that you will get better in the future. Affirm that you are healed now. A total change in consciousness is required. Realization of our identity with the one Spirit, is all we need.

Exercise for Week 28 (*Forgiveness*)

All evil that manifests through people has its origin in the universal carnal mind. Understanding this we can separate the individual person from the evil.

The universal carnal mind believes in two powers. It is a belief in a selfhood and a power apart from Spirit. In the Spiritual kingdom there is only One Power and there is no evil. The only evil that exists is the impersonal evil that arises when we forget our true self and believe in the false power of the universal carnal mind.

Regardless of the errors in our lives, we are not responsible for them. Error is a universal belief we have accepted as our own. We have chosen to see our lives as containing evil. Once we change that perspective, we can change our lives. We have temporarily believed that error is our personal sin. We are hypnotized; and until we awaken, we remain caught up in the errors of worldly beliefs.

The only evils and sins are those in our dark unconscious mind. The light of truth illuminates the illusion of evil and sin. We can then clearly see that it is not our personal sin but the hypnosis of the world at work. The belief in personal sin disappears when illuminated by the light of truth.

> **"There is no such thing as personal evil or personal sin."**

Don't personalize evil by believing that individuals are evil. We can forgive others when we understand that there is no personal evil. If we punish others we stoop to operating on the same level of fear and force that they are on. Punishing individuals will not cure the hypnosis of the world. This hypnotic illusion is the real source of what we believe to be evil.

The only power is the power of the Spirit. However, when we believe in other powers, we give them power and control over us. Only by believing in evil can these negative powers control us. Once we withdraw the belief we are free of its effect. Spirit is infinite and all-powerful, and no other power is real.

Exercise for Week 29 (*Forgiveness*)

Belief in guilt and blame are hindrances to our own spiritual growth. Let us choose to free ourselves from either blaming others or blaming ourselves.

> "People are doing the best they can for the awareness they have."

When we remember that people are only living up to their understanding of Reality, we can forgive their trespasses because they don't know what they are doing. They are living in a hypnotic dream and are really not responsible for the actions they take.

People can't properly judge a course of action based on partial evidence. And if they don't know the truth of their being, they cannot have the complete evidence. The results will be off, but we must not condemn those who are still in the dark. We should choose compassion and forgive them as others have forgiven us.

If we see others committing an error, let us realize that their belief within their hypnotic world is the real culprit. People can only react according to the level of their understanding of the truth.

Exercise for Week 30 (*Forgiveness*)

Most of humanity does not yet see the truth. They are lost in hypnotic illusions, and this distorted viewpoint causes wrong action. We cannot pass judgment on those who don't understand. They act according to their current limited understanding of truth. If they knew better they would do better.

Don't allow the actions of others to affect your choice of action. To remain free, we must forgive those who act without knowledge of the truth.

> "I will forgive those who do not yet see the truth."

The true identity of each of us is the perfect Spirit. Therefore we are all the same and there is truly nothing to forgive. The law of Spirit is forgiveness, compassion and doing unto others as we would have others do unto us. No matter what others appear to be doing, forgive them.

Exercise for Week 31 (*Forgiveness*)

If we tear a sheet of paper, the two torn edges become opposites. Where one has a hill the other has a valley. Many people will look at one edge and judge it as different than the other edge. Yet it was the same sheet of paper before it was torn. Both edges were created from the same sheet of paper and were once one.

We constantly judge events and people. We consider things to be good or bad, success or failure, more or less. These are the illusions of the world as seen through a mind that perceives Reality as sets of opposites. In our growth from childhood, this concept of opposites was useful to make sense out of a confusing stream of information bombarding our consciousness. However, this view of the world gets in the way of understanding spiritual Reality.

> **"I will not judge others."**

When we look at another person, let's not look at his outward human appearance. Instead look beyond, to Spirit within him, and remember that his true being is Spirit. This week do not form negative judgments against others.

When we judge others according to the appearance they make, we will not gain freedom, but will be caught in the false illusions of life. When we stop judging others, we free ourselves from illusion. We will see Reality more clearly and understand the truth of Spirit.

This is also our key for getting along with other people. Remember back before we began to study about Spirit. Remember the problems we created for ourselves. Remember how we reacted to life with fear. We didn't know any better then. Today most people still don't know any better.

Exercise for Week 32 (*Forgiveness*)

Our reluctance to forgive is an obstacle to our spiritual growth. We deserve to be free of the limitations and baggage that came with holding grudges. Ask your mind to step back and review without judgment. Ask Spirit to come forth and teach you the peace and harmony in forgiveness.

When we see others as wrong, then we judge. As soon as we see others as operating under the perfect law of Spirit, we also release ourselves from judgment. We thus free ourselves to operate from the higher spiritual law.

"Forgiveness will bring me closer to Spirit."

It is true in life that what we sow determines what we reap; we receive the same thing that we give. When we judge others we invite judgment from others. Our attitude will bring more negative occurrences, which will lead to even more judgment. When we sow forgiveness, we will reap peace of mind which will bring us closer to Spirit. When we forgive others we are also forgiving ourselves. When we no longer judge others we no longer judge ourselves.

Exercise for Week 33 (*Forgiveness*)

We can forgive and undo our past as if it never occurred. In fact the past never really occurred, because we saw it through a judgmental filter. We selectively remember events. We change the meaning and color the results.

We need not suffer for this false past. Let us cut loose our anchor to the past. The false past need not control our present. It doesn't matter what sins we think we have committed. Let's forgive ourselves now and let go of our past.

> **"I forgive myself and release my past."**

It is not your sin or wrong thinking that has caused you suffering. Suffering did not begin in you, so don't judge yourself. Suffering and error are impersonal, so forgive yourself for everything you imagined you did wrong. Error is just an illusion that disappears when you remember the infinite positive power of the Spirit.

Exercise for Week 34 (*Love-Peace*)

This week we will claim the heritage that is our birth right, the peace of Spirit. We have the right to be released from the suffering and ignorance of the material world. We can be assured that Spirit will bring us the peace and prosperity we deserve.

> "Spirit, let me see problems differently and enter into peace."

There often seem to be thousands of problems assaulting us. Let's step back and realize the spiritual peace that will allow our trials to evaporate into the nothingness from which they came. Seek this peace whenever the troubles of the material world encroach on your inner peace.

It's difficult to solve problems on the level of the problem. A better solution is to go beyond these problems into the Reality of Spirit which is our true being. At this level all our problems have already been solved by Spirit. We need only go beyond the worldly methods to see that our problems have, in Reality, been solved. The peace that we are entitled to has only been masked by problems we assumed were insurmountable.

Exercise for Week 35 (*Love-Peace*)

It has been written: "My peace I give unto thee: not as the world giveth." This refers to the love and peace that are beyond the logical concepts of the material world. It is a higher peace than that afforded by the pleasures of the mind and body.

> "The love and peace of Spirit are within me."

Rejoining our true nature of Spirit allows love and peace to flow through us. Rejoining allows us to undo anything in our past, as if it had never occurred. In truth it never did actually occur. It was only our reaction to specific events, or dreams. The love and peace were always within us. Even when we dreamed about attacking others, the truth within us was always of love.

Exercise for Week 36 (*Love-Peace*)

We are not alone in the limited self that our mind created. Instead we are part of Spirit, and Spirit feeds us the love that we desire. The self that our past conditioning created does not exist except in our mind. We created this limited self, and now we are expending most of our energy in sustaining it. But this self does not bring us love and peace. Instead it brings us separation and worries. We may have noticed that all the goals that our old mind has given us have not brought us the love and peace that we seek. The achievement of one goal is quickly replaced by the desire to achieve another. Meeting the goals of our old conditioned mind will never quell our longing for love and peace.

> "The love and peace of Spirit nourish me."

Let's remember that we are perfect exactly as Spirit created us. The love and peace of Spirit are ours to have, and there is nothing we need to do but to accept this flow from Spirit. Let's not separate ourselves off from this flow of good. Just as the branch that is cut away from the tree will wither and die, we are not alive without the flow from our Spirit source. When we are in the flow of Spirit, love and peace will truly nourish us.

Exercise for Week 37 (*Love-Peace*)

This very moment, the experience of peace and joy is available to us. This is not dependent on any other person or human power. From the beginning of time our dominion over our peace and joy has existed within us. However, we have allowed this domination to slowly slip away as we put our trust exclusively in human power. But we can regain our dominance right now. We can choose to receive the perfect peace and joy of Spirit. There is no need to wait. We can receive peace and joy this very moment.

> "The perfect peace and joy of Spirit are mine now."

Spirit is infinitely powerful and all other power is an illusion. Spirit is all good; evil, lack and limitation are illusions.

Exercise for Week 38 *(Abundance)*

Spirit answers all sincere calls. The call, however, must be for something spiritual. Only then can we be assured of an answer. It is possible that Spirit may not be interested in giving us a new Rolls Royce automobile, etc. Spirit will, however, give us all that we really need.

> "I need but ask and I will receive."

Seek first the Spirit and all other things will then be given to you. We are always with Spirit, and all that Spirit has is ours. Once we accept this truth, Spirit will set us free and provide a more abundant and joyful life.

Exercise for Week 39 *(Abundance)*

Spirit is the infinite source of our supply. If we lose part or all of our material supplies, Spirit can immediately recreate them. There is no limit to the gifts that Spirit can create. Its powers are infinite, beyond our imagination. It can create the entire universe and even more.

> "I claim the infinite gifts of Spirit."

All that Spirit has is yours. It is Spirit's good pleasure to give you the universe.

Exercise for Week 40 (*Present*)

Past events need not affect our present self. We can break out of these historic chains at any moment that we choose.

> "I let the past and future go. I live in the present."

Barriers to our spiritual progress are our own preconceived lacks and limitations. These barriers are rooted in our past and future thoughts. These barriers include the belief that something has to be different before we can fully know Spirit.

There is nothing in our past that needs to be overcome. We can forgive anything that happened in the past. Instead of blaming others, let's look for the hidden gift, the lesson of life. Every situation has a gift that can help us understand Spirit better. We can know Spirit now, regardless of our perceived past.

Planning for the future prevents us from living in the moment. In this very moment we can have the peace of Spirit. We can know Spirit now.

Exercise for Week 41 (*Prayer*)

It is important to give thanks for the life that we lead. It's not that Spirit needs to hear our thanks. Rather we must remember our gratitude for the opportunity to live and grow. The practice of expressing appreciation on a regular basis offers us an immediate connection to the joy and abundance of Spirit.

> "I thank Spirit for the gift of life."

This week, in gratitude for life, let us lift our hearts above despair and worry, and become joyful for the gift of life. Let's celebrate our life and give thanks to the beauty of our being.

Exercise for Week 42 (Prayer)

This week, let's be still and listen to that quiet, small voice within us. Let's allow it to guide us. Let us quiet our usual mind chatter and listen for that voice of guidance. This will lift us above the hypnotic world and allow us to receive the guidance that we seek.

> "I quiet my mind and receive guidance from Spirit."

Spirit is currently doing everything for us. Our daily practice brings us to the awareness of the perfection that Spirit is now achieving. Through prayer we can awaken to the truth that we are not now and never were alone. We are comforted and protected by our spiritual guidance.

Exercise for Week 43 (Prayer)

Some people believe that they can pray for a new color television and Spirit will provide it. Others even pray for the specific model and color of the automobile they want. Some ask for more rain and some ask for less. In a war each side prays for victory. Spirit does not answer this type of prayer. Prayers that ask for material favors from Spirit are futile. This type of prayer comes from mental power and not of the kingdom of Spirit. The prayers that Spirit does answer are those of the spiritual kingdom. These prayers should be for more spiritual knowledge, or for the ability to hear and understand Spirit better.

> "Spirit, let me know you correctly."

You shall know the truth of yourself as a spiritual being, and this truth will set you free.

Exercise for Week 44   (Prayer)

All who seek the truth of Spirit will reach it. We will not fail to know this if we really want it. All prayers asking for knowledge of the truth are answered. When we ask to know the truth of Spirit correctly and more fully, we will receive this knowledge. Spirit knows exactly what we need for our growth.

> "Seeking, I cannot fail to know the truth of Spirit."

The world of form is our classroom to learn the truth. It makes available to us lessons for spiritual growth. Everything can be used as a teacher. Every circumstance can lead us to the truth.

Exercise for Week 45   (Prayer)

Spirit created various ways to come into focus. One of the most powerful is the meditation called self-remembering. Our decision to use these methods of recalling our true identity is essential to our liberation.

We must slow down our thought process, quiet our racing mind, be still, and listen to the truth. The loud chatter of the world only brings confusion and lack of meaning. Let us listen to the truth of who we really are, and not base our identity on who others say we are. Let's be still and listen to the truth.

> "When I am still and listen,
> I hear the truth of Spirit."

The place where you now stand is holy ground. You don't need to go to a church or sanctuary. Wherever you are, Spirit is. All you need do is be still and acknowledge your true identity, created in the image of the Spirit.

Exercise for Week 46   (*Listen*)

When we are enmeshed in human problems that seem unsolvable, let us take time out and still our mind. Let us remember our true identity as part of Spirit. Let us relax our mind, open our awareness and listen for the directions of Spirit.

Let's put ourselves in the hands of Spirit, which will direct us toward the correct path for our growth.

> **"I allow Spirit to direct my life."**

Spirit is at work now, even as we are reading this. At this very moment, we have the opportunity to allow Spirit to direct our life. Let us surrender to the love and peace of Spirit.

One important lesson to learn in spiritual life is "Surrender to Spirit." Surrendering is difficult because our logical mind thinks it knows better. But this week, let us disregard the logical mind. Let's surrender to Spirit's direction for our life. Spirit goes before us to make the crooked places straight.

Exercise for Week 47   (*Purpose*)

Our greatest purpose in life is to remember our true identity as part of Spirit, and listen for the directions of Spirit. Spirit has a plan for us and we will get the opportunity to learn it. Even if we ignore Spirit, we will continue to be given future chances.

We will remember our purpose, but occasionally we will also forget. The path to spiritual illumination is not straight up. There are both peaks and valleys in our path. Often we will forget, and think we are lost. But we will remember again and again. Our overall path is upward. We will gradually remember our purpose more and more frequently, and for longer periods.

> "I remember my purpose."

Our purpose is not to live our lives to fulfill human desires. Our purpose is not to satisfy personal goals of supply or power. Our purpose is not to achieve personal gain. No, our purpose is to allow the will of Spirit to be performed through us.

Spirit is served when we remember our true identity. Spirit is not separate and apart from our identity, but part of and within each of us.

Exercise for Week 48   (*Purpose*)

Let us live more and more in conscious union with Spirit. Everything that we need will be provided. Spirit will draw to us the teachers and experiences that we need.

> "I live more and more in Spirit."

Our separation from Spirit is not real, but only an illusion. We dream that we are alone and separate, but we never really are since we are always part of Spirit.

Once we are able to see through the illusions of the world and perceive our true oneness with Spirit, we will never again be so lost in these illusions. We may frequently find ourselves back in these illusions, but we will remember how to get home more quickly.

The path towards freedom is sometimes obscure, and we will no doubt stumble and fall along the way. Yet the path does spiral upward. At times it may seem that our new knowledge is very fragile and easily lost. We may think we are right back where we started, but we will remember the truth again and again more and more often. Our natural state is to communicate with and abide in Spirit. This is our enlightenment, our salvation.

Exercise for Week 49   (*Purpose*)

This week we will practice remembering Spirit on a regular basis. Let us begin by periodically stopping whatever we are doing (within reason) and thinking about Spirit. It need take only ten seconds, but remember Spirit regularly. We might time our reflection with some regular event such as the chime of an hourly clock, the bark of the dog next door, etc. Remember that we are part of Spirit and no longer alone.

Other techniques can provide a trigger in our outer awareness the same way. We might affix a small colored dot to the face of our watch so that whenever we check the time, we remember our connection with Spirit. We could also affix the colored dot to anything that we periodically use throughout the day.

> "I remember my connection to Spirit throughout the day."

Our attitude towards life should be to listen to the directions given by Spirit. When we are committed to spiritual growth with all our heart, our path will be revealed.

Exercise for Week 50   (*Healing*)

We can see the beauty and health of the true world. We can right the upside-down, crazy world of our dreams and nightmares. All we need to do is ask to know Spirit more completely. Have faith that everything we need to know will be revealed, but remember it takes faith. Belief in Spirit is required even at those times when our logical mind says no!

> "I am blessed and healed by the power of Spirit."

Spirit will never leave or forsake us. It is not necessary to live by physical beauty, strength, mental knowledge or ability. Spirit is within us, and all that Spirit has, we have. This realization brings all that we will ever need. If we put our faith in the power of the infinite Spirit, we will be blessed and healed. We can truly experience heaven on earth.

Exercise for Week 51   (One)

This week's spiritual meditation will remind us of our true identity. Spirit resides within us and is our true identity. To remember our higher self is to forget who we think we are.

We are more than just a human. We are one with the infinite Spirit that always was and always will be. The leaf of a tree is more than just a leaf. It is a leaf but it is also part of the tree. Similarly, we are unique human individuals, and are also part of eternal Spirit. When we remember this, we need no longer be enslaved by human law. We already are the physical manifestation of Spirit. We are in perfect union with the One Spirit.

Let us acknowledge now that we are eternal and infinite, not limited to our mind and body. Never doubt the everlasting love of Spirit, because we are one with that Spirit.

> "Spirit and I are one."

From time to time we will forget ourselves, and then realize that we need new guidance. When the illusions of the world close in on us, we should shut our eyes for a moment and silently reaffirm our connection to Spirit that is within us and is part of us. Let us affirm that we and Spirit are one, and our true nature is incorporeal, infinite being. We dwell and have our existence in Spirit. We are not separate from Spirit. When we acknowledge Spirit as inseparable from ourselves, we will be blessed and healed.

Exercise for Week 52 (*Teacher*)

We may want to repeat the fifty-two spiritual meditations again. We may want to do them alone or with a friend. We need not be the perfect master to teach the truth. We may continue to experience times when we forget our true being. Still, we can teach what we know. This teaching illuminates the darkness of material existence in both ourselves and in others.

> **"I am a teacher of the truth."**

Teaching does not mean inflicting our words on those who don't want to hear. Instead let us teach by example through our compassionate presence, telling only those who really want to know about the truth.

Let us teach what we would learn better. But we mustn't charge blindly ahead and attempt to teach those who cannot yet hear. If our beliefs are still too new and fragile, they can be shattered by the world's hypnotic reaction.

We must not attempt to tell others that they are wrong in their world view. They will resist us. Trying to force the truth on others could prevent them from being able to hear it. Instead, live the life of Spirit, demonstrating your understanding of the eternal truth. Let the light of Spirit shine through us. When others come to us and ask our secret, then share.

But even then, share slowly. Few people can immediately conceive our jump to a greater Reality. Let's teach the truth, but don't teach beyond the ability of our student.

Let us allow Spirit to go before us to bring light to the darkness and make the crooked places straight. Spirit will guide us in when, whom and how to teach.

Daily Meditations

It's said that there is a time for everything, a time to be born and a time to die. But there is more. There is a moment beyond time, a moment when you know your true identity. For many of you, that moment is now.

Remaining aware is vital to preventing disease, lack and limitation from regaining control of your experience of life. You can continue to live a life of health, happiness and abundance by regularly remembering your true identity. The hypnotic effect of life in material bodies constantly suggests that we are separate and apart from Spirit. Periodically recall that you are one with Spirit, and not separate and alone. This will protect you from slipping back into the hypnotic trance that most humans accept as their world view.

Begin each day celebrating your true identity and affirming the one true power in the universe. Throughout the day, remember again and again. This is the most important meditation you can do on your spiritual path.

> **Be silent and listen to the magnificent Universe.**
> **Accept Spirit as infinite and all-powerful.**
> **Ask Spirit to direct your life.**
> **Remain aware of your true identity, united with Spirit.**

It was with great joy that Spirit created the world. Spirit saw all that was made and beheld that it was very good. It is Spirit's good pleasure to give you everything you need. It is Spirit's good pleasure to give you the Universe.

Recovery Work

There are times when we get caught up in the stuff of life. As we accept truth more and more into our lives, we are caught up less and less. But some things will be difficult, such as loss of a job or lover, and challenges of poor health and death. What do we do at those times when we are really feeling down and life seems to us so negative or hopeless? When times are really difficult, use one of the following meditations. Choose the one that works best for you and use it as often as necessary. Any of these may be useful to you at various times of your life.

> "Spirit, let me see this differently."

> "I turn it all over to Spirit."

> "I am not this problem. I am free."

> "There is a greater plan for me, and I do not understand everything."

INDEX

Index

Abdominal 132
Abraham Lincoln 250
Abundance 380
Acidophilus 50
Acids 35
Acne 81
Acrylics 93
Activity scale 62
Acupressure 142, 196
Acutane 81
Addiction 214, 215, 265
Additives 47
Adrenal glands 144
Adrenaline 144
Aerobic Exercise 160
Affirmations 282
Aging 172
AIDS 111, 190, 191, 219
Air Pollution 105
Alcohol 211
Alpha waves 167
Alzheimer's 175, 244
Amino-acids 24
Amnesia 246
Amphetamines 215, 222
Amyl nitrate 221
Ancestral memories 235
Angina pectoris 121
Anima 235
Animus 235
Antibiotics 202
Antigen 111
Antioxidants 38
Antisocial Personality 248
Anxiety 245, 258
Archetypes 235
Arteriosclerosis 120
Asbestos 100
Ascorbic acid 34
Aspirin 198
Asthma 130, 196
Auto immune disease 111
B cells 110
Back Pain 132
Barbiturates 215

Baths 73
Behaviorism 236, 276
Benzedrine 222
Beta-carotene 32
Biofeedback 152
Bipolar Disorder 250
Birth Control 187, 208
Blood pressure 119, 196
Blood sugar 124
Brahma 310
Bronchitis 208
Buddhism 314
Burn-out 147, 246
Butterfly 360
Caffeine 72
Calcium 36
Caloric contents 29. 60, 64
Cancer 113, 115, 11 209, 212
Cannabis 216
Carbohydrates 26
Carbohydrates 26
Carbon monoxide 100
Carcinogens 99
Cardiovascular fitness, 158
Carl Jung 171, 235
Carl Rogers 236
Catholic Church 339
Cells 21
Cellulite 65
Cementum 89
Cerebral cortex 231
Cervix 116
Chamomile 168
Change 276
Chemotherapy 117
Chiropractic 137
Chlamydia 188
Chloroform 221
Cholesterol 29, 208
Christianity 334
Chronic pain 141, 196
Chronic stress 143
Cirrhosis 213
Clothing 91, 95
Cluster Headaches 141

Co-Dependent 264
Cocaine 215, 216
Codeine 218
Colds 128
Color 225
Colors 225
Communication 270
Connective tissues 21
Conscious mind 232
Contamination 99
Cool-down 159
Corona Virus, 128
Coronary Bypass 122
Cortex, 85
Corticoids 144
Cotton 94
Crack cocaine 217
CSF's 118
Cuticle 85
Darker self, 235
Darvon 141
Daydreams 172
Death 261
Decibels (dB) 227
Delusional (Paranoid)
Demerol 141, 218
Dentin 89
Depersonalization 246
Dermis 77
Dexedrine 222
Diabetes 124
Diets 58
Dilaudid 141
Discs 132
Dissociative Disorders 246
Distilled Water 71
Doctor 194
Dorsal muscles 132
Dostoevski 250
Down's syndrome 244
Drugs 200, 204
Drugs 206
Dynorhins. 141
Eastern Orthodox 340
Eggs 50

Ego 233
Electra complex 234
Emotional Balance 293
Emotional Issues 256
Emphysema 208
Enamel 89
Endocrine glands 144
Endorphins 141
Enneagram 237
Environment 98, 244
Envy 259
Epidermis 77
Epinephrine 198
Eric Berne 240
Error 365
Esalen Massage 156
Estrogen Replacement 181
Evil 372
Exercise 112, 157, 160, 177
Fasting 65
Fats 27, 41
Fear 257
Feet 135
Fetal alcohol 213
Fiber 27
FIght or flight 143
Fish 49
Fitness 158
Flip-Flop 288
Flossing 90
Flu 129, 130
Fluorescent Lights 223
Food allergies 40, 57, 61
Forgiveness 275, 374
Formaldehyde 103
Freeman 263
Fructose 26
Generic Drugs 206
Genital stage 234
Gestational diabetes 126
Glucose 26
God 301
Gonorrhea 189
Gospels 335
Gout 212

Grains 41
Gray matter 231
Group therapy 242
Guru, 310
Hair 85, 86, 212
Halcyon. 170
Hallucinogens 219
Halogen Lights 224
Hans Seyle 143
Happiness. 356
Hashish 216
Hatha yoga 165
Headaches 138
Healing 387
Health and Wellness 267
Health Foods 48
Heart 119, 208, 121, 123, 198
Herbal Baths 73
Herbal medicine 196, 197
Herbs 198
Heroin 141, 215
Herpes 188, 189
Higher Consciousness 283
Hinduism 310, 313
HIV 190
Holmes and Rahe 145
Holy Trinity 339
Honey 44
Hot flashes 180
Humanistic 236
Hydrogenated Oil 41
Hyperactivity 222, 244
Hyperglycemia 126
Hypertension 120, 198, 213
Hypnosis 286
Hypoglycemia 26, 44, 126
Hypothalamus 144
I am 362
Ibuprofen 197
Illusion 366
Immune deficiency disease 111
Immune s109, 110, 112
Influenza 129
Insomnia 168

Insulin 124
Iron 37
Irradiated Foods 42
Isokinetics 163
Isometrics 162
Isotonics 162
Ivan Pavlov 236
Iyengar yoga 165
Judge 375
Karma 312
Kegel's exercises 187
Kosher 329
Kundalini yoga. 165
L-tryptophan 168
Law of Attraction 287
Lecithin 27
Lessons 357
Librium 170, 221
LIfe expectancy table 178
Lifting 134
Light 223
Light bulbs 224
LInen 94
Listen 272, 384
LIthium 250
LIver 204
LIver disease 213
Loneliness 263
Longevity 172, 175, 178
Love 364
Love-Peace 378
Low birth weight 244
LSD 220
Lung cancer 207
Lymph nodes 111
Lymph system 111
Lymphocytes 110
Macro-minerals 35
Macrobiotic Diet 55
Macrophages 111
Major Depression 249
Malaria 198
Maltose 26
Manic-depression 250
Marijuana 216

Maslow 236
Massage 154
Medical Check-up 195
Meditation 150, 151
Meditations 295, 351, 352
Medulla 85
Memory 277
Menopause 174, 180, 182
Mental Illness 242
Mental retardation 244
Mescaline 219
Migraines 140
Milk 50
Mineral Water 71
Minerals 35
Money 279
Monounsaturated Fats 28
Mood Disorders 249
Morphine 141, 218
Moses 250
Muscle Strength 158
Muscular Endurance 158
Muscular tissues 21
Mushrooms 221
Nail Care 88
Narcolepsy 222
Narcotics 218
Natural sunlight 223
Negative Thought 280
Nerve tissues 21
Neuroses 243
Neurotransmitters 244
Neutralizers 72
Niacin 33
Nicotine 207
Nightmares 172
Nitrites 43
Nitrogen dioxide 100
Nitrous oxide 221
Nonoxynol-9 191
Nor epinephrine 144
Novocain 217
Nutrients 22, 23
Nutrition 53, 176
Nylon 92

Oedipus complex 234
Olefins 94
Omega-3 50
One Spirit 362, 388
Opium 218, 141
Oral cancers 209
Oral stage 234
Organ transplants 124
Organochlorines 103
Organs 21
Osteoporosis 36
Osteoporosis 174, 181, 213
Pain 141, 142
Pancreas 124
Pandemic 128
Panic 245
Pantothenic acid, 33
Pap-smear 116, 195
Paranoia 253, 255
Paraquat 216
Parkinson's Disease 175
Patanjali 165
PCB's 100
PCP (Phencyclidine) 220
Penicillin 198
Percodan 141
Perfect 358
Periodontal disease 89
Persona 235
Personal conscious 235
Personality Disorders 248
Peyote 219
PH Factor 77
Phallic stage 234
Phenols 104
Phenothiazine 255
Physician 194
Pills 221
Pituitary glands 144
Plaque 89
Pleasure principle, 233
Plutonium 101
Polarity Therapy 156
Polyester 93
Polyunsaturated Fats 28

Positive Thinking 279
Post-traumatic Stress 245
Posture 134
Potassium 37
Prayer 381
Present 381
Preservatives 43
Problems 378
Promoting agent 114
Prosperity 277
Prostate gland. 115
Proteins 24, 25, 54
Protestant Church 340
Psyche 235
Psychoanalysis 233
Psychological Dependency 215
Psychology 232
Psychopath 248
Psychoses. 243
Pulp 89
Purpose 385
Pyridoxine 33
Quaaludes 222
Quadriceps 132
Radon 104
Rayon 94
Reality 234, 353, 356
Reality Therapy 241
Recreational Drugs 215
Reflexology 156
Relationships 274
Relaxing Baths 73
REM 167
Reye's Syndrome, 130
Rhino Virus 128
RIboflavin 33
Rishis, 309
Rolfing 156
Root canal, 89
Safer Sex 192
Salt 45
Samhita, 310
Saturated Fats 28
Sauna 75

Schizophrenia 254, 255
Second-hand smoke 207
Self 235
Self-Help Networks 241
Senile dementia 244
Senility 175
Sexual Behavior 183
Sexual diseases 188
Sexual Organs 182
Sexuality 182, 184
Shadow archetype 235
Shi'ites 332
Shiatsu (Acupressure) 156
Shoes 96
Showers 74
Siddartha Gautama, 314
Sigmund Freud 171, 223
SIlk 95
Simple Carbohydrates 26
Simple phobias 245
Sin 372
Skin 77
Skin Allergies 81
Skin Care Products 78
Skinner, B. F. 236
Sleep 166
Sleep Apnea 169
Sleep Rhythms 167
Sleep-walking 169
Sleeping Pills 170
Smoking 207
Snoring 169
Snuff 209
Social phobias 245
Sociopath 248
Sound 226
Sounds in Decibels 228
Spandex 93
Spinal cord 132
Spine 132
Spiritual 351
Spiritual Quest 300
Spiritual truth 370
Spring Water 70
Starches 26

Steroids 222
Stress 143, 244
Stress 147
Stress and Longevity 175
Stress management 147
Stroke 120, 213
Strokes 208
Sub-conscious 232
Subcutaneous tissue 77
Substance Abuse 215
Sucrose 26
Suffering 355, 365
Sufis 332
Sugar 26, 44
Suicide 249
Suicide Potentiality 252
Sulfites 43
Sulfites 212
Sulfur 37
Sulfur dioxide 100, 102
Sun and Skin 83
Sun Light 224
Sunnis 332
Sunscreens 84
Support Groups 241
Swedish Massage 156
Sweeteners 45
Synthetic fibers 92
Syphilis 189
Systems 21
T cells 110
Tai Chi 166
Tantra 318
Teacher 389
Teeth 88
Tempeh 56
Tension Headaches 139
Teratogens 99
The Traveler 263
THiamin 33
Thorazine 221
Thymus 110
TInnitus. 227
Tobacco 209
Tofu 56

Toothbrush 90
Toothpaste 90
Toxins 99
Trace elements 35
Tranquilizers 202
Transactional Analysis 240
Trust 364
Tumor Growth 114, 118
Types of Therapy 240
Ulcers 212
Unconscious 235
Undifferentiated
    schizophrenia 254
Upanishads 310
Urethane or ethyl
    carbonate 212
UV-A rays 83
UV-B rays 84
Valium 170, 221
Vedas 310
Vegetables 51
Vertebrae 132
Vitamins 32, 112
Warm-up 159
Water 67
Water Pollutants 71
Water Softeners 72
Weight 57, 66
Weight Range 59
Whirling dervishes 333
Wool 95
Wrinkles 82
Yoga 165
Zen Buddhism 319